# Dancing with the Muse in Old Age

## Priscilla Long

coffeetownpress

Kenmore, WA

coffeetownpress

A Coffeetown Press book published by Epicenter Press

Epicenter Press
6524 NE 181st St. Suite 2
Kenmore, WA 98028.
www.Epicenterpress.com
www.Coffeetownpress.com
www.Camelpress.com

For more information go to: www.Epicenterpress.com
Author Website: www.priscillalong.com

Dancing with the Muse in Old Age
Copyright © 2022 by Priscilla Long

Cover artwork: *"Crossroads 2, 050520"* by Carol Nelson. Mixed media on panel, 8 inches by 8 inches by 1.5 inches.

Library of Congress Control Number: 2022940371

ISBN: 9781684920204 (trade paper)
ISBN: 9781684920211 (ebook)

Printed in the United States of America

Dedicated to two dear friends,
Flynn Donovan and Amanda Irons Donovan

And to the memory of
Alda Irons (1915–2014),
poet and beloved mother-in-law

# Also by Priscilla Long

*Holy Magic: Poems*

*Fire and Stone: Where Do We Come From?*
*What Are We? Where Are We Going?*

*Minding the Muse: A Handbook for Painters,*
*Composers, Writers, and Other Creators*

*Crossing Over: Poems*

*The Writer's Portable Mentor: A Guide to Art, Craft,*
*and the Writing Life* (Second Edition)

*Where the Sun Never Shines: A History of*
*America's Bloody Coal Industry*

*The New Left: A Collection of Essays* (Editor)

# Contents

# Introduction

Creating—making, inventing, imagining—is our human birthright, no matter our age. So why focus on old age? We are an aging society. We are all aging and in my own case it has gotten to the point of 79 years old. For me—for all of us—there couldn't be a better time to consider how to approach our forthcoming or existing old age.

*Dancing with the Muse in Old Age* works against ageism and for creativity. It reflects the new ways of looking at old age: as a potentially dynamic and productive time full of connections to others and deeply satisfying work, whether paid or unpaid. It offers numerous models of people who grew to be very old while also living remarkably creative and productive lives. Some were able-bodied; others were disabled in one way or another.

There are any number of ways of being creative and productive in old age. Here I focus primarily—but not entirely—on the arts. This is because I have lived much of my life in the arts. Even as a much younger woman working as a printer, as I did for fifteen years, I wrote in my journal each morning and wrote poems—or what I thought were poems. Thus was I involved in the arts.

But this book is for everyone who is aging. The lives of the dozens of vital, engaged, and even brilliant elders presented in this book model for us all how to grow old, no matter what our goals and endeavors. These aged persons—whether they play the piano or compose poems or dance or paint or write novels or memoirs or take photographs or design a garden or fight fires (yes), or begin college at age 94, or work for justice—keep on growing, learning, and creating. Even disability does not stop them. And trust me when I say that there was a whole other list of elders I could have used. In no way was I scraping the bottom of the barrel to find persons in old age and in very old age doing vital, dynamic, and even transcendent work.

That we find models for what we hope to do or be—people we can identify with—is no minor matter. As a young writer growing up, virtually all the books I read were written by men. Indeed, I thought writers *were* men—something I am not. This hindered my progress. Many of us find ourselves challenged to find role models who resemble ourselves. In writing this book I sought, and found with very little trouble, a great variety of people who were thriving in old age, mostly, though not entirely, from within the United States. People of color. White people. People of different origins, genders, regional and class backgrounds.

Old age is a prime time to flourish in creative productivity. It is also a prime time to *begin* creative work. As the National Institute on Aging recently reported, "participating in the arts creates paths to healthy aging."[1] Old age is in fact an excellent time to begin *any* new work, whether paid or volunteer, whether in the capacious world of the arts or in some other world. The elders presented in this book, who thrive in the face of ageism, are evidence.

Ageism poisons creativity. And ageism—the deep and often unconscious prejudice against old age and against the old—is, in our American society, rampant. We are saturated with it. Otherwise, why would people be so reluctant to state their age? Why is it the height of rudeness to ask? Because it's bad to be old and the older you are, the worse it is! And you may very well face discrimination. An AARP survey of 3,900 people over the age of 45 found that more than 90 percent viewed age discrimination as common, nearly two-thirds having seen or experienced it personally.[2]

Ageism hurts us all. As we'll see, it hurts the young. And self-inflicted or internalized ageism is an important *cause* of decline. Let me repeat that. *Self-inflicted ageism is an important cause of decline.*

Most of us harbor at least some negative attitudes toward aging. It's hard to avoid considering how thoroughly ageism saturates our culture. (I am speaking here of mainstream American culture.) I am aware of how ageism has affected me in how pleased I've felt when people have expressed surprise at my age, having thought I was younger. In my heart of hearts, I must believe that young is better than old. It is a personal project of mine to thoroughly assimilate the notion that old age can bring with it advantages, privileges, and pleasures not afforded by the younger ages (see Chapter 6).

What about the issue of revealing one's age? My identical twin sister was always a bear on the subject. *Please do not reveal our age! Thank you!* Then I wrote a creative nonfiction piece, an abecedarian, titled "O Is for Old." This appeared in a literary journal.[3] Trust me. You cannot write a piece titled "O Is for Old" without revealing your own age. But Pamela was okay with this, since it was a literary journal and "nobody will read it anyhow." But then, guess what? She received the prestigious MacArthur genius award for her amazing scholarship on the history of technology. Our age, 71 at the time, was broadcast around the world. I think she was the oldest or one of the oldest to ever receive this honor. In any case all kinds of people wrote to me to say congratulations on my sister's award. But they would add, as if it were a mistake to be corrected: "But...they said you were 71!" I have now begun the practice of stating my age whenever it comes up or is appropriate. Guess what? I am now 79, and guess what? I can still type!

In old age, creative work can thrive. And in doing creative work, the person in old age can thrive. In this book I explore old painters, old writers, old filmmakers, old poets, old composers, old choreographers, old dancers, old photographers, old musicians, old sculptors, old printmakers, old designers. I am interested in artists and in everyday creators who become productive or remain productive into very old age and who in old age produce beautiful and meaningful works, whether world-renowned or known only to a few friends.

The fact that many creators who appear in these pages are well known or even famous (a few worked for decades with little or no recognition) should in no way overshadow the many non-famous vital older adults in our communities who are active, who are learning and developing, who are contributing to their families and to their communities, and who are creating. Some lesser-known and virtually unknown creators also appear in these pages.

The arts, of course, are not the only place where the very old have made very significant contributions. Consider science. A pioneer of positive aging, psychiatrist Gene D. Cohen, points to the Austrian zoologist Karl von Frisch (1886–1982), who discovered dancing in bees, who received the Nobel in 1973 at age 87, who composed his classic work *Animal Architecture* at age 88.[4] Another aged creator in science was John Fenn (1917–2010). Fenn worked along diligently but with little recognition until Yale University forced him to retire at age 70. He then went to Virginia Commonwealth University, opened a new lab, continued what turned out to be breakthrough work, and won the Nobel in chemistry in his mid-80s. Fenn published his last paper at age 90.[5] Barbara McClintock (1902–1992) studied the genetic structure of maize. She was a meticulous and innovative scientist, who, in her early 80s, in 1983, received the Nobel. She continued as a leader and active researcher at the Cold Spring Harbor Laboratory in Long Island until her death at age 90.[6]

I also think of Francis Crick (1916–2004), co-discoverer of the structure of DNA, who thereafter turned to the study of the brain. Of him the neurologist Oliver Sacks (1933–2015) wrote, "When he was told that his colon cancer had returned, at first he said nothing; he simply looked into the distance for a minute and then resumed his previous train of thought. When pressed about his diagnosis a few weeks later, he said, 'Whatever has a beginning must have an ending.' When he died, at age 88, he was still fully engaged in his most creative work."[7]

These brilliant old creators for me serve as models of how to grow into old age if one should be so lucky as to get to old age. Their very lives pulverize the stereotype of old age as a time of decrepitude and decline.

Look at the visual artist Sam Gilliam (b. 1933) barreling ahead with his customary virtuosity in his late 80s. Termed "one of the great innovators in postwar American painting,"[8] Gilliam was associated with both color field painting and abstract expressionism, making a series of formal breakthroughs beginning with his renowned drape paintings: huge off-the-stretcher canvasses hung and draped like curtains or clothes on a line. His experiments and innovations and gorgeous color work has continued ever since. Of pyramid-shaped sculptures shown as part of a 2020 exhibit at New York's Pace Gallery, art critic Peter Schjeldahl wrote, "Like everything else in this show of an artist who is old in years, they feel defiantly brand spanking new."[9] In his hometown of Washington DC, the Hirshhorn Museum gave Gilliam a major retrospective in the spring of 2022. This African American artist was nearing 90 years of age. He continued to work despite health challenges, going to dialysis three times a week. "Well," he told an interviewer, "You get four hours to contemplate and do nothing and then a full day to work. It doesn't stop my work."[10]

Another case in point: Lawrence Ferlinghetti (1919–2021). A poet and prime mover in the Beat (he preferred, "wide open") poetry movement. Founder of San Francisco's City Lights Books and City Lights Publishers. Ferlinghetti composed more than thirty books of poetry including *Coney Island of the Mind* (1958), which has sold a million copies. He composed plays and novels, and he was a painter. His last book was the free-associating autobiographical novel, *Little Boy*. The publication date was March 24, 2019, the day he turned one century old.[11]

Or consider the Canadian writer Margaret Atwood (b. 1939). She has written, so far, seventeen novels, sixteen books of poetry, ten books of nonfiction, eight collections of short stories, and three graphic novels. Asked whether her writing got any easier with age, she replied that it did not: "It's the same blank page with nothing on it." Asked whether there were aspects that got harder, she replied, "I can't tell you that yet. I'm not old enough." She was 81 at the time. In this interview she also insisted that everyone has creativity: "It's a human thing."[12]

I believe that the philosophy of the dancer, potter, and master teacher Paulus Berensohn (1933–2017) has something to say to us all. In his late 30's, Berensohn wrote a book about making clay pots by pinching (off the wheel), a book which became required reading for any potter. But it also became hugely popular outside that obvious market. *Finding One's Way with Clay* is about making art and its relationship to the human spirit. The technical exercises in the book pertain to potters but the philosophy of making art pertains to everyone. Where Berensohn uses the word "clay," substitute any material at all:

> These exercises….are concerned, acutely, with the growing relationship of the potter to his clay; with bringing more and more personality, imagination and inspiration into play; and with tapping sources deep within the experience of the potter to inform the forms he makes. I don't believe it to be a talent that we either have or don't have. We all breathe, we are all alive, we all have unique qualities. Yet it takes hard conscious and unconscious work for most of us to connect these facts with what we make, to find *our* pot as we also seek our dance and our song.[13]

As we begin or continue doing our work, possibly moving into a new, unaccustomed area, whether in the arts or elsewhere, Berensohn's thoughts may help us to hold on, to hone, to learn, to have patience, to keep on.

Another thought that may give courage to those of us aging into creative work is that of the poet Marvin Bell (1937–2020): "Art is a way of life, not a career."[14]

And finally, artist and art therapist Shaun McNiff writes, "Art and creativity are the soul's medicines—what the soul uses to minister to itself, cure its maladies, and restore its vitality."[15]

*Dancing with the Muse in Old Age* considers aging (and ageism) in terms of demographics and resources in the United States and beyond; the current science on aging and the brain and on aging and happiness. A chapter titled "Resource Drain or Resource?" explores Social Security and the question of whether the bourgeoning numbers of old people are going to bring down the economy. (The short answer: We are holding up the economy.) A chapter on aging and creativity challenges the notion of "peak ages of creativity"—alleged to be ages 39 to 42. In the final chapter we explore the advantages of being an *old* creator.

Whatever age we are, whatever our vocation or avocation, our understandings around aging can profoundly affect our own flourishing as persons and as creators. It is my hope that, within each of our lives, this book will help tilt the balance against ageism and toward creativity.

## Note on Nomenclature

The lexicon referring to old age is fraught and contested. Some insist that the word *elderly* and *elders* is respectful, whereas the word *old* is not. Others make up terms, such as *olders*—anything to avoid saying "I am old" or "you are old." All is fallout from the way ageism pervades our culture. None of us is immune. Consider the expression "90 years young." What underlies this kindly intended phrase is the notion that it's better to be young than to be old. My entire work here is to challenge such an idea. I'm only 79, but I like the word *old.* I have chosen to use it here, at least much of the time. It brings to my mind the phrase *old soul.* To be called an old soul is a very touching compliment. I like *elder* also, especially when it refers to wise and knowledgeable old ones, such as in Native American usage. I like the word *senior* less, except when it refers to a discount. But we are all different here, and I invite you, my reader, to cross out any term not to your liking and insert one of your own (unless you are reading a library book).

## Composing Our Lives: Old Age

What do we want for our old age? At the end of each of these chapters I pose a series of questions for you to explore in relation to your own life.

So much is not up to us. To begin with, we don't know how much longer we have to be alive—one day or one decade. Finances may be a worry. How do we pay the bills as we get older and older? How do we live the life to which we are accustomed or to which we wish we were accustomed? We may be dealing with health issues or pain or living with a longtime disability or learning to live with a new one. We may be grieving the loss of someone dear to us. But also, we may have more time, more opportunities to contribute to our community, to learn, to create.

There's a lot that we *can* control. We can plan the next decade rather than just letting it happen. Of course, plans change. On planning our lives, Mary Catherine Bateson, author of *Composing a Life* and *Composing a Further Life*, writes, "if you think you know what you are going to be doing in five or ten years, you're wrong. But if you don't have an opinion on it, you're in trouble. In other words, go toward the future with a plan you're willing to let go of."[16]

I suggest obtaining a notebook—a simple composition book would be perfect. Then take each of the questions below, or any one that interests you and write on it for five or ten minutes without stopping, without lifting your pen off the page, without worrying about correctness or neat handwriting. This is called discovery writing, and there are no correct or incorrect answers. And yes, I do suggest writing by hand, the idea being to keep the hand moving, the science being that more parts of the brain are activated when writing by hand than when tapping keys. But this is up to you.

This project, this exploration, begins the process of composing an old age that you would love to live. The questions under "Composing Our Lives" at the end of each of these chapters often begin with an exploration of what the reality is, within your own life. What is true for you right now? What do you love about your life? What do you deplore? For there's no way to get from here to there without a clear idea of what "here" means in your own case. And there is also no way to get "there"—your dream of a fine old age—without the destination, your goals and dreams, articulated, even though they may shift and change as you go along.

For each of these writing prompts, write for five or ten minutes.

1   What are your own negative and positive attitudes toward old age, toward old people, and toward your own old age? After writing, circle and then list the main points.

2.  Do you habitually reveal or conceal your age, and why? There may be a good reason to conceal: Age discrimination is real. But might it also be about your own internalized shame and negative feelings about growing old? Explore.

3.  Do you see models, people whose old age you wish you could emulate, at least in part? Such models might be members of your own family or people you know. Or they can be people known to you, an author, an actor, a teacher, a cook, a gardener. What characteristics do they have that you might want to emulate or strengthen in your own life?

4.  What would be, for you, a satisfying old age?

5.  Which elements of this life do you have now? Which elements might you work toward?

Alma Thomas, age ca. 79, in studio, 1971. *Photograph by Ida Jervis, © 1971, Anacostia Community Museum, Smithsonian Institution.*

# 1. Creating While Aging

*Being an artist is a way of life....It is something one has a passion for, does...and can do it literally until they pass away. It's an old age thing. You become better with age.*
—Faith Ringgold, visual artist, at age 82[17]

We are growing older. In 2021, more than 16 percent of the United States population is age 65 or older; by 2030, this number is expected to rise to more than 20 percent.[18] The ballooning population of old people has partly to do with the aging of baby boomers, that extra-numerous post-war generation born between 1946 and 1964. But it also has to do with a long-term trend of increased longevity. People are living to older ages. And, worldwide, longevity is increasing while birthrates are falling.[19] The new shape of society—one with proportionally more old people—will not pass with the passing of the baby boomers. This is the case despite the setback of COVID-19. In 2020 and 2021 the worldwide pandemic reduced life expectancy in the United States and around the world by two to three years.[20] This is tragic, but in the long run it will not reverse the trend.

In the United States, since 1900, average life expectancy at birth has increased dramatically. In 1900, for white men it was 47 years, for white women, 49 years, for Black men, 33 years, for Black women, 34 years.[21] In the twenty-first century in the United States, the average life expectancy at birth for white males was 76.1 years, for white females, 81. For Black males life expectancy at birth was 71.5 years and for Black females, 77.9. (Longevity has increased for everyone, but systemic racism continues to challenge the life expectancy of people of color.) Hispanic newborn boys, who were not counted in 1900, could expect to live for 79.1 years; Hispanic newborn girls, for 84.2 years.[22] This trend of increased longevity (considering the past century) is a worldwide phenomenon.[23]

What made these extra years happen?

During the first half of the twentieth century the low average life expectancy had largely to do with the fact that death was common at all ages, including in infancy, childhood, and young adulthood. Dying in childbirth was not unusual. And, in 1900 many children—around a fourth of all children born—died before the age of 5.[24]

Between 1900 and 1930, the widespread acknowledgment of the much earlier discovery that germs cause disease resulted in hand washing, efforts to keep flies off food, food sterilization, cleaner water, and the practice of isolating the sick. In addition, according to Steven Johnson in his book *Extra Life*, vaccination became widespread. Johnson writes, "The best estimates hold that roughly a billion lives were saved thanks to the invention and mass adoption of vaccination over the past two centuries...."[25]

In the late 1930s, sulfa drugs were introduced to fight bacteria, and during World War II penicillin was introduced. Both helped people live longer. More recently—for those who take them on—improvements in lifestyle (diet, exercise) have resulted in longer lives and in healthier lives. In medicine, there have been great advances, particularly in cardiac care.[26] The result of all this: an enormous difference in the number of people who lived to grow up and have children of their own.

There are more older people in the world, and they are living longer. In 2010 there were 1.9 million Americans over age 90. By 2016 in the United States there were 82,000 centenarians—persons 100 years or older.[27] Centenarians, one researcher found, can walk up and down stairs. Meaning, they are active. They also "tend to have a sense of purpose in their lives."[28] About one centenarian, the late neurologist Oliver Sacks tells this story: At age 109 she had to enter an old-age home due to diminishing vision. But once her cataracts had been removed, once she could see again, she removed herself from the place to return to independent living. Her reasoning: "Why should I stay here with all these old people?"[29]

Longer lives give us more time. More time to do. More time to create. More time to change and learn and grow.

More time allowed the Minnesota-based master potter Warren MacKenzie (1924–2018), who had previously thrown perhaps 100,000 pots, to continue throwing pots. Of MacKenzie, his United Kingdom–based Goldmark Gallery wrote in his last year, "inseparable from his studio, at 94 he is still to be found at his foot-powered treadle wheel throwing the loose, lively pots that once made him one of America's most famous potters."[30]

More time allowed the Caribbean poet and playwright Derek Walcott (1930–2017) to compose, in the ten years before he died at age 87, two more plays and two more books of poems. A *New York Times* reviewer wrote that in the poet's penultimate book, *White Egrets*, Walcott "produced some of his best work." It is "a book of loss and regret, a majestic settling of accounts, a monument to a lifetime of writing and friendship."[31]

More time allowed Diana Athill (1917–2019), well known in her younger years as a London-based editor—most famously of Jean Rhys and V. S. Naipaul—to publish her second book of short stories at age 94. Athill wrote extensively about her own life and its old age, which continued until she died at age 102. In her late 80s, in a book titled *Somewhere Towards the End*, she wrote about how vital it was that she came into writing:

> The activities I escape into are mostly ordinary things which have become more valuable because I am old, enjoyed with increased intensity because of the knowledge I shan't be able to enjoy them for much longer; but easily the best part of my old age, has been, and still is, a little less ordinary. It is entirely to do with having had the luck to discover that I can write. I don't suppose that I shall carry it as far as my friend Rose Hacker, who at the age of a hundred is the oldest newspaper columnist in Britain...but it looks as though it will still be with me when (if!) I reach my ninetieth birthday, and it is impossible adequately to describe how grateful I am for that.[32]

At age 98, Athill published a memoir, *Alive Alive Oh! and Other Things That Matter*. A review in the *New York Times Book Review* described this last as "an invitation to sit a spell with an intractable and witty friend who's pushed even further into what the poet May Sarton termed the 'foreign country of old age.'"[33]

More time allowed the Lebanese American poet, novelist, and visual artist Etel Adnan (1925–2021) to continue writing and painting into her 90s. In the spring 2018 issue of *Paris Review*, which featured her current artwork (she was then 93), curator Nicole Rudnick wrote, "So numerous are her paintings, drawings, films, tapestries, ceramics and murals that I imagine it must be impossible to see them all; so brisk and vital are they that I am always eager for more—and amazed by the beauty she discovers each time."[34] In 2021—the artist was 96—New York's Guggenheim Museum presented an exhibition titled "Etel Adnan: Light's New Measure."[35]

Longer lives give late starters—creators whose lives were otherwise occupied or preoccupied during their younger years— more time to develop. Anna Mary Robertson Moses (1860–1961), formerly known as "Grandma," was a hard-working farm wife who raised five children. She said, "I just didn't have time to paint before I was 76." Her painting career did not erupt from nowhere; she'd always had creative hobbies, particularly her elaborate pictorial embroideries. But, due to disabling arthritis in her hands, she could not continue to embroider. So, she began to paint. Her painting flourished between her start during her 70s and her death at age 101.[36]

The painter and superb colorist Alma Thomas (1891–1978) was not precisely a late starter, but before her 70s her life was largely taken up with teaching art to children. She was born in Columbus, Georgia, attended Howard University, and got a master's degree from Columbia University, studying sculpture in both places. She then taught art to children in Washington, DC, "thirty-five years in one room." She reflected, "I enjoyed those thirty-five years. I devoted my life to the children and I think they loved me...." In 1964, she was offered a painting retrospective at Howard University. She was 72 and recovering from a terrific attack of arthritis. But she took up the challenge and at that time began painting the abstractions done in vivid color that she is known for. "From then on," she said, "I just painted." Recognition of her work came quickly, with "her banner year" being 1972 (she was 80 years old). She exhibited her painting at the Whitney and New York art critics noticed it. She died at the age of 86 as an internationally recognized artist.[37]

Another creator whose day job took up most of his time in his younger decades was the author Richard Adams (1920–2016). He worked in the British civil service and wrote on the weekends. In his 40s, he began composing his novel *Watership Down* for his children. It was published in 1972, the year Adams turned 52. It became a bestseller and two years later Adams left his job to become a full-time author. He continued writing until his death at age 96.[38]

The poet Sarah Yerkes (b. 1918) had two previous careers, the first in landscape architecture and the second in sculpture. After sculpting became too physically challenging, Yerkes turned, at age 96, to poetry. At age 101 her first book of poems, *Days of Blue and Flame*, was published. An article about her is titled: "Is this the oldest debut author in history?"[39]

## Being Well While Old

Our ageist stereotypes *equate* old with ill, old with decrepit, old with physical and mental decline. Yet the majority of people over age 85 do *not* require assistance in daily living[40] and some of these *provide* assistance. Today there's an increasing cohort of very well, very old people. There's even a term for them: SuperAgers. The MacArthur Foundation Research Network on an Aging Society reports that from 1982 to 1994, the number of elders unable to perform daily tasks *decreased* by almost 3.6 percent, the result being 1.2 million *fewer* disabled elders in 1994.[41] This trend continued, although at present, as we shall see, we are backsliding.

We do know that disability does not prevent a person from making significant and even transcendent contributions to art or to the community. Consider the painter Henri Matisse (1869–1954), the dancer/choreographer Martha Graham (1894-1991), the jazz musician/producer Quincy Jones (b. 1933), the poet Stephen Kuusisto (b. 1955). Would we even dream of shunting such world-class creators into an impairment statistic? Yet Matisse used a wheelchair, Jones uses a wheelchair, Graham suffered from severe arthritis, and Kuusisto is blind. The World Health Organization estimates that about 15 percent of the world's population live with a disability of one sort or another.[42] Some are old. Some of these old disabled persons are world-class creators.

Whether or not we are able-bodied, as we age, our bodies begin to show wear. If they didn't, we could join the tardigrades, microscopic animals that apparently do not die, or a species of jellyfish that, under threat, reverts to an earlier stage of biological development and begins again, or sentient beings called green hydras that live in fresh water. They can be killed of course but do not appear to age or die as a biological necessity.[43]

These creatures may or may not be immortal, but we are mortal. Our skin ages. For some of us, our vision will get weaker or our hearing will get worse. Half of all persons over 75 suffer at least some hearing loss. One-sixth of all persons over 75 have vision loss. Indeed, as neuroscientist Daniel J. Levitin reports in his book *Successful Aging*, 90 percent of people over age 55 wear eyeglasses.[44] But listen. I have worn eyeglasses since I was 3 years old. (Before that I wore an eye patch.) This has never prevented me from reading a book, writing a poem, or teaching a class. And let's keep in mind that younger people who live with a disability are, like everybody else, also aging.

What of memory loss? According to Laura L. Carstensen of the Stanford Center on Longevity, "dementia risk doubles with every five years after 65."[45] A 2011 National Institute on Aging (US) report found that 25 to 30 percent of all persons aged 85 or over have dementia. In 2018 the US office of Health and Human Services reported that 33 percent of persons over age 90 had dementia. And, according to the World Health Organization, 5 to 8 percent of the world population over the age of 60 has dementia. Dementia is not, WHO emphasizes, a normal part of aging.[46]

Here is a good place to stop and say that although memory loss is not to be wished for, if it does happen it is not the end of life nor of the world. People with memory loss can actually develop enhanced creative abilities (due to greater disinhibition). They may become especially good at improv theater, due to living more in the present moment. This is demonstrated by Seattle's Re-Ignite the Mind Improv Theater. People with memory loss also turn out to be very good at visual art, as demonstrated by an exhibition of watercolors titled "The Art of Alzheimer's: The Artist Within" mounted a few years ago at Seattle's City Hall. The organizer of the exhibition said, "While most stories about dementia are ones of sadness, the 51-painting exhibition creates a new narrative—a story of hope and joy." An article about the exhibition reported that "approximately 50 close-knit and supportive Alzheimer's community members turned out for the event…celebrating the artists and helping ensure their journey of memory loss isn't experienced alone."[47]

In addition to the positive development of creative and caring communities being formed around people with memory loss, there is growing knowledge and hope for retaining one's mental sharpness. For the generation born before 1946, dementia rates, for reasons not entirely understood, fell dramatically. Over the 12 years from 2000 to 2012, the dementia rate in Americans aged 65 and older fell by 24 percent, so that 11.6 percent of this population had dementia in 2000, whereas in 2012 the rate had fallen to 8.8 percent. This means one and a half million persons who would have had dementia under the 2000 rate, in 2012 did not have dementia. Carstensen notes that each cohort (of Americans) that reached age 90 had been healthier than the one before.[48]

And a large study, the "Health and Retirement Study" at the University of Michigan, led by Hui Zheng, found cognitive functioning steadily improving within populations born before 1947.[49] Most importantly, lifestyle factors (see ahead) "may help to prevent one-third of dementia cases."[50] So writes neuroscientist Daniel J. Levitin.

But if healthy lifestyles can prevent dementia, unhealthy lifestyles can foster it. In the United States, in addition to COVID-19, poor economic conditions, including increasing inequality of wealth and unequal access to healthcare, have eroded gains in longevity. We are going backwards. The causes of many deaths in middle age—among people of all races—are suicides, drug overdoses, and alcohol-related deaths, as well as diseases such as diabetes. Our current obesity epidemic works against longevity.[51]

The Health and Retirement Study at the University of Michigan found that for those born after 1947, there was an alarming level of cognitive decline, beginning as early as age 50. The reasons, according to study author Hui Zheng:

Lower household wealth; less likelihood of marriage; higher levels of loneliness, depression and psychiatric problems; and an increase in cardiovascular risk factors such as obesity, physical inactivity and diabetes among boomers.[52]

Zheng notes that cognitive function may have links to aspects of what he calls "modern life," such as the increase in economic inequality and feeling less connected to friends. "Part of the story here is the problems of modern life, but it is also about life in the U.S.," he said. He mentions the cost of health care in America and the lack of universal health care that other nations provide.[53] But, he continues, "research suggests mental decline may be reversible with changes in individual behavior."[54]

This news about mental decline in the baby boomer cohort is very bad, but is it news about aging? Does mental decline come naturally with age? The steadily improving cognitive health of generations previous to the boomers tell us that, no, this is not about aging.

The lives of vital, active, even athletic old people counter the notion that age equals decline. So, here goes.

In 2018, Katherine Beiers, age 85, completed the Boston marathon.[55] In 2019 another old competitor to finish the Boston marathon, Larry Cole, was also age 85. In 2018, Canadian Betty Jean McHugh, age 90, continued to run marathons. She began running in her 50s. She considers the age 90 to be "just a number."[56]

Not to forget Spokane-based Sister Madonna Buder (b. 1930), aka "the Iron Nun," who by her late 80s had competed in 400 triathlons, forty-five of them Ironmans (you swim 2.4 miles, bike 112 miles, and run 26.2-miles).[57] Now that she is in her 90s though, she's had to slow down. On her daily routine she swims a half-mile, rides a bike for twenty miles, and goes for a three-mile run.[58]

As I write these words an email arrives from my friend the writer Jim Herod (b. 1937), age 81, mathematics professor emeritus. He had just completed a 10k race (beating out his 70-year-old competitor). Herod began running as a paperboy delivering the *Selma Times Journal* to his customers in Orville, Alabama. Occasionally his bike would break down, prompting him to run his route. He continued running through high school, college, graduate school, the army, and throughout his career as mathematics professor at Georgia Tech University. So, running is nothing new. Herod just keeps running. His writing though, has shifted from papers with titles like "Series Solutions for Nonlinear Boltzmann Equations" to short stories, memoirs, local history, and blogs.[59]

In September 2017, Colorado climber Robert Kelman, age 87, became the oldest person to climb Devil's Tower, in northeast Wyoming. He summited Devil's Tower two years after open-heart surgery.[60] And Seattle's Stimson Bullitt (1919–2009), always a lover of the mountains of the Pacific Northwest, summited Denali, North America's highest peak, at age 62. At age 70 he took up technical rock climbing. At age 79 he climbed the north side of 9,415-foot Mount Stuart. At age 83 he successfully executed a difficult climb known as Illusion Dweller at Joshua Tree National Park. Stimson Bullitt continued climbing until about two years before his death at age 89.[61]

How can an 85-year-old scale a mountain? How can a 90-year-old run a marathon? They can because they want to. They can

Jim Herod, age 80, November 25, 2017, 10-kilometer race at Old Lock One, Tombigbee River, Alabama.

because they think they can. They can because they train. As cosmetics entrepreneur Mary Kay Ash (1918–2001) put it, "If you think you can, you can. If you think you can't, you're right."[62]

Let me clarify: It's not that any one of us could or would want to run a marathon. But these aged athletes make it impossible to say that this or that person is *too old* to run a marathon. It is true that our old body is less flexible, more prone to injury, and slower to heal. Old athletes modify their training accordingly. But, much age-related deterioration, write Anders Ericsson and Robert Pool in their book *Peak*, "happens because people decrease or stop their training." The authors point out that as an increasing number of older people train to run marathons, at this point "a quarter of marathon runners in their sixties can be expected to outperform more than half of their competitors between the ages of twenty and fifty-four." They point to Don Pellmann (1915–2020), who in 2015 became the first person 100 years old or older to run 100 meters in fewer than twenty-seven seconds.[63]

Whatever thing we might want to take up, we are not *too old* to take it up. Thinking you can is crucial. And nowhere does *thinking you can* have more force than in the arena of creative work.

Powerful creators who are old or even ancient abound. I think of Stanley Kunitz (1905–2006), who at age 95 became the tenth Poet Laureate of the United States. That year his collected poems received the National Book Award. He continued composing poems until his death at age 100. Shortly before his death his assistant asked him how he had repeatedly used the power of his mind to overcome obstacles. His answer: "I don't know, but it's been a principle all along to do what I can and more. And it's amazing that if you believe in that, there's almost nothing that stands in your way except your own restrictiveness."[64]

I think of dancer and choreographer Martha Graham, who revolutionized dance; who continued to dance into her 70s; who created 181 original dances, twelve of them in her last decade; who choreographed her last work, "Maple Leaf Rag," at age 96.[65] I think of the painter Wayne Thiebaud (1920–2021), actively painting in his late 90s. "What keeps you going," Thiebaud said, "is the thrill of experiment and expectation. That's what you do as a painter. You live on hope...that next picture."[66]

These old athletes and old creators possess a key attribute of people who experience what is known as optimal aging: They have a passion or enthusiasm great enough to occupy at least three hours a day.[67] (The other attributes are lowering stress, connecting with others, and regular exercise—especially walking and weight training.)

The stereotype of old as decrepit is just that—a stereotype. Some of us are old and sick or disabled. (Some of us are young and sick, young and disabled.) Some of us are old and vigorous, old and active, old and very accomplished. Some of us are old and disabled but also active and very accomplished. Ill health and disability can strike at any time of life. Physical decline is inevitable; death is inevitable. Poor health in old age does happen, but it is not inevitable.

There are diseases that are particularly associated with older age—cancer, cardiac disease, diabetes... So yes, we might fall ill or down. We might also live through setbacks and illnesses, just as many centenarians have done. We might recover and go on living for years or even decades.

A 2014 study found that chronological age is no longer a proper metric forecasting population health, dependency, and costs to society, since substantial numbers of older individuals are living "healthy and active lives and...are largely indistinguishable from their younger contemporaries."[68]

## Disabled Creator / Great Art

But suppose we do become disabled? Suppose life throws us some untoward limitation? The first thing to say is that, like everyone else, disabled persons of all ages are aging. Some older persons live with a disability because they have been disabled since they were younger. Other older persons become disabled in older age.

Artists begin making a work within the confines of a *chosen* limitation. A painter starts painting on a canvas of a particular size. That is a limitation. A poet setting out to write a sonnet chooses a limitation: fourteen lines and a volta—that big turn in thought or argument. The composer of a sonata will think of three parts—exposition, development, recapitulation.

So what of limitations visited upon us by illness or old age? The fact is that a life of creativity—a life of artmaking or photographing or poem-making or novel writing or filmmaking—does not *require* us to be able-bodied.

In her 70s and 80s the painter Alma Thomas had severe arthritis. A decade before her death at age 86 she said, "I'd like to make my canvasses bigger, like Sam Gilliam, but my arthritis is so bad that I can't get up on a ladder." Besides this, in 1974, when she was in her early 80s, Thomas broke her hip. So what did she do? A friend related, "She used to paint with the paintings on her lap because she couldn't stand up long....At the very end she had herself wedged in, to be able to stand up to paint, she was so weak." What Thomas herself said was, "Do you see this painting? Look at it move. That's energy and I'm the one who put it there....I transform energy with these old limbs of mine."[69]

Hungarian-born Eva Zeisel (1906–2011) lived to be 105. She was an industrial designer and a ceramicist, designing everyday objects such as bowls and cups and plates. As a younger woman she spent five years in the Soviet Union and then sixteen months in a Stalinist prison, twelve of them in solitary confinement. Eventually she got to America. Her show at the Museum of Modern Art in 1946 was the first one-woman show at MoMA.

In her 90s Zeisel went blind from macular degeneration. But she continued to design using her hands and balsawood and she continued to get big commissions.

Was it more difficult to work like that? To an interviewer she answered, "The process—getting shapes out of air—is always the same."[70]

The singer-songwriter Johnny Cash (1932–2003) was 71 years old when he died on September 12, 2003. His hard-drinking, hard-driving life was hard on his body. In the early 1980s he underwent stomach surgery to correct problems caused by years of amphetamine use. His career had turned stale and uninspired. In 1987 he underwent heart surgery. In the late 1990s he was diagnosed with Shy-Drager syndrome, a catastrophic nervous-system disorder that causes loss of fine motor skills, mask appearance of the face, difficulty chewing and swallowing, dizziness, fainting, difficulty walking, difficulty speaking, changes in the voice, and a monotone speaking voice. Later he was re-diagnosed with "autonomic neuropathy." Same symptoms, different label.

In his last decade, the great singer, with the help of a great producer, Rick Rubin, embraced rock music and went on an alternative rock tour. He made six new albums. The first won a Grammy. The albums include grim and powerful songs such as "God's Gonna Cut You Down." In 2002, the year before his death, Cash released the penultimate album—an astonishing eclectic range of covers and original songs. Four months before his death, June Carter Cash, the love of his life, died. The next day, Cash said to his producer, "I need to have something to do every day. Otherwise there's no reason for me to be here." Cash worked every day for three more months. A week before his death he completed the final track of his final album. His voice is broken. The songs are mournful, slow, painful, full of grief.[71]

Johnny Cash has never been more powerful.

John Huston (1906–1987) the filmmaker, actor, writer, and director of such films as *The Maltese Falcon* (1941) and *The African Queen* (1951), directed his last film, *The Dead* (1987), based on the famous short story by James Joyce, from a wheelchair. He was suffering from emphysema and died shortly after it was completed.[72] The New Yorker film critic Pauline Kael, in a rave review of this film, wrote:

> Huston directed the movie, at eighty, from a wheelchair, jumping up to look through the camera, with oxygen tubes trailing from his nose to a portable generator; most of the time he had to watch the actors on video monitor outside the set and use a microphone to speak to the crew. Yet he went into dramatic areas that he'd never gone into

before—funny, warm family scenes that might be thought completely out of his range....He's given [the James Joyce story] a marvelous filigree that enriches the social life. And he's done it all in a mood of tranquil exuberance, as if moviemaking had become natural to him, easier than breathing.[73]

The Impressionist painter Pierre-Auguste Renoir (1841–1919) was, for the last thirty years of his life, progressively disabled with rheumatoid arthritis. In the last years the pain was severe, and yet he kept painting. His son, the filmmaker Jean Renoir (1894–1979) wrote movingly of his father: "His hands were terribly deformed. His rheumatism had made the joints stiff and caused the thumbs to turn inward towards the palms, and his fingers to bend towards the wrists. Visitors who were unprepared for this could not take their eyes off the deformity."

Renoir could no longer walk. He had to be lifted out of his bed and onto his wheelchair. His skin became so sensitive that holding a paintbrush in his hand injured it, so a soft piece of cloth was put in his curled palm and he gripped the brush rather than held it. But, as his son wrote, "The more intolerable his suffering became, the more Renoir painted." His eyes remained acute, his arm steady.

On his last day an infection developed in the painter's lungs, and he could not leave the bed. "He asked for his paintbox and brushes, and he painted the anemones...for several hours he identified himself with these flowers, and forgot his pain. Then he motioned for someone to take his brush and said 'I think I am beginning to understand something about it.'"[74] He died that night. He was 78 years old.

The painter Henri Matisse lived for 84 years. After being operated on for intestinal cancer at the age of 71 (in 1941), he could no longer leave his wheelchair or bed—and *this* is when he began his amazing cutout series. He constructed the group of works comprising *Jazz* by cutting shapes out of painted drawing paper, and, with the aid of assistants, pinning and repining them to his wall, endlessly adding and shifting components. He completed *Jazz* in 1946.[75] Among the other masterworks of his old age is the Dominican chapel at Vence, France. Matisse worked on all aspects of the small chapel, from its architecture to its stained-glass windows to its large mural drawings on the tile walls to its wrought-iron spire. He began work on it in 1948. He was then 78. He completed the chapel and it was consecrated in 1951.[76]

During this period of Matisse's late work, Picasso and his companion, the painter Françoise Gilot (b. 1921), would visit him. In *Life with Picasso* Gilot writes:

> Matisse was confined to his bed for three-quarters of the day but that didn't dampen his enthusiasm for the project. He had paper fixed to the ceiling over his bed, and at night, since he didn't sleep much, he would draw on it with a piece of charcoal attached to the end of a long bamboo stick, sketching out the portrait of St. Dominic and other elements of the decoration. Later, he would roll around in his wheelchair and transfer his drawings to large ceramic squares covered with a semi-mat enamel on which he could draw in black.[77]

But what about dance? Isn't dancing a young person's art? The dancer, actor, and choreographer Carmen De Lavallade (b. 1931) has this to say:

> Most dancers today will stop dancing when they're in their 40s. They start thinking of themselves as old at 40. And when I was coming up I was watching Martha Graham and José Limón and they were more than 40...It never dawned on me to stop, I mean, I have to adjust, I think we adjust but I always found...when you're young and you have that facility it's FUN to use all that energy but as you get older, certain things take over and it gets more tuned. You don't HAVE to throw your leg over your head to say what you want to say. The vocabulary changes....

One time, De Lavallade continues, she was in a film (she was in her 70s) and during the shoot she had to go up and down a staircase for five hours. When she got home her legs were, she said "not speaking to her." In two days she had a solo performance to execute. The piece she was to perform contained both movement and words. She had formerly loved the vigorous dancing part and paid little attention to the words. But in this emergency, she thought:

> Well I've got to change, nobody knows—it's a solo—so I can do what I want—*in comes creativity!* Well, it's really about the words, isn't it? So the words took over and the body was secondary. And I liked it better, it was richer and warmer, and …all of a sudden I heard the words, really for the first time…

During the performance she moved, she danced, she wasn't stationary. But her movements were more subdued and in the new emphasis on the words she found a new richness in the dance.[78]

The jazz pianist Dave Brubeck (1920–2012), who died at age 91, was advised by his doctor to *not* quit performing. At age 80, after returning from a European tour with his wife, having played a set every night, Brubeck told a writer that "he composes every day whether sick or well, and plays if he feels well, and if he is sick he plays until he feels better."[79] In very old age Brubeck would creak onto the stage hauling his oxygen tank, sit, with some difficulty, at the piano, and proceed to give a brilliant performance. He seemed to be in better shape *after* performing than before. He said, "You can be so beat up that you can scarcely walk on stage but when you get to the piano the excitement kicks in, you forget about being tired."[80]

In 2007, Joan Jeffri, director of the Research Center for Arts and Culture at Teachers College of Columbia University, extensively interviewed 213 elderly visual artists (between ages 62 and 97) living in New York City. The interviews were conducted in English, Spanish, and Chinese and the artists were Black, white, Asian, and Hispanic. The study found:

Astonishingly, the resilience of artists in relation to their art is a testimony to old age. All the artists we interviewed visited their studios on a frequent and sometimes daily basis, even if it took 1.5 hours to walk the three blocks to the studio. When the medium became too taxing—such as large-scale sculpture or paintings, not one artist talked of giving up art; s/he simply changed the medium.[81]

For musicians, playing fast may become increasingly difficult in old age. But playing fast is not everything. The saxophonist Sonny Rollins (b. 1930) spoke of hearing his great predecessor Coleman Hawkins (1904–1969) when Hawkins was near the end of his life. Rollins heard Hawkins one night "when he was sick and he really couldn't play all the notes that he usually plays. He only played certain notes but the notes he played were great. He was playing less notes, but each note had such depth and power that it was a revelation."

Sonny Rollins also spoke of his own experiences as a performing jazzman in older age. Speaking in the 1990s—he was in his late 60s—he was, according to his biographer, continually asked to play the kind of music he played in the 1950s. "They don't understand," he said, "that I have a different philosophy; I am trying to change all the time..." Rollins worked on his music constantly, growing and developing, but it was also the case that he had less stamina. "That might be another reason not to go back to playing the way you did a long time ago. It may be physically impossible because of age....I can no longer practice fifteen hours a day like I once did." He added that he had to prove every time he played before an audience, that he could still do it. He had to prove "that I am still capable of playing and maybe even playing better." His biographer, Eric Nisenson, adds: "If you think that Sonny means his own playing is weaker, you probably have not heard him recently." He was no longer comfortable playing at fast tempos but had not lost any technical facility. His music, Nisenson wrote:

is a summary of all he has learned, and explored, during the fifty years of his professional career. Getting older has not made it harder for Sonny to play with a sense of openness and freedom. Instead, endless avenues are open to him every time he plays. He is still discovering new areas, fresh musical concepts, and deeper aspects of himself as grist for his art.[82]

For some artists, disability can bring painful times. Martha Graham had to give up dancing after her last performance in 1969, at age 75, due to severe arthritis that particularly afflicted her hands. She plunged into depression and alcoholism. "Without dancing," she said, "I wanted to die." Three years went by before she reemerged to direct her company, teach, and choreograph.

She put her last years to energetic creative use. A biographer writes: "Still vigorous in her eighties, Martha taught classes at her school almost daily. She supervised rehearsals, coached individual dancers, reconstructed some of her older masterworks, and continued to choreograph new works."[83] Before her death she created more than twenty new works along with thirty revivals.

Merce Cunningham (1919–2009) got his start in Graham's company. Cunningham, who died at age 90, choreographed to the end, finishing with "Nearly 90." In a 1981 interview with the dancer and his domestic partner and collaborator John Cage (1912–1992), Cage remarked, "I noticed that when Merce became 40, critics in London objected to his continuing to dance, because they thought that dancers should be younger. But now that he's… um… even older [Merce was 62] no one seems to object any longer to the fact that he dances…."

Merce says (joking), "They don't *voice* their objections…"

"I think," Cage continued, "they are becoming interested in seeing how long this whole thing is going to go on…." Both laugh.[84]

It went on for twenty-eight more years. Merce Cunningham choreographed and ran his studio, teaching and coaching his dancers up until his death. He himself danced well into his 80s. The documentary film, *Merce Cunningham: A Life in Dance* by Charles Atlas is a riveting portrait of an old creator. In the mornings, says Cunningham, with an amused look on his face, "the principal problem is to get up—everything hurts." He first does exercises in bed. Then "teeters" into the kitchen and fixes his oatmeal and tea and talks to his cats, both in English and in French (they don't answer). He then draws and writes in his journal (the film shows Cunningham's strangely beautiful drawings of animals). He then "does an hour of further exercises." He then goes to the studio, where he directs his dancers. At the end of the film, we see Cunningham dancing, using a bar, a beautiful thing to behold. He says, "My interest in movement as in dancing is just as fascinating to me now as it ever was, if not more so."[85]

Old age can be a time of vigorous health and creativity. Or it can be a time of challenging disability and creativity. Either way creativity can flourish.

## Ageism: Its Toxic Effects

It cannot be stated too often: Internalized ageism—whether conscious or not—is an important *cause* of decline. Researchers Sarit A. Golub et al. write that "stereotypes about aging are processed mindlessly by individuals in their youth and…this mindless encoding may lead to erroneous perceptions about the elderly and even the enactment of learned stereotypes as one ages."[86] Jonathan Rauch, author of *The Happiness Curve: Why Life Gets Better After 50*, wrote, "Evidence suggests that children form negative attitudes toward aging as early as the fourth grade….Those implanted stereotypes are carried within us like rotten seeds, sprouting decades later into deprecatory self-images and comments. When we act on the stereotypes, and transmit them to others, we make them self-fulfilling. Experiencing an ordinary memory glitch, we think nothing of saying 'Sorry, I had a senior moment.'"[87]

One study primed one group of subjects with images of aged decrepitude (the screen flashed images too fast for conscious awareness) and primed a second group with images of aged vitality and intelligence. Afterwards, the group primed with decrepitude wrote with significantly shakier handwriting.[88]

In another study, a group of 20-year-olds primed with negative stereotypes of old age were timed as they walked to the elevator. These young adults walked quite a bit slower than the control group not so primed. A similar study had persons aged 63 to 80 play a computer game in which some were primed with positive images of old age and some with negative. Afterwards, the ones primed with positive images walked faster—much faster.[89]

Yet another study suggested that the *belief* that memory deficits come with old age can *cause* memory deficits. The study primed subjects with negative and positive images of old age. Words flashed were *incompetent, decrepit, diseased* and, in contrast, *guidance, sage,* and *accomplished.* The result: "Older participants exposed to the positive age stereotype primes performed significantly better on the memory test than those older participants exposed to the negative age stereotype primes."[90]

Most importantly, a study tested the memories of old people living in two places where the elderly are highly esteemed—in the American Deaf community and in Mainland China. In these communities the memories of the old were equal to those of the young. Both groups outperformed American hearing elders.[91]

Americans who can hear live in a culture shot through with ageism, some of which we've inevitably internalized. How could we not in our youth-obsessed culture in which ageist statements are made publicly and without embarrassment? Facebook CEO Mark Zuckerberg: "Young people are just smarter."[92] Which, if true, makes it odd that in the United States twice as many founders of *successful* technology businesses are over 50 than are under 25.[93] And with the painful advent in 2019 of the worldwide COVID-19 pandemic, which tends to make older people more seriously ill, the publicly expressed ageism is at times hard to tell from fascism: Lt. Governor Dan Patrick of Texas announced his view that old people should volunteer to die to save the economy.[94] California Governor Gavin Newsom's administration advised hospitals to prioritize younger people with greater life expectancy for care during the coronavirus outbreak. Although this was quickly retracted, it is pretty shocking nonetheless.[95]

Ageism hurts us all (including young people, see ahead) and it harms our future well-being. But having a positive view of aging and of those who have grown old does more than make a person feel better about growing older. As Ashton Applewhite reports in her book *This Chair Rocks: A Manifesto Against Ageism,* "People with positive perceptions of aging actually live longer—a whopping 7.5 years longer—in large part because they're motivated to take better care of themselves."[96]

The way forward into thriving in old age involves continuing or learning to honor ourselves and our lives in the midst of our current challenges. It may involve transforming a situation in which we have always put others first. It may involve dealing with or healing from trauma. It may involve working with and overcoming long-held negative ideas, such as "I am too dumb" or "I am too old" to do this or to learn that. It is *never* too late. In her book *Keep It Moving* the dancer/choreography Twyla Tharp (b. 1941) writes, "Age is not the enemy. Stagnation is the enemy. Complacency is the enemy. Stasis is the enemy."[97]

## Ageism Hurts the Young

Persons in youth or middle age who are full of ageist biases deprive their own selves of a promising future. Instead of seeing possibilities expanding as they grow older, they see possibilities shrinking. They are driving themselves into the dead end of thinking they will be unable to do this or that when older or old. And if you think you can't...

Indeed, a young adult who harbors ageist attitudes jeopardizes his or her very life in older age. Longitudinal studies by Becca R. Levy and her team at the Yale School of Public Health found that "young adults holding more-negative age stereotypes were twice as likely to experience cardiovascular events up to 40 years later than their young adult peers holding more-positive age stereotypes, after adjusting for relevant covariates including family history of cardiovascular disease."

There are other unfortunate consequences for younger people holding ageist attitudes. When these young people grow older, their negative attitudes regarding old age exacerbate chronic stress, which harms the body. And ageism affects behavior: people with positive views of aging tend to take better care of themselves in terms of exercise, nutrition, and health care. Finally, Levy and her team have found that "negative age stereotypes predict detrimental brain changes decades later, including the accumulation of plaques and tangles and reduction in size of the hippocampus"—that brain organ essential for memory.[98]

Jonathan Rauch (*The Happiness Curve*) points to negative attitudes toward growing old—the expectation that old age will be a time of humiliation and decrepitude—as feeding what is commonly termed the midlife crisis. "Why do so many people imagine that if they are not satisfied with their lives in midlife, they never will be? Why do they believe that time is growing short at age fifty….? Why, looking ahead, do they see a future of decline? Very largely because the stereotypes about late adulthood backflow into middle age."[99] It's not so much that the person in crisis is thinking about old age. It's more about "how my life has turned out," which is another way of thinking of middle age as the concluding chapter.

In the words of psychiatrist Gene D. Cohen, "If potential in later life is denied, then we do not plan or prepare for it. With awareness of it, our sense of opportunity, challenge, and responsibility is altered in a positive way."[100]

For myself, let me say this. I can't predict the future. But right now, I'm happy—very happy—to be in my late 70s. I'm in the prime of life, fruitfully immersed in the process of writing poems, essays, short stories, books. Never have I been more productive. I continue to teach. I'm connected to good friends, family members, my partner, and to many fellow poets and writers in my community. After a recent year of recovering from a broken ankle, I feel fine—healthy and strong. I'm not an athletic type, far from it, but I dutifully walk my five miles per day. I lift weights. I do yoga, (though not as much as I should). I live by myself, happily so. I write these words not to boast or pat myself on the back or any such thing. I write them to counter the negative narrative about age and about aging I hear again and again during the course of any given week. It shocks me. I'm here to say that this common-as-dust negative narrative is not my narrative. It's not "just how things are." It's not the narrative of the numerous aged and even ancient creators presented in this book. These artists, whether able-bodied or disabled, whether well-off financially or just barely getting along, inspire me and inform me of what might be possible for me in very old age. It is my hope that you the reader can also take hope and inspiration from their lives and work.

## Composing Our Lives: Old Age

Two principles are key to composing a deeply satisfying old age. The first is to live and work toward our goals in a spirit of self-compassion, treating ourselves as we would a good friend. The second is to make any desired lifestyle change a bit at a time, to proceed in small steps. Crash diets don't work. If we intend to set a new course or change direction or embark on a new plan, if we want to change our lifestyle, the transition is likely to be gradual, done in small steps. For this reason, I pose the question: How could I improve this matter by 5 percent? These two principles—self-compassion and a commitment to gradual shifts—also make an excellent foundation for doing creative work of any kind.

For each of these writing prompts, write for five or ten minutes.

1. Are you in the habit of negative self-talk, sarcasm when it comes to your own life or self or body? What sorts of things do you tell yourself? Do you think or say things about yourself that you wouldn't dream of saying to anyone else? Do you put yourself down? What kinds of things do you say to encourage yourself?

2. In what ways might you become a better friend to yourself? How might you treat yourself better by 5 percent?

3. Write for ten minutes doing nothing more than encouraging yourself in every possible way.

Bessie, left, and Sadie Delany in the cover photo of the book *Having Our Say:
The Delany Sisters' First 100 Years* By Sarah L. Delany, A. Elizabeth Delany and
Amy Hill Hearth (copyright 1993). *Photo by Brian Douglas; photo copyright by
Amy Hill Hearth. Used by permission of Amy Hill Hearth, copyright 2022.*

# 2. Brilliant Old Brains

*Alex Katz is on fire.*
—Calvin Tomkins, writing of the 91-year-old painter[101]

The phrase "senior moment" implies that senility arrives with old age the way taxes arrive with April. Yet many old people and even very old people have excellent memories. When a young person forgets where they put their keys, we don't attribute this to their age. Nor should we when an old person forgets their keys. Suggestion: Let's dump the phrase "senior moment."

Forgetfulness is an occasional visitor to persons of all ages. But that's not even the main point. The main point is a study led by linguist and cognitive scientist Michael Ramscar, at University of Tubingen in Germany.[102] Ramscar and team programmed a computer to simulate the human brain. They then loaded this computer with more and more experiences, information, and vocabulary until they got an approximation of an older person's brain. The more loaded up with information the computer was, the slower it was at coming up with words and with the names of things.

The computer was not in decline. It had more associations, more connections, more information to sift through. In calling up a name or a word, it had a bigger job to do. Michael Ramscar stated that when he started, "I was a firm believer in the dotage curve."[103] But because the simulations mapped cognitive processes so accurately, he was forced to acknowledge that he didn't need to invoke decline at all.

Older brains are fuller brains. They are replete with more information, more experience, more vocabulary. In addition, older brains work differently from younger brains. Young people tend to use one side of the brain or the other, depending on the task. Old people tend to use both sides of the brain on any task. This according to a study at Duke University of both young and old brains.[104] Old brains are more synchronized. More hyper-connected. Better—in theory at least—at high-level creative work. Older brains have more associations, which benefit creative work and give the older brain a larger resource base.

Here's an experience I had forgetting the names of things. I'm a gardener, and on most days I go into the garden, if only to gaze at the plants. But one rainy October evening, walking down the street, I slipped on a leaf, turned my ankle and broke it. I underwent surgery involving a titanium nail pounded into my malleolus and a brace screwed into my fibula. There followed the cast, the knee cart, the boot, the walker, the crutches, and finally the walking stick. Entering the garden was risky due to uneven terrain. When I finally returned, I could not recall the name of two or three plants that I myself had planted. Later, though, I sat down with my journal and listed seventy-five plants in my garden whose names I *did* remember. So, I ask you, which of these moments—forgetting the names of three plants or remembering the names of seventy-five plants—counts as the *more* senior moment?

## Keeping Our Wits About Us

We know that we cannot control our fate. But we can influence it. We can work to protect the health of our brain. Indeed, the creator immersed in creative work, who also connects with likeminded peers, goes a long way toward a lifestyle that supports vitality and mental acuity in old age. Researchers have learned a lot about daily practices that support a vibrant and creative old age. These are, in short:

• learn
• exercise
• if you smoke, quit
• eat right

- reduce stress
- connect with others
- pursue goals with passion

## Learn

John Medina, molecular biologist and author of the book *Brain Rules for Aging Well*, calls what we must do "aggressive learning." Learn a new language: Bilingual persons do significantly better on cognitive tests, "regardless of the age at which the language is learned."[105] Learn a musical instrument. (I've taken the hint and begun lessons on my old-time banjo, abandoned forty years ago.) Read books—voraciously. "If the brain is to remain healthy," wrote the neurologist Oliver Sacks, "it must remain active, wondering, playing, exploring, and experimenting right to the end."[106]

An even more emphatic point of view has been put forward by neuroscientist Rachel Wu and her team at CALLA (Cognitive Agility Across the Lifespan via Learning and Attention) at University of California, Riverside.[107] In their view, the best defense against cognitive decline is cognitive development. It's not about maintenance. And cognitive development happens in adults the same way it happens in children. The learning environment required is the same. Begin with intellectual engagement. Which involves the following:

- Input from the immediate environment, rather than using past knowledge or experience.
- Individual scaffolding. We need to learn in steps and at our own pace.
- Growth mindset. The belief that abilities are not fixed or limited. They develop from the effort and dedication of the learner.
- A forgiving environment. This environment is supportive and non-perfectionist and sees the making of mistakes as part of the learning process.
- A serious commitment to learning. Eschew a "hobbyist" attitude in which one quits when things become difficult.
- Learning multiple skills at the same time, as children do.

This last point gave me pause. Should one become a dabbler? A dilletante? But I can see it another way. I practice my banjo for about an hour a day. Now, I own a DVD "Teaching Company" course on music theory. It has been sitting on the shelf. Learning music theory is a different skill, one to which I aspire, and I doubt it would hurt my banjo playing! But if I alternate days studying music theory with days practicing my instrument, I would be practicing only half as long; my playing would undoubtedly deteriorate. But what if I practiced banjo every day, as usual, and studied music theory one day a week? My knowledge of music theory would develop slowly, but so what? It would develop. Nothing lost, everything gained.

Wu and her associates find that adults become increasingly specialized as they grow older, and as a result, learn less and less. Their notion is to reverse this trend.

In Italy, Giuseppe Paterno (b. ca. 1924), at age 93, entered the University of Palermo to study history and philosophy. He was born into "a very poor family, everything we had was spent on keeping us fed." Despite being a fanatical reader, he had to quit school at age 14 to help support the family. He later married, helped raise two children, and worked for forty-two years as a surveyor on the Italian railways. His retirement afforded him the opportunity to return to his love of philosophy and, eventually, to enter university. Paterno said:

A month in, I contacted the head of the faculty. I was having doubts: everyone else on the course was so much younger than I was; there was so much technology involved I didn't understand. He told me that I must continue, that I have a gift and should persevere. It gave me the strength to carry on.

Soon I didn't feel any different to the other students. I'd read and study just like them. Unlike the others, I used a typewriter to write my thesis rather than a computer. But that didn't matter, the result was the same. Three years later, six weeks before my 97th birthday, I graduated top of my class.[108]

Paterno now plans to go for a master's degree in philosophy. He reflected, "My time at university has changed me for certain. It's as if my brain has evolved; I've started to speak a different language. If I'm discussing the newspaper with my friends, I can articulate myself with greater precision....I'm still the same man I've been for coming up to a century, just with a few minor upgrades."[109]

Any artist going in a new direction is puzzling, playing, exploring, and experimenting. This artist may face a steep learning curve, not a bad idea. Washington DC sculptor Marilee Shapiro Asher (1912–2020) had her first show in Chicago in 1938 and her work has sold for decades in DC galleries. In her late 80s, she began to find sculpting in heavy bronze too physically challenging. She switched to digital photography, taking a class at the Corcoran School of Arts and Design, and then found a teacher to continue teaching her Photoshop. In her 90s and 100s, using a walker to assist her in getting around, she continued to make art. Asked, at age 106, if she would ever stop, she said, "You can't stop even if you wanted to!"

Asher was ever-curious about the world around her. She stated, "I'm fascinated by what's going on in science, in physics, in breakthroughs of all kinds. It's a big regret about dying, I won't know what's going to be!"[110]

At the age of 67, the painter David Hockney (b. 1937) turned from oil painting to watercolor, feeling its greater immediacy. To an interviewer Hockney explained:

> The thing is it does take a while to master the techniques—having to work, say, from light to dark, because unlike with oils, you won't be able subsequently to daub a light color over a dark one. Everything has to be thought out in advance—and I realized it would take time to master all this. I had to ask myself, was I going to be willing to take six months to learn all this? Well, I was and I did, and it took even longer, mastering the medium, innovating new techniques, but by the end I'd broken into this looser, more immediate way of being present to my material.[111]

Now in his 80s, Hockney has turned to making art on his iPad, with a *New Yorker* cover done using this technology appearing in December 2020 and an exhibit of digital works in Paris. At age 83, Hockney explained to an interviewer, "I did say I was drawing on the iPad, but actually I'm painting on it. I've got two hundred and twelve paintings done this year with only eight more to do....Then I'll have done two hundred and twenty paintings for 2020."[112] He also planned to go back to painting with paint.

Anna Mary Robertson Moses constantly prodded herself to learn. More than a half-century after her death, her reputation is shifting from that of a quaint folk artist to an artist whose "all-at-once compositions are indeed modern" in the words of *New Yorker* art critic Peter Schjeldahl.[113] Moses, following her enormous fame and commercial success, resisted pressure to repeat what people loved, what they wanted. A biographer wrote:

> Time and again she tried to tackle problems that posed a challenge, as though to prove to herself that she could still learn and progress. Such experiments often resulted in extraordinary achievements. She continued to the very last her earnest endeavors at "improving" instead of just making it easy for herself.[114]

In his book *Successful Aging*, neuroscientist (and musician) Daniel J. Levitin writes about Andrés Segovia (1893–1987), who launched a new tour at age 93. In an interview the great guitarist stated that he still practiced five hours a day. Why? "There's this one passage that has been giving me a little bit of trouble." Along the same lines, at age 80 master cellist Pablo Casals (1876–1973) was asked why he practiced so much. "Because," Casals replied, "I want to get better!"[115]

"Trying something new later in life," wrote Levitin, "like competitive sports, business enterprises, or artistic endeavors, can dramatically increase both your quality of life and how long you live."[116] Nell Irvin Painter (b. 1942), one of the nation's distinguished historians, author of seven scholarly books, professor of history at

Princeton University, recipient of numerous awards and honors, said goodbye to her academic career at age 64. She entered art school. Thus began a decade of aggressive learning within an entirely different world, in which she was required to move out of her "former realm of historical truth into visual meaning."[117] Painter writes of her experiences as an old art student in her book *Old in Art School*.

The sociologist Sara Lawrence-Lightfoot, for her book *The Third Chapter: Passion, Risk, and Adventure in the 25 Years After 50*, interviewed middle-aged to early-old people with distinguished or even brilliant professional careers, but who became dissatisfied and left everything behind to begin again. Of course, they took with them their values, their experience, and their wisdom, such as it was. Their new endeavors required intense new learning.

One example was "Josh Carter" (Lawrence-Lightfoot changed the names of her subjects). This man was an accomplished journalist, a well-paid and highly respected newspaper executive. He was also a stealth fiction writer. He increasingly felt that despite his "huge salary," he had outgrown his job. He quit (gracefully) and turned to writing fiction, enjoying the slower days and greater control of his time. But soon this new life became not enough. He possessed a "gorgeous Steinway piano" and would sit down to "revisit classical pieces he had played all his life." After several months of growing dissatisfaction, he made the big switch. He began piano lessons with the best jazz pianist in the city—a brilliant taskmaster—and Carter was up to the task. Not that he expected to become a great jazz pianist but that he began each day practicing scales for three hours and then practicing further for another hour. This older creator did not give up writing by any means. But he took on a new kind of learning, the kind, as he explains, that involves "thinking with your body."[118]

The New York–based painter Harry Shapiro (1899–2002) remained obscure as an artist but gained public attention as he turned 100—as a vital, mentally acute centenarian. In his pre-retirement years he worked as a commercial artist drawing dresses and such for catalogs. He painted on the side. "I ate at two tables," he said, "commercial art and fine art."[119] As a centenarian, he was pictured in *Life* magazine and became the subject of a National Public Radio broadcast. He was studied by the New England Centenarian Study and by the Albert Einstein College of Medicine. His mental acuteness was tested by Marjory Silver of the New England study, and he passed tests, such as repeating back eight numerals, which many younger people fail. Of him Silver said, "What was really typical about him was his constant learning. He was constantly thinking of new things. He loves to learn. He describes himself as a little boy, loving to learn things, and that lasted his entire life, and consequently, every time he learned something, his brain was building up more ability to learn. He was building new pathways, new connections between the neurons..." Shapiro himself said: "I think the reason I've lasted so long on this earth is because of my love of painting and music and literature... things that lift the spirit of man up."[120]

Creative work itself exercises the brain. "Every project you undertake," wrote Levitin, "requires...some way of looking at the world differently, and then acting on it."[121]

In my experience making a new work is a matter of, first, intending. At this moment I intend to compose a book of poems titled *Somewhere / Nowhere / Here: Cartographies of Home*. It involves the idea of home, of homing, of nesting, of location and of dislocation. It involves remembering home—my homes—past and present, and my own search for a home. It involves researching ideas of home in art, since some of the poems will be ekphrastic—based on an artwork. It involves looking at the loss of home, the painful human dislocations and migrations disrupting the world today. It involves a long period of working on the poems, their forms and language. It involves workshopping the poems with my longtime Third Sunday workshop, sharing them and learning from the critiques of these old friends and fellow poets. Finally, I will read individual poems at open mics around town, or on Zoom. I will send them out to literary magazines to be considered for publication. I will send out the completed book to publishers for consideration. Making art is absorbing, engaging, challenging, exhilarating, and yes, it exercises the brain.

## Exercise

What we must wrap our minds around is physical exercise. Thirty to sixty minutes a day of brisk walking is enough to make a rather staggering difference in terms of retaining our wits. Let me revise that. According to the book by Eric B. Larson, MD, and Joan DeClaire, *Enlightened Aging*, a large study of seniors age 65 and older found that "people who exercised more than fifteen minutes three days a week had a 30 to 40 percent lower risk of Alzheimer's disease and dementia than those who exercised less."[122] And in *Brain Rules for Aging Well*, John Medina reiterates, "greater physical activity means greater intellectual vigor, regardless of age."[123] For persons living with a disability, moving in whatever ways possible contributes to strength and health.

Nicholas Delbanco, in his book on old artists, *Lastingness*, notes how many conductors and orchestra leaders live to old age—from Arthur Fiedler (1894–1979) to Arturo Toscanini (1867–1957). Conducting is, not coincidentally, vigorous aerobic exercise.[124]

In his 90s, the prolific painter Alex Katz (b. 1927) "keeps in shape with a daily regimen of swimming and rigorous exercises," wrote Calvin Tomkins in a *New Yorker* profile. Katz said, "I used to do two hundred sit-ups, three hundred pushups, and a hundred chins....I can't do as many now." Still, he continues to do sit-ups, pushups, and chins. And he makes art, including large public commissions such as the "nineteen five-foot-high paintings, transferred to glass by artisans, and embedded in the walls," which are turning the New York City F train's 57th Street station "into a playground for Katz's boldly colorful high-intensity art."[125]

Before the COVID-19 pandemic, dancer and choreographer Twyla Tharp reported daily to her gym. Working out, now at home, is practically her religion. She says, "I am by now addicted to exercise."[126]

Mick Jagger (b. 1943) of the Rolling Stones trains for some three hours a day for five or six days a week. He jogs, kick-boxes, bicycles, and does weight training under the guidance of a trainer. He also meditates. He does yoga. All of which is required as he continues to work at age 78: His performances involve athletic-level dancing and strutting about onstage at high speed, during which he is estimated to cover twelve miles in a single performance.[127] He just can't be panting and out of breath!

Wayne Thiebaud painted every day, and he played tennis every day too. At age 98 he continued "to get up before first light every day to work in his upstairs studio." Around noon he went out to play doubles on a nearby tennis court. By 2 p.m. he was at work in his midtown (Sacramento) studio. Late in life Thiebaud began painting clowns. The images are magical and tragic, and in a strange way, frightening. They constituted a new body of work first exhibited after the artist turned 99.[128]

The musician and performance poet Patti Smith (b. 1946), when asked what she did to prepare for a stage performance, replied, "I would roam the streets for a few hours."[129] Indeed, walking improves creative thinking. "Walking opens up the free flow of ideas," reports a study in the *Journal of Experimental Psychology* titled "Give Your Ideas Some Legs: The Positive Effect of Walking on Creative Thinking."[130]

The illustrator and children's book author Maurice Sendak (1928–2012) was, according to his friend Twyla Tharp, "a great walker." He and his German shepherd walked "every day for the last twenty years of his life." During his daily constitutional Sendak would "allot at least an hour to find just one novel color or form, one discovery each day."[131]

Swimming works. The acclaimed painter Peter M. Sacks (b. 1950) swims two miles a day, summer and winter (in a wet suit).[132] Berkeley pianist Lily Hearst (1897–2005), who was active and well-respected but not well-known, at age 105 practiced piano and played piano at the senior center every day. She was an active skier until, at age 88 a car hit her and broke both her legs. She swam every day until age 105. Her story is told in the book *Aging Artfully* by Amy Gorman.[133]

I am one of the world's most un-athletic people. My favorite sport is reading a book. I cannot catch a ball and have never been able to catch a ball. I could go on, but I will spare you. However, I have read the science. I am moving more! This is not only about going to the gym or doing jumping jacks or some such every day. It is about going up and down stairs, walking to the store or to work, walking over to speak to your coworker rather than hitting *send* on an email. A book on aging I've found helpful is *The New Rules of Aging Well* by Frank Lipman and Danielle Claro. They have a section titled "Do Your Own Chores":

> You don't want to confine your activity to the time you're able to spend in the gym. It's much more important to be moving all day long....So look for and relish opportunities throughout your day to move, in ordinary ways: squatting to dig through a low drawer, stretching to reach a high shelf, hoisting mulch from the back of a car, helping a neighbor move a picnic table. The everyday work of real life—taking out the trash, moving things around in the garage, mowing the lawn—is the kind of activity that keeps the body nimble and strong.[134]

Lipman and Claro suggest that doing our own chores, rather than outsourcing them, will help us move more.

Any exercise at all is better than none. For substantial health benefits, federal guidelines recommend 2.5 to 5 hours a week of moderate-intensity exercise or 1 hour and 15 minutes to 2 hours and 30 minutes of vigorous to intense exercise. Add to this, weight training at least twice a week, and balance exercises. Exercise—in whatever ways possible—benefits all people, including those living with disabilities.[135]

## Quit smoking

Of course we know this. And I am in deep sympathy with smokers—I used to be one. And there's the point of view of comedian George Burns (1896–1996) with his invariable cigar.

He was asked, at age 97, "What does your doctor say about your smoking and drinking?" "My doctor," he quipped, "is dead."[136] The poet Donald Hall (1928–2018), who lived to age 89, smoked Kent cigarettes (after giving up his cigar), in old age, nearly setting himself on fire any number of times and once wrecking his car while searching for a burning cigarette dropped while driving.[137] But forget George Burns and Donald Hall! Even Keith Richards (b. 1943) of the Rolling Stones, at age 75, quit smoking, difficult as that was.[138] Did I mention that we should quit smoking?

## Eat Right

The Delany sisters, Sarah "Sadie" Delany (1889–1999) and Bessie (Dr. Annie Elizabeth Delany, 1891–1995), were ordinary middle-class centenarians until their memoir, *Having Our Say* (written with Amy Hill Hearth), spent two years on the *New York Times* bestseller list. Sadie states: "About thirty years ago Bessie and I started eating much more healthy foods. We don't eat that fatty Southern food very often. When we do, we feel we can't move! We eat as many as seven different vegetables a day. Plus lots of fresh fruits."[139]

Whatever our diet of origin, whether some form of soul food as for the Delany sisters, or some other cuisine, we can all modify toward more healthy eating. We all know the mantra—more vegetables, more beans, more lentils, more whole grains, more nuts and seeds, more fish, less or no junk food. Eat at home more. Of course, we've *been* eating at home more since the COVID-19 pandemic began upending all our plans. And we have, as a nation, been gaining weight (on average, between seven and twelve pounds).[140] Likely the rise in baking at home has resulted in our scarfing down more cookies, more cakes, more homemade breads. So, what to do? Here again, slow change may work its slow magic. Can I subtract a cookie and add a vegetable?

This is not to say that eating right is always simple, or even, at times, much of a choice. If you are among the food-insecure—as are 10.5 percent of American households amounting to 13.8

million households)—it is not simple. If you are among the 5.5 million persons 60 years or older in the United States who "often go hungry," it is not simple.[141]

## Reduce Stress

Let's say you are out walking your dog in the woods and you startle a bear and this bear, despite your dog's best effort, attacks. What happens in your body? Your adrenal glands, springing into action, produce cortisol, which spurs the production of adrenalin, which tenses muscles, narrows blood vessels, and fully prepares you to counterattack, or, better, run. But what if, with no bear in sight, you are under chronic stress, a worrier, continually stressing out over this or that. Your body is producing cortisol constantly. Cortisol is bathing the neurons of your hippocampus and in fact killing them. And there is more. The brain produces a protein, BDNF (brain-derived neurotrophic factor) that protects its neurons. In experimental animals, chronic stress turns off the gene that produces BDNF, which the hippocampus requires. (I feel for these lab animals.)[142] The lesson: Chronic stress contributes to dementia.

Certain life events arrive with a load of stress. A terminal or serious diagnosis. Divorce, or the death of a close friend or spouse or child. The loss of a job and the resulting financial anxiety. Chronic poverty and the anxiety it fuels. The duties and burdens of caretaking (not to forget that caretaking can also be infused with love and can add meaning to life). Who does not get stressed out by the dreadful events and tragedies reported in the daily news? For some (I am one) a cluttered home stirs up stress. So does having more to do than I can possibly get done in the day. Add your own.

Sitting quietly for even a short time every day with all digital media turned off, breathing deeply, meditating—all reduce stress. There are all sorts of meditation classes with various philosophies, including secular ones (for people of any faith or no particular faith), and there are mindfulness classes. The Northwest Mindfulness classes I attend grew out of Mindfulness Based Stress Reduction founded by Jon Kabat-Zinn at the University of Massachusetts Medical Center. A book of his I find useful is *Mindfulness for Beginners*. There are also yoga classes, Tai Chi classes...any one of these may be helpful.

## Connect with Others

Perhaps nothing is more vital to our well-being as we age. In old age we need companions, cronies, pals, good friends, close connections, whether to relatives or others or both. Someone to gossip with, to confide in. We need to connect not only with peers our age but with people younger than ourselves. We need to participate in our community or communities *actively*—the opposite of just letting things happen.

When you are in college, say, friendships come as part of the territory, at least usually. And later, as a busy person with a full-time job plus raising a family, it works fine to be socially passive. In fact, who has time to be anything else? But in older age, especially as we roll with common, life-transforming punches— retirement or job loss, the inevitable deaths, a change in a significant relationship, a new disability—social passivity is not a workable idea. We may gradually fall into isolation. Isolation, it is said, is as dangerous as drunk driving. Barriers such as a lack of mobility may make it hard to get out of the house. But this is a difficulty to be gotten over, under, or through, a problem to solve, not an impassible wall. Indeed, since the pandemic, many of us have been more or less stuck in our homes. The use of Zoom or Skype or other video media has made meetings, classes, and social occasions more accessible.

Is there someone you are fond of but have neglected? Is there a cause involving social justice or a political candidate or an environmental issue or an economic issue you feel strongly about? Might you join a local group that is working on that issue? Do you enjoy gardening or might you? Could you volunteer to help with a city greening project or join a garden club or a native-plant society? Is there a place in the community you could volunteer? A food bank or a literacy program? Is there a class that would fascinate you?

An excellent resource for people beginning or continuing to learn a skill is the book *Peak* by Anders Ericsson and Robert Pool.[143] It's a book about engaging in "deliberate practice" (rather than mindless practice) toward achieving top form in any given field. To keep motivation high through the stages of learning, the authors suggest joining a group with like interests. And if no such group appears to exist, they suggest *forming* such a group. What a fine idea—not only toward keeping up motivation within some new endeavor but toward joining or helping to form a like-minded community.

Such communities are completely common in the arts. Sarah Yerkes, the poet whose first book of poems, *Days of Blue and Flame*, debuted when she was 101, resides in the Ingleside retirement community in Washington, D.C. Yerkes spoke about the people who drew her to poetry:

> In this poetry workshop I started going to—it was because
> I liked the people who were in the group. A lot of people,
> in life as well as at the Ingleside, have done so many other
> different kinds of things, but they haven't been wildly
> creative. So when a group of potential soulmates turns up,
> I join them.[144]

In his memoir, *Words Without Music*, composer and musician Philip Glass (b. 1937) describes the numerous theater, music, and film associations that have enriched and informed his life. These go from rehearsing and performing with his own music ensemble, to a three-year stint assisting his friend the sculptor Richard Serra (b. 1938), to composing music for films, an intensely collaborative activity. He gives a glimpse of his life in the late sixties:

> I worked full-time with Richard for almost three years. I
> enjoyed the work and it was a great parallel activity to my
> composing for the ensemble, not to mention the theater
> work that I was also doing for Mabou Mines. There was
> enough flexibility in his schedule so that I could still tour
> with the ensemble and perform in and around New York

as the opportunity arose.[145]

Glass discusses his lifelong friendships with musicians, poets, artists, and spiritual seekers from around the world. His life in music has been immersed in sociability and friendship. The community of like-minded creators is both an advantage and a necessity of the creative life. A necessity because one's fellow creators question, probe, praise, criticize, talk shop, and basically live in the same world. Creating in isolation can lead to reinventing the wheel because one had not heard of the wheel.

But we have a problem. The older one gets, the more one's peers and good friends, one's beloveds, precede one in death. Each death leaves a giant hole, and some are devastating. We survivors are the rememberers. We remember and honor and elegize—and we grieve. But we must go on living. Sadie Delany was 106 years old when she lost her beloved sister Bessie, who died at age 104. After she lost Bessie, Sadie wrote:

> Losing your sister after having lived together for more than one hundred years, well, it's a pretty terrible thing. It's like you opened the front door of your house and stepped inside, only there was no house, just a hole in the ground and you keep falling and falling....But what are you going to do? Lay down and die? Jump off a bridge? Somehow or another you live through it. You keep breathing. It's out of your hands. Your body does it whether you want it to or not. Next thing you know you've gotten through the first day, the first week, the first month.[146]

"Nothing can change time," Patti Smith reflected, "or change the fact that I would be turning seventy in the Year of the Monkey [2016]. Seventy. Merely a number but one indicating the passing of a significant percentage of the allotted sand in an egg timer, with oneself the darn egg. The grains pour and I find myself missing the dead more than usual."[147]

Missing the dead is going to be part of it, an increasing part of it, as our significant others come to the end of their lives. I myself can already count nearly twenty of these beloved dead. I catch myself in thoughts like, "I must ask Jerry what he thinks of…" Or, "Waverly would know…" Then I remember.

In his essay "This Old Man," the writer Roger Angell (b. 1920) makes a long affectionate list of his dead, "almost beyond counting, and we want to herd them along, pen them up somewhere to keep them straight."[148] And there in *his* list is one of *my* old friends, a high school friend long out of touch. His list is "almost beyond counting" because he was, at that writing, 93 years old.

Patti Smith tears off a page of her calendar to arrive at the date of her wedding anniversary, "twenty years without him, which prompts me to pull an oblong box from under the bed, opening the lid long enough to smooth the folds of a Victorian dress partially obscured by a fragile veil. Sliding the box back into its place, I feel strangely off-center, a moment of sorrow's vertigo."[149]

Until we become someone else's loss, our inevitable losses mean that younger friends, younger colleagues, and younger peer artists are essential to our well-being and creative thriving. And cross-generation relationships benefit the young as well as the old. Here is Wayne Thiebaud, at age 98:

> I'm working with about eight students from around the country, who come to show their work. They have already graduated and are out in the world. They want to come and talk about their work and about painting. So, I've been doing that [and] I force them to talk critically about my work. They are hesitant at first to do it but once they get at it they are pretty good! They give me a lot of variations and ideas.[150]

Some families make art together across generations, and in this special way older and younger family members partake in sustained meaningful interactions. The jazz pianist and composer Dave Brubeck and his wife, Iola Whitlock Brubeck (1923–2014), a lyricist and librettist, had six children of whom four became professional musicians. Brubeck's biographer wrote:

> If you want to spend more time with your teenage children,
> one sure way to know where they are every night is to play
> jazz with them. Beginning in 1973 [Brubeck was in his
> mid-50s], Brubeck toured with three of his sons—Darius,
> Chris, and Dan—as Two Generations of Brubeck and the
> New Brubeck Quartet, his initial reluctance to embrace
> their newfangled cultural reference points—which
> included rock, funk, and soul music—quickly forgotten.[151]

Brubeck continued performing with his sons throughout his life—the youngest, cellist Matthew, became old enough to join up in the 1980s. Brubeck absorbed the influences and predilections of their generation as they continued to learn from their father and from other musicians of his generation.

Another powerful illustration of old and young artists working together is the documentary film *Places/Faces* (*Villages/Visages*), in French with English subtitles, by the eminent 89-year-old filmmaker (and photographer) Agnès Varda (1928–2019) and the eminent young (early 30s) photographer JR (b. 1983).[152] The film won the L'Œil d'or award at the 2017 Cannes Film Festival. In it Varda and JR drive around to small villages in JR's truck, searching out people to photograph. JR's truck is equipped to print out large-format photos. They paste these enormous prints on the local buildings and barns. The reactions of the people photographed—they have been *seen*, *recognized*—and their communities are very moving. The film is also about the relationship between filmmaker and photographer as they go about making the film. Not to be missed on the DVD is the interview with Varda and JR about their process. The tender friendship and intellectual vibrancy between them is palpable.

## Pursue Goals with Passion

Purposes and goals ebb and flow. They are not one single thing. Are you glad to get up in the morning, happy to get on with your plans? What are your plans? Or do you get up to follow habits and routines unthinkingly? Does your day involve "passing the time," possibly watching a lot of television? A life's purpose comes down to this day's purpose. For you, what is this day's purpose?

"The act of creating," writes Nicholas Delbanco in *Lastingness*, "becomes a *source* of vitality rather than a drain on it."[153] In her 90s, the art photographer Imogen Cunningham (1883–1976) worked seven days a week, ten hours a day. (She was primarily a portrait photographer, so her work involved relating to people constantly.) Asked what her philosophy of life was, she replied, "The goal of life is to get a lot of work done every day." In her introduction to Cunningham's book of photographs titled *After Ninety*, Margaretta Mitchell writes, "The fact that the photographer, beginning in her ninety-second year, worked steadily until her death on 24 June 1976, seeking her subjects, photographing them, selecting and supervising the printing of the photographs, wrapping and sending complimentary prints to sitters is astonishing."[154] Mitchell was writing in the 1970s. Today an older artist's energy and focus seem more common and less astonishing, but Cunningham remains a model of the creative life.

The composer Elliott Carter (1908–2012) wrote music at a steady pace from his adolescence until he died at the age of 103. In his early years he composed very slowly, making thousands of pages of sketches for each score, and spending several years on each new work. But beginning in his mid-70s, according to his *New York Times* obituary, he began composing "at a brisk pace."[155] He died in November 2012, having completed his last piece in August. From *The New York Review of Books*: "More than half of his 150-odd works—including his longest work for orchestra, concertos (or concertinos) for clarinet, flute, horn, violin, cello, and piano, as well as his only opera—were completed after his 85th birthday."[156] He composed his opera, "What Next?," at the age of 90.

At age 104, the Cuban American painter Carmen Herrera (1915–2022) was a poster artist for persistence. She continued to work every day. Although she painted with great dedication and brilliance for her whole life, mostly in New York City, she received little or no recognition (due to some combination of sexism and the fact that she was of Cuban origin) until she received her first one-artist show at age 69. Even then, she did not sell her first painting until age 89. But finally recognition came. A 2009 *New York Times* headline reads: "At 94, She's the Hot New Thing in Painting…"[157] On the occasion of her 2017 Whitney retrospective—she was 101 years old—Adam D. Weinberg, director of the Whitney Museum of American Art, wrote that Herrera had created "a stunning body of work that places Herrera firmly in the pantheon of great postwar abstract painters…" He further wrote:

> Herrera's career reminds us what it takes and means to live as an artist. It cannot be merely a search for recognition. Being an artist is a commitment to the process of discovery, making, and invention. It is often a slow, confusing, difficult, and psychologically challenging endeavor. It takes tremendous grit, courage, and persistence, and the ability to sustain one's efforts in the face of intense criticism—or worse, little or no recognition. It is not for the faint of heart.[158]

Herrera herself said, "Don't be intimidated about anything."[159] She also said, "I don't want to be considered a Latin American painter or a woman painter, or an old painter. I am a painter."[160]

William Butler Yeats (1865–1939), who lived for 71 years, composed great poems throughout his life. But his last three years—he was in poor health—saw a surge of productivity. In that time he composed seventy poems, including masterworks such as "The Circus Animals' Desertion,[161] in which he evaluates his own life's work:

> Those masterful images because complete
> Grew in pure mind but out of what began?
> A mound of refuse or the sweepings of a street,
> Old kettles, old bottles, and a broken can,
> Old iron, old bones, old rags, that raving slut
> Who keeps the till. Now that my ladder's gone

I must lie down where all the ladders start
In the foul rag and bone shop of the heart.

Here is the master of his craft, toward the end of his life, looking back. And isn't that one of the tasks of old age—to look back at where one has been? And isn't one of the advantages of being an *old* artist to be *that* skilled at the craft?

Of course, passionately pursued goals need not be art-oriented goals. I like the story told by Angela Glendenning (b. ca. 1934) of Staffordshire, England. She found herself to be entirely uncreative in any traditional art or craft: "I have no hobbies. I cannot sew, knit, paint, act, make music or do crafts." But "what I am good at is going the extra mile to support the underdog, the neglected, the damaged and the deprived." After her husband died, she felt very unsure for a time. Then her niece Sarah required a kidney transplant and Glendenning decided to donate her own kidney. This took time, attention, and many doctor visits, and then the surgery. The kidney transplant failed (later Sarah got a kidney that worked).

Glendenning then got involved with a kidney patients association and a transplant association and she hooked up with a young Sudanese physician who had been touchingly kind to her and her husband during her husband's last illness. As a way of repaying his kindness she created a fundraising project to bring a kidney dialysis machine to his town in Sudan. She called this *Angela's Just 70 Project* in which she ran seven miles, walked seventy miles, swam a mile, canoed for seven miles, cycled seventy miles, rode a horse for seven miles, and climbed seven tors (rocky peaks). She raised enough money to send two dialysis machines to Sudan. She then became involved in immigrant rights and other social justice causes, in the process acquiring close and caring friends from around the world.[162] Here is one woman's creativity—outside the arts—leading to a deeply satisfying old age.

As creating—making—is a source of vigor and energy, so its interruption or disintegration becomes, for the creator, a source of anguish. In his 70s Igor Stravinsky (1882–1971) composed a burst of new, innovative work. But in his 80s a series of strokes felled him. He said:

> Like childhood—my childhood—old age is a time of humiliation. The most disagreeable is that I cannot work long at sustained high pressure and with no leaks in concentration. But there are others. My slips in writing are no longer rare and my manuscripts have to be vetted.... Since I am not permitted to sit for long at the piano, I must compose most of whatever I can compose in my head. This is hampering because the instrument nudges my imagination into position; and ironic because I am writing my first solo-piano piece since 1925. Yesterday I worked at the piano for the first time in five months. The feel of dust on the keys was upsetting.[163]

Stravinsky was unable to compose much at all during the last five years of his life. "The vacuum which this left has not been filled," he wrote, "but I have been able to live with it, thanks, in the largest measure, to the music of Beethoven."[164]

Anna Mary Robertson Moses, at the age of 100, began to have falls. She continued to paint and after her 100th birthday completed more than twenty-five pictures. Her family decided that she would be better off and safer at a nursing home. On July 18, 1961, they took her to one of these. She was very unhappy. She wished to go home. She wished to have her paints. The family doctor forbade it. He felt that "she would not rest if she had her paints." She told one visitor, "As soon as I get back home, I will start painting again."[165] She never did get back home. She died in the nursing home on December 13, 1961. She was 101 years old.

## The Brain Itself

Nothing about the brain is static. Every time we learn something new, the brain changes. It changes constantly until the day we die. Our brain is plastic. This is the core discovery of the revolution in neuroscience that has occurred during the past three decades. Another finding is that, contrary to previous belief, the hippocampus, a seahorse-shaped brain structure quintessential to making long-term memories, can produce stem cells—new cells—in middle and old age.[166] It can do this—given learning and given exercise.

Further, an injured brain seeks workarounds. Given learning, given exercise—it is impossible to say these two words too often—it rewires itself to bypass damaged or dead brain tissue. This neuroplasticity is explored in detail in Norman Doidge's *The Brain's Way of Healing*.

But the brain can also die, neuron by neuron by neuron. Don't try this experiment: Sit in front of a TV. Don't move around much. Don't socialize much either. See if you do not, after a few years, become cognitively impaired. Why? Your neurons—some 86 billion at last count[167]—are dying off. And the connections between them—the average neuron has seven thousand connections; some have as many as one hundred thousand connections[168]—are deteriorating. Your hippocampus may be shrinking. When it comes to our brain, use it or lose it is no joke.

The good news is that "exercise training increases the size of hippocampus and improves memory," according to research reported in PNAS (Proceedings of the National Academy of Science of the United States).[169]

But here's the bad news. A National Health Statistics Report (June 28, 2018) noted that only 22.9 percent of United States adults aged 18 to 64 meet federal guidelines for exercise (see p. 47).[170] Further, a Center for Disease Control and Prevention report (November 9, 2018) noted that only 28 percent of adults over 50 years of age meet these guidelines. This leaves 31 million adults age 50 and over who are inactive.[171] And the COVID-19 requirement for many employees to work from home, despite advantages such as less commuting, has only made people more sedentary. One study found that working from home is associated with two more hours per day of sitting.[172]

Given these sobering statistics, I wonder about other sobering statistics on dementia and stroke and so on. For instance, one study reported that one-fourth of all people over 70 have at some point a "silent" (unnoticed) stroke.[173] To what extent do such events index age and to what extent do they index the long-term effects of a sedentary lifestyle?

Sadie Delany and Bessie Delany, the renowned centenarian sisters, did their exercises every morning. At age 106 Sadie had this to say about a few of her sedentary friends: "Some of our friends that are twenty, thirty years younger come in here and tell me they're worried about me, but to tell you the truth, I think I look better than they do. They come huffing and puffing up the steps and I'm thinking, *I hope you don't die in my parlor.*"[174]

Exercise, she says, "is important. A lot of older people don't exercise at all."[175]

Sadie Delany had it right. As learning and exercise stimulate the brain and keep it healthy, so lack of learning and lack of exercise impair it—no matter what your age. But for those willing to take the hint, the news is very good indeed. I quote from *Stahl's Essential Psychopharmacology* by the psychiatrist Stephen M. Stahl:

It is interesting to note that so far, the only intervention that has been consistently replicated as a disease-modifying treatment to diminish the risk for MCI [mild cognitive impairment] or Alzheimer's disease and that can slow the progression of these conditions is cognitive activity. Thus exercising the brain in a "use it or lose it" paradigm appears effective....Even physical exercise may be effective....[176]

Obviously, some things are just out of our control. For example, early-onset Alzheimer's, the rare form of this devastating disease, has little to do with lifestyle. It is genetically determined. And much is yet to be learned about the more common type of Alzheimer's and other forms of dementia, such as Lewy body dementia or vascular dementia. Yet for everyone, including those living with the challenges of memory loss, time spent on creative activities—writing, painting, dancing, photographing, or whatever—improves quality of life. Such is the discovery of the burgeoning "creative aging" movement, which is, according to the organization Lifetime Arts, "the practice of engaging older adults…in participatory, professionally run arts programs with a focus on social engagement and skills mastery." This movement toward making art in old age is not, in other words, about "making macaroni necklaces."[177]

Ina Bray is a vibrant older woman I met during a PowerPoint talk I gave at Horizon House, a Seattle residence for seniors. She related the story of her husband, James N. Bray (1932–2016), who had a Ph.D. in finance from UCLA, who taught at various universities, who eventually formed his own small financial-advising business. In his late 70s he began having memory problems. With the onset of pneumonia at age 80, his vascular dementia became acute. He lived for four more years. Ina took Jim to an organization called Elderwise that uses a spirit-centered (instead of body-centered) philosophy of dementia care, including respect for the person's choices, story-telling, conversation, good food, and regular times of working with art materials along with others. At first Jim wanted nothing to do with this art business; he had hated painting in kindergarten and saw no reason to like it now. But ultimately, he was persuaded to try. He became totally absorbed; it became the center of his world. More than that, he began producing comely and graceful abstract paintings. The art sessions added richness and meaning to his life.[178]

A professional urban herb-farmer and writer, Thomas DeBaggio (1942–2011) was at the age of 57 diagnosed with early-onset Alzheimer's Disease. He'd been a walking encyclopedia of plant names, an expert and author on the cultivation of herbs. Within the context of the successful herb business he was running with his wife in Virginia, he became increasingly unable to remember the names of the plants. After the devastating diagnosis, he decided to write down his memories, as long as he had them, and his experiences. The resulting books, *Losing My Mind: An Intimate Look at Life with Alzheimer's* and *When It Gets Dark: An Enlightened Reflection on Life with Alzheimer's*, are moving and heartbreaking. His struggle to write, which he managed with increasing difficulty—along with his appearances on NPR and the Oprah Winfrey show—helped to lift the veil of shame and humiliation that still surrounds this disease. For me it was refreshing to read an account, not *about* people with dementia but *by* someone struggling with it. His will to create this personal record of his painful decline gives him a kind of redemption, or so it seems to me.

Dementia happens. The American composer Aaron Copland (1900–1990) lived until age 90, but, due to the onset of Alzheimer's disease, he stopped composing years before. As he himself expressed it, the end of his creative life "was exactly as if someone had simply turned off a faucet."[179] Dementia terminated the brilliant, innovative work of the visual artist Miriam Schapiro (1923–2015), who died at age 91.[180] The painter Willem de Kooning (1904–1997), famously kept on painting while suffering from Alzheimer's late in life. His last paintings were exhibited in the midst of controversy: Was this his work or that of his assistant?[181] (Or, I wonder, had painting for de Kooning become part of proprioception, bodily knowledge like riding a bicycle, the last to go in Alzheimer's. Besides, we are becoming increasingly aware of how artistically creative people with memory loss can be.)

Before Alzheimer's set in, Iris Murdoch (1919–1999) composed twenty-six novels, a book of short stories, a book of poems, five works of philosophy, and several plays. Her last years of dementia are movingly portrayed in John Bayley's book *Iris: A Memoir*. Bayley was Murdoch's husband.

Dementia happens and persons falling into dementia should be treated with love, care, and respect. They should retain choices and relationships and access to social and creative opportunities. We should rejoice in what Marigrace Becker, program director for a University of Washington brain wellness center, calls a "new story" of what it means to live with dementia, through art, fitness, and other programs.[182]

But we should not allow our concerns about dementia to hose the reality, emphasized by Laura Carstensen of the Stanford Center on Longevity, that "people are functioning better cognitively as they get older," that "people in their 80s are testing like people in prior generations tested at 65,"[183] that we are increasingly cognizant of the roles of exercise and learning in preventing dementia. We should not allow the statistic that about 36 percent of persons 85 or over had dementia (in 2021) overwhelm the fact that 64 percent of persons 85 and over (in 2021) did *not* have dementia.[184] Dementia and our very legitimate concerns about it should not become a rationale to fuse our notion of old age with dementia: An old person is more likely to be mentally acute than to have dementia.

Here's another thing to consider. Aging begins at birth, continues throughout life, and occurs in an economic, social, and cultural context that either supports an eventual satisfying old age or challenges it. Conditions may not determine, but they do influence.[185] Poverty, despair, a lack of nutritious food, loneliness and isolation at age 30 or 50 affects one's ability to shape a healthy and creative old age. The historical time one is born into has an effect. When I was 14 years old, during the 1950s, I lived with my grandparents for a year. These good people did not exercise at all and I think they thought it was bad for you.

So, we can't control everything. And we don't know what the future will bring. But there are good reasons for people of any age to keep going strong, to learn, to exercise, to keep on creating or to begin creating. There are good reasons for us to take care of ourselves as if we expect to really hit our stride at age 100.

# Composing Our Lives: Old Age

For each of these writing prompts, write for five or ten minutes.

1. To what extent do you go about your life using your already-acquired knowledge, brilliance, wisdom, and experience? What new areas of learning are you engaged in? What new areas might you be interested in?

2. If you were offered a chance to take a class or classes or even go back to school to get a degree that life did not afford you at an earlier time, what would the subject matter be? What would you major in?

3. Do you believe in your heart of hearts that you are too old to enter a new area of learning? Keeping in mind that there's no need to be clever or to learn fast, what are the ways you might set this demon aside to enter a field that has long fascinated you?

4. Are you swift on your computer? On your phone? You may be one of the many elders who are aces at the new media. But if this area could use work, describe which apps or tools you might like to learn. Check out OATS (Older Adults Technology Services).

5. How much do you exercise every day or every week? Can you keep track for a week? Can you improve these numbers by 5 percent?

6. What are your eating habits? How can you improve your eating habits by 5 percent?

7. Are you living with chronic stress or with daily unspecified or shifting anxiety? Describe. If you could be more free from worry, where would you put this energy?

8. What steps could you take to reduce your stress by 5 percent?

9.  How rich and satisfying (or impoverished and unsatisfying) would you judge your social connections to be?

10. If you could improve this area of your life by 5 percent, what would you do?

11. What are your main purposes in life? What is your purpose today?

12. If you could improve this area of your life by 5 percent, what would you do?

Marilee Shapiro Asher, age 101, working in her studio, August 19, 2014. *Photo courtesy Linda Hansell.*

# 3. The Happiness of the Old

*I feel many things more intensely than ever before, and for me life grows more fascinating.*

—Pablo Casals, cellist, age 93[186]

The conventional wisdom is that when you get old, you get old and lonely, old and sad, old and isolated, old and depressed. Even happy elders—which, as it turns out, is *most* elders—believe that *other* elders are lonely, sad, isolated, and depressed.[187]

The conventional wisdom is mistaken. More typical is the view expressed at age 88 by the Santa Fe painter Marcia Muth (1919–2014): "I find that my eighties have been even more fun than my seventies were."[188] In 2006, she and her wife, Jody Ellis (1925–2018), a musician, were elected as living treasures of Santa Fe, New Mexico. They each lived into their 90s; they each were vital prime movers in their arts and book communities.[189]

## Happiness Is Usual

Happiness has been much studied, and we know a lot about it. There are three kinds to consider. First, happiness right now. How are you feeling at this moment? How did you feel yesterday? This is hedonic happiness, a kind of happiness related to pleasure. Second, life satisfaction. How would you rate your life satisfaction, from No. 1—I'd rather be dead, to No. 10—terrific! This is evaluative well-being. Third, there's the kind of happiness one gets from meeting goals, living with a purpose, seeking and finding meaning. This is eudemonic well-being. It comes from an Aristotelian notion of ethical or right behavior or right action leading to happiness.

On average, happiness over a lifetime occurs in a U curve.[190] Young people, people of college age are happy. (This is an *average*. We've all known the miserable adolescent... Nevertheless, this U-curve is a strong, consistent finding.) The dip comes in middle age, about age 40. A time, for many people, of stress and restless dissatisfaction, and this pit can materialize despite achievements and financial solvency. But as older age approaches, people get happier, more content, more satisfied. Generally speaking, old people are happy people. A Brookings Institute study found that the relationship between age and happiness—"often referred to as the 'U-curve'—is particularly striking due to its consistency across individuals, countries, and cultures."[191]

Older adults, according to neuroscientist Daniel J. Levitin, have a positivity bias.[192] We tend to attend to positive things. This comes under selective attention. Brain regions associated with selective attention are quite active in older people. Sonny Rollins, known as "jazz's greatest living improviser," who "time and time again created something miraculous out of thin air," was forced, in 2014 at age 84, to quit playing his saxophone due to pulmonary fibrosis, a diagnosis disastrous to one whose life was using his breath to play the horn. Is he unhappy? Seated under a large painting of Buddha in his home in Woodstock, New York, he spoke to David Marchese of *The New York Times*: "Happy is not the word," he said. "but I'm the most content I've ever been. I have most things figured out." He continued:

> The reason my retirement happened quietly was because my health problems were gradual. I didn't expect them. I wasn't quite sure that I would never be able to play again. It took me a while to realize, Hey, that's gone now....When I had to stop playing it was quite traumatic. But I realized that instead of lamenting and crying, I should be grateful for the fact that I was able to do music all my life. So I had that realization, plus my spiritual beliefs, which I've been cultivating for many years. All that work went into my accepting the fact that I couldn't play my horn.[193]

Happiness among the old is common and usual. And happiness—perhaps, as Sonny Rollins suggests, contentment is a better word—tends to increase from a low point in middle age despite disabilities and losses. The studies that have uncovered this U-curve are numerous and enormous. One was a Gallup poll of 1.5 million Americans, asking "whether they experienced a lot of struggle in their life yesterday." Another is the survey done in the United Kingdom by the National Office of Statistics to measure subjective well-being. The annual survey queries more than 300,000 people. And there's the Gallup World Poll, "whose survey set of 160 or more countries covers about 99 percent of the world's population."[194] And there are others. All these studies consistently show that happiness starts high, dips to a low around age 40, and slowly rises thereafter, into old age.

## Poverty, Depression, and Loneliness

Poverty, though, makes for unhappiness.[195] Poverty is stressful, and we know that chronic stress damages health.[196] In the United States, according to the National Council on Aging—these figures were compiled before the worldwide pandemic made it worse— more than 25 million adults over the age of 60 are economically insecure (they live on less than $30,000 per year). Ten million Americans over 50 live in dire straits: in poverty as defined by the federal government—$12,490 annual income for a one-person household and $16,910 per year for a two-person household.[197] Ponder this: About half the persons who patronize food banks come from a household with a full-time worker. These low-paid, full-time workers are unable to earn enough to purchase groceries for the family.[198] Depression is growing among older Americans (16 percent among those 65 or older, according to a 2019 survey), and poverty can bring it on, since older adults who live with food insecurity are three times more likely to sink into depression.[199]

This is tragic and undeniable, as well as being a national disgrace. But there is another side to this coin, as we'll see in the coming chapter. Please contemplate these numbers: Americans over the age of 50 "have a combined annual personal income of over 3.9 trillion and control 77 percent of the total net worth of US households."[200] So, poverty and depression exist, but we should not use them to further a bleak view of old age.

To invert the depression statistic, 84 percent of elders are *not* depressed. In one happiness study researchers looked into the sales of anti-depressants among a million Britons and found that middle age (the 40s) was the age of peak anti-depressant prescriptions. They extended the study to twenty-seven European nations and found ditto. They then studied prescribed mental-health drugs in the US states of New Hampshire and New Mexico. Here they found "the biggest probability of consuming medication occurs in the age bracket 45–49."[201] Once again, unhappiness in middle age. Of course, who among the aged poor can afford an anti-depressant drug?

And what of loneliness, said to be a condition of the old? No matter your age, loneliness is bad for health and well-being, as bad as smoking, as bad as obesity, as bad, no doubt, as reckless driving. Prolonged loneliness is dangerous for anyone—teenager, college student, the newly divorced 45-year-old, and yes, any old person, bereaved or not. The immune systems of lonely people, especially those who experience loneliness over several years, reports Laura Carstensen of the Stanford Center on Longevity, "tend to overexpress an array of inflammation genes, which control immediate tissue-repair processes but also drive the wear and tear we call aging. If you compared two fifty-year-olds, one with a happy social life and one who felt isolated, the lonely person would have an 'older body' in that it would show greater chronic inflammation."[202]

But to associate loneliness with old age is part of a misconception that sees old age as a time of misery, decline, isolation, and loneliness. The National Council on Aging did a fascinating study on American perceptions on aging in 1974 and again, for comparison, in 2000. The same questions were asked on each survey of 1,155 persons age 65+. These were all people living in the community, not in institutions. One question was: Is ____ a problem for me personally? Loneliness was one of the categories. In 2000, 21 percent said loneliness was a problem for them personally (down from 36 percent in 1974). This is a lot of lonely people, though many fewer than in 1974. But consider the next question: How serious a problem would you say____is for most people over 65 these days? In 2000, 84 percent of the responders felt that loneliness was a big problem for most people over 65 (down from 94 percent in 1974). Here what we see at work is negative attitudes toward aging. People, including old people, think loneliness is much more of a problem for old people than it actually is.[203]

And there is this: Often legitimate concerns about loneliness are placed alongside statistics on how many people in the United States live in single-person households: 28 percent of persons over age 65, or 13.8 million people as of 2019.[204] I live in a single-person household. I live happily and quite connected to others. I love living by myself; only some sort of dire disability would persuade me to do otherwise. Could we please drop the association between living alone and being lonely? Indeed, studies have found that they are not connected.[205]

## Friendships in Old Age

Our dear ones, our loves, our friends and good buddies go a long way toward making life worth living. The problem is, the older we get the more Old Man Death (or, as some would have it, Madame Death), has occasion to call upon one or another of our close friends or family members. Consider that for most centenarians, not a single person remains alive who knew them *back when*.

This is only part of the reason that the social circle of elderly people tends to shrink. In Laura Carstensen's words, "You can expect to have fewer—but deeper—connections in old age." The old tend not to be social butterflies. They do not enjoy random parties or blind dates. But this does not make them hermits, although they may enjoy their solitude. Carstensen suggests that the minimum number of close relationships a person should have is three; fewer than that is way too fragile.[206]

I suggest that one of the tasks of old age is to attend to friendships, to nourish the ones we are blessed with, and to be open to new ones. It's vital to construct a world for oneself larger than one's own individual existence. And—any vibrant personal community will include people of all ages.

Artists and people who live in art worlds tend to be connected. Arts communities enjoy high connectivity, or so I gather from my own experience in Seattle writing and poetry circles. Over the years you get to know other poets at readings, in classes and workshops, at conferences, and by working closely with one or another poet friend.

One study found this also to be the case among visual artists. In *Above Ground*, the study of New York City aging visual artists, Joan Jeffri reported that "the average personal network size for aging visual artists is 29." Jeffri also found that older artists tend to have stronger relationships with other artists than with family.[207] Whatever the case, meaningful connections and close relationships are endemic to arts communities.

The photographer Imogen Cunningham worked up until the week of her death at age 93. A few months before Cunningham's death, the curator of photography at the Stanford University Museum of Art paid a call to her San Francisco home:

> We [the curator and her husband] were there to look at some photographs. The phone was ringing every few minutes. Each ring meant somebody was making a date with Imogen. Finally, getting on toward dinner time, three very attractive young men came to call and take her out to dinner. Off she went. That was the life she lived.[208]

## The Wonder of Life

Intimate associations are no doubt aided by the greater emotional steadiness that tends to come with old age. "Age is associated with improved emotional experience and emotional stability," writes Laura L. Carstensen. "Negative emotions are experienced less frequently. We regulate emotions better, avoiding extreme highs and extreme lows."[209] With age may come shifts in our brain chemistry, according to neuroscientist Daniel J. Levitin, causing us to become steadier. "Some older people," he writes, "describe a 'burning off' of previously distressing mental states." Levitin reports that in his 70s the singer, songwriter, poet Leonard Cohen (1934–2016) was amazed to find that his chronic depression, which no medication had helped, simply evaporated.[210]

Certainly, for me, the "extreme highs and extreme lows" of my 20s and 30s are history. I can look out my October window at the yellow ocher leaves of the Pacific ninebark I planted last year, seen against the thick mossy branches of my neighbor's old cherry tree, and this all by itself gives me a contented feeling. Even more so when a flicker alights or one of our resident Steller's jays. Sitting at my desk writing has most always made me happy, especially early in the morning. (Still, for me, the anxiety of ambition has yet to retract its nasty claws.)

The choreographer and dancer Twyla Tharp, at age 76, required major surgery on her hip, which in turn required her to learn to walk again, not to mention dance again. Her recovery was slow, painful, and at times humiliating. But she did recover. She writes:

> By the sixth month following surgery I began to take great solace in small known things....the intense pleasure of turning an avocado in my hand, the absolute triumph in feeling the sun on my neck, a marvelous glimpse of the moon in the evening sky. For about the millionth time I decided to start learning to cook. Amazed and awed to be alive, the quotidian became my comfort zone.[211]

Tharp is not alone among the old to be amazed and awed to be alive. At 93, cellist Pablo Casals reported on his current happiness:

> For the past eighty years I have started each day in the same manner....I go to the piano and I play two preludes and fugues of Bach. I cannot think of doing otherwise. It is a sort of benediction on the house. But that is not its only meaning for me. It is a rediscovery of the world of which

I have the joy of being a part. It fills me with awareness of the wonder of life, with a feeling of the incredible marvel of being a human being. The music is never the same for me, never. Each day it is something new, fantastic and unbelievable.[212]

Art contributes to the richness of life, to its beauty and its meaningfulness. I would say it contributes to happiness. The Washington, D.C. sculptor Marilee Shapiro Asher continued making art until she died at the age of 107. (In 2020, the year of her death, she contracted Covid-19.) Asher was introduced to clay in her early 20s: "The feel of it—the clay—that you could do with your hands what you wanted with the clay—was thrilling." At age 106 she felt the same way: "Very often I start from something material, something I see that looks very interesting and I want to play with it. I do believe that art is the highest form of play." [213] In her memoir, *Dancing in the Wonder*, she wrote: "In the studio, with an ongoing project in which I am absorbed, time does not exist. If I stopped to think about it, I would have to say that I am happy."[214]

Another rather cheerful aged artist was Diana Athill. In her late 90s, she composed her memoirist essays, *Alive, Alive Oh!*. In one essay she tells how she made the rather momentous decision to move into an Old People's Home. She chose a London establishment where residents were provided with their own apartments and where they were treated with care and respect, and in no way lost their freedom. Athill had to drastically downsize, and could only move a few of her beloved possessions to her own room at the new place, including only 300 of her 1,000 books (the books were the hardest part). Once there, though, she kept her old friends, made new friends, gardened with these new friends, freely went about London as before, attending cultural and political events. And she continued to write.[215]

One of the foremost abstract painters of the twentieth century, Agnes Martin (1912–2004), felt energetic and cheerful in old age. At age 88 she said, "I think about nothing but painting. The older I get the more I *like* to paint. It grows on you."[216] Her paintings, many of them large canvasses consisting of shimmering stripes or sometimes grids, "depict states of mind, states of existence," explained her friend and dealer Arne Glimcher. "They were ecstasy, joy, happiness, innocence. They were landscapes of the mind."[217] These paintings do not reproduce well; they need to be seen. I myself have had the opportunity to attend only one exhibition of her work. I was mesmerized, calmed, could not stop looking.

Martin, despite her enormous critical acclaim and eventual commercial success, had a difficult life. Specifically—and never publicly disclosed before her death—she was early diagnosed with paranoid schizophrenia, hospitalized several times throughout her life, and throughout her life received both psychiatric treatment and antipsychotic medication.[218] Nevertheless, she painted. And when she painted, as Arne Glimcher noted, she was not ill. Her writings and public lectures took on a zen cast: "If you can imagine you're a rock / all your troubles fall away," she wrote in a piece titled "Beauty Is the Mystery of Life."[219] She was widely admired and became a public figure and a kind of art saint.

Martin exerted enormous control over her public image. She painted every day but destroyed much of her work, not in fits of pique but as an editor of her oeuvre. She insisted that her art had nothing to do with her biography, which, as Glimcher noted, was not true.

But her old age truly was happier. In her last decade, in Taos, New Mexico, she painted every morning, and then went to lunch with one or another friend. This was a tsunamic change for a person who had been shy and reclusive. She began giving her paintings titles such as "Happy Holiday" (1999), "Lasting Love" (1999), "Lovely Life" (1999), "Affection" (2001), and "I Love the Whole World" (1999). "She had a wonderful old age," said Glimcher, "and I take great pleasure in that and comfort in that."[220]

Another artist who experienced contentment in old age was Wayne Thiebaud. In his early 90s he said: "Working becomes your own little Eden. You make this little spot for yourself. You don't have to succeed. You don't have to be famous. You don't have to be obligated to anything except that development of the self."[221]

At age 85, the year before she died, the abstract painter Alma W. Thomas was asked by an interviewer how she painted now. "I make a lot of little color sketches," she replied. "I have hundreds of them. And I keep up with what is going on. I buy all of the art magazines, and many of the new books. And I go to exhibitions. I like to feel myself part of this day in time." The titles to Thomas's paintings reflect her philosophy and outlook. She felt there was enough ugliness out in the world, "people struggling, having difficulty, and then you have to come back and see the same thing hanging on the wall. No. I wanted something beautiful that you could sit down and look at." Her painting titles include: "Garden Blue Flowers: Rhapsody"; "Wind Dancing with Spring Flowers"; and "Earth Sermon: Sun, Beauty, Love and Peace."[222]

## Difficulties and Hard Times

Of course, happiness in old age is not universal. May Sarton (1912–1995), who died of breast cancer at the age of 83, was, in her old age, often unhappy. She just did not feel well. She'd had strokes. She had breast cancer. She was in a lot of pain. She got depressed. Yet she continued to compose poems and books. During her lifetime she authored sixteen books of poems, nineteen novels, thirteen nonfiction books, many of them journals, and two books for children. Her last book, *At Eighty-Two: A Journal* is full of warm reminiscences, notes on a seemingly endless parade of friends who come to visit and to help out, and vivid observations on her garden, on Pierrot (the cat), on dinner with friends, and on readings and signings and honors. But it is also full of pain, depression, fatigue, and discouragement. "The sun is out but I am having a very hard time," she writes. "The antibiotic is sickening."[223]

The novelist and literary critic Doris Grumbach (b. 1918) turned 70 in 1988. In her memoir/journal *Coming into the End Zone*, she writes of "the odium of growing old" and in other passages, deplores her age, deplores the "dread event" of her 70th birthday, deplores her older body, writes of being grateful for the arrival of small bits of information to her "floppy disc" intelligence, which is often "down." I first read Grumbach's *Coming into the End*

*Zone* when I was about to turn 70 (in 2013). I felt a bit shocked at how *old* Grumbach sounded at age 70. (She subsequently wrote six more books and recently turned 102.) Now that I am 79 and rereading *Coming into the End Zone*, she still sounds, at age 70, *ancient*, as if she were about to turn 110. The difference between her memoir of turning 70, written in 1988, and Patti Smith's much more upbeat memoir of turning 70, *Year of the Monkey*, written in 2016, tells how profoundly old age is changing.

The cover of Grumbach's *Coming into the End Zone* displays an antique automobile stalled in an overgrown pasture. We are antique, stalled, and out to pasture? Yet Grumbach's writing is also lucid and erudite. And despite her frequent references to her own decrepitude, she notes how much more acute she has become at observing her surroundings ("the sun going down…the head of the old horse eying us from the…barn.") "When I was young," she writes, "I was hardly aware of where I was….Why was I so oblivious? I can put it down to only one thing: self-absorption."[224]

The business of outgrowing self-absorption, of growing into a fascination with "everything that is out there" may be a developmental benefit of growing into old age. For me, certainly, it's an element of happiness.

## The Pursuit of Happiness

To be happy in old age is a legitimate goal, or so it seems to me. In his book *The Virtues of Aging*, Jimmy Carter (b. 1924) writes, "What should be our major goals as we prepare for our later years? You may be surprised to learn that I think one of the most important is our own happiness."[225] And if Carter is any example, creating, making, is part of the flourishing well-being that is happiness. Carter builds furniture, makes paintings, and writes books (thirty-two so far) as well as engaging around the world in human rights work and conflict mediation.

Happiness is not something we can will into existence. And neither is it a fixed quality. But just as regular exercise optimizes conditions for health, so an engaged and productive lifestyle optimizes conditions for happiness. Happy, engaged, productive elders such as Jimmy Carter model for us all how to grow into old age.

The Harvard Study of Adult Development (called the "Grant" study) followed the psychological development of 268 Harvard sophomores beginning in 1939. The men included in this very significant longitudinal study are now in their 90s. One of them reflected:

> I think it is enormously important to the next generation
> that we be happy into old age—happy and confident—not
> necessarily that we are right but that it is wonderful to
> persist in our search for meaning and rectitude. Ultimately,
> that is our most valuable legacy—the conviction that life is
> and has been worthwhile up to the limit.[226]

Psychiatrist Gene D. Cohen proposed a developmental stage that tends to occur in older people in which "we feel more urgently the desire to find larger meaning in the story of our lives through a process of looking back, summing-up, and giving back."[227] This felt desire explains the urge to write memoir among the many older writers in adult education writing classes.

## Remembering, Recovering, Making Meaning

Looking back, remembering, and articulating one's life and its meanings is an aspect of eudemonic happiness. And composing a memoir is also a way of giving back to the larger community. Dorothea Nordstrand (1916–2011) comes to mind. She was a Seattle resident who spent her last couple of decades—she died at age 95—composing reminiscences of her hard-working, working-class family, who moved from a mountain homestead in northeastern Washington State to Seattle when she was 3 years old. I was privileged to be her editor for her many stories that appear in the online encyclopedia of Washington State history (HistoryLink.org) and for the resulting book, *Pork Neckbones, Sauerkraut & Rutabagas, Memories of my Green Lake Girlhood*. Nordstrand's memoir holds more than the story of one family: It also remembers the past of a unique place and its community.

The Delany sisters, Sadie and Bessie, composed their memoir *Having Our Say* after they had both turned 100 years old. Their book glimpses not only the lives of the accomplished, devout, resilient, witty sisters and their large middle-class African American family, but also the challenges of the segregated America in which they grew up.

Much less protected by his family was the legendary jazz trumpeter Clark Terry (1920–2015). In his vivid autobiography, *Clark*, Terry details his struggles growing up in St. Louis as the seventh of eleven children whose mother died when he was 6 or 7 years old. In his memoir he wrote, "Whenever I played 'Sometimes I Feel Like a Motherless Child' later on in my career, I felt every note."

Terry's father supported the children and beat up none of them except for Clark, whom he beat on a regular basis. His father also opposed Clark's desperate dream to play the trumpet. When Terry was 12 years old his father threw him out of the house. He went to live with his older sister and her jazz-playing husband. But there were mother-figures (his older sisters) and kind moments. Long before, the neighbors, who could no longer abide the sound of the trumpet Terry had fabricated out of trash—he played when his father was at work—got together to buy him a real, if old, instrument.

But Terry's book is a lot more than a coming-of-age story. He joined the segregated Navy to play jazz, practicing obsessively in the toilet room after he had finished cleaning it. He later played in various bands and bars across the unbearably racist United States. His story becomes not only his story but America's story. And yes, Clark Terry, who was, in the first place, ever-resilient, ends up full of contentment, a happy man.[228]

Another writer who looked back was Leonard Woolf (1880–1969), author, publisher, political theorist, civil servant, and husband of Virginia Woolf. Woolf spent his last decade, in his 80s, writing his autobiography in five volumes. He completed the fifth volume, *The Journey Not the Arrival Matters*, the year he died at age 88.

Part of remembering has to do with revisiting and integrating traumatic experiences. "Art," wrote Goethe, "deals with what is hard to bear and with what is good."[229] In his last book Woolf recounts in painful detail Virginia Woolf's mental illness and her suicide by drowning, which occurred on March 28, 1941. The chapter "Virginia's Death" recounts the event, but it is more than that—a long (96-page) reflection on who she was and their life together and on the terrible times of the world war in which they lived. (They lived with German bombers heading for London flying low over their country home. The couple held regular discussions on what they would do if Hitler landed, which was entirely possible.)[230] Woolf's account—like that of Pablo Casals, who lived through the same war in Spain and who, in *Joys and Sorrows*, recalls its desperate times—is far more than a personal account, despite how personal it is. It's a window into the history of the twentieth century at that time and in that place.

A writer who in old age was finally able to deal with what was hard to bear, and to begin writing again after decades of artistic silence, was the author of the classic American novel, *Call It Sleep*, published in 1934 when he was age 28. Henry Roth (1906–1995) grew up in a Yiddish-speaking immigrant family on the Lower East Side of New York. *Call It Sleep* was praised in reviews, except for one review in the Communist Party publication *The New Masses*, which condemned it. Roth, drawn to Communism, cared mainly about the one negative review. The novel sold few copies, but in the early 1960s enjoyed a revival. That is when I read it as a college student. It is an amazing and profound American novel. At that time Roth was discovered farming in Maine. He had not written a word in decades.

Henry Roth's fiction is not autobiography, but it was deeply based in his own life experience. His "fragile sense of self," as a *New Yorker* writer called it, was battered by his loyalty to the Communist Party and its curt dismissal of his book (he later changed his view of the CP), by the virulent anti-Semitism that he experienced daily after the family moved from its Lower East Side Yiddish-speaking world to Harlem, by uneasy family dynamics, and at the core, by the terrible secret he carried and condemned himself for, his incest with his sister beginning when he was 12 and she was 10, which lasted for years, and his subsequent adolescent incest with his 14-year-old first cousin.[231]

Art uses whatever is at the core of one's being—somehow. By this I do not mean that art is autobiographical, but there is a kind of energy that art uses that gets jammed up when a high wall must be built around some central core secret. In old age, Henry Roth was able to face his past and begin writing again. Between the ages of 73 and 89 he wrote six novels, which, writes psychologist Becca Levy, "allowed him to come to terms with past actions he regretted as he faced his own mortality."[232] Of these last works one critic wrote, "Roth stands at the intersection of the American and the Jewish more fully than the more famous, more assimilated, Jewish writers of a later generation." And, "he writes in the face of departing memory and approaching death with a vitality that exceeds much of contemporary fiction."[233]

What does this have to do with happiness? Articulating one's life experience, creating what one was meant to create, fulfilling one's earliest ambitions and dreams—such is an incubator for contentment.

Another writer who in old age returned to past trauma was Maya Angelou (1928–2014). In her 86 years Angelou published some thirty books. That would be seven autobiographies including the marvelous *I Know Why the Caged Bird Sings*, twelve books of poetry, three books of essays, two cookbooks, and ten children's books. She was also a dancer, a composer, a director, a performer, and a singer. In the last year of her life she composed her last memoir, *Me and Mom and Me*. This book honors her mother but also remembers how her mom abandoned her children when Maya was 3 and her brother 5. She brought them to their grandmother in Arkansas; they weren't returned to their mother until Maya was 13 and her brother 15. Though the grandmother raised them with great love, the maternal rejection was a huge life event. Old age is a time to return to old times and old wounds in order to integrate traumas and put them behind you. This is what *Me and Mom and Me* does.[234]

In her book *The Third Chapter*, Sara Lawrence-Lightfoot found that her subjects, professionals who radically changed careers late in life, often had to face down childhood traumas to follow their dreams. Lawrence-Lightfoot writes:

> Many of the men and women I interviewed spoke passionately and longingly about how the Third Chapter is a time when they have finally been able to face the deep injuries of their childhoods—assaults that they have ignored, repressed, or fled from for most of their lives. They find that confronting these early injuries allows, in the words of one person, the "ancient wounds to lose much of their hurting." Revisiting these "old burdens" allows them to move on to the next chapter in their own lives, and allows them to recognize and repair those hurts that were—wittingly or unwittingly—passed on to the next generation.[235]

Some of these wounds had to do with humiliating comments by teachers or parents regarding the child's yearning for creative expression or to enter some creative pursuit. A successful public-health doctor who had spent his life fighting malaria had, as a child, loved opera. He had begged his mother for voice lessons, but her lesson was that opera was for sissies. Nearing the age of 70 he began (secretly) taking voice lessons. A graphic designer running a successful business had been informed by an eighth-grade art teacher that she would "never be an artist." She was devastated and dropped her art. Late in life she began to defy that news to paint large watercolors with wild bursts of color. Another artist had had to throw off her childhood reputation as a stupid underachiever. Slowly and over time she became a highly respected quilt maker.[236]

Most of these creators were not going to become famous or even well-known. But they were spending their late years learning, honing their craft skills, and living their dreams.

Children, adolescents despite their strivings for independence, and young adults remain close to their upbringing and captive to its values, teachings, relationships, and circumstances, for better or worse. Parental desires for their offspring have a huge influence. I was a war baby (born 1943) and grew up into the sixties and became an activist in the civil-rights, anti-Vietnam War, and women's movements. (Notwithstanding the cliché, the peace-and-justice activists of the early sixties were war babies like me, not boomers.) The conventional view here is that we were acting in accordance with our generation and not in accordance with our parents' generation. But many of my fellow young activists were "red diaper babies" or they were the offspring of labor union activists or Quaker pacifists or New Deal reformers or the like. Far from being in conflict, the generations were in accord.

I was not a red diaper baby. I was born of religious parents who had nothing to do with activism. But as I see it now, my activism accorded with my parents' antiracist values, with their strong values about honesty, about paying your bills no matter what, about standing for the right thing. And I wrote, more or less secretly. My parents did not really value or encourage creative expression and it took me a long time to grow into being a writer.

And what of the trauma of violence so many of us have experienced, whether on the street or on the battlefield? How many studies of creativity, whether of old or young creators, discuss the shattering impact of violence on a person's creative process and practice? None that I have read. As a college student on a co-op job in New York City I was assaulted and raped by a violent stranger. After that traumatic experience I went on with my life and studies but became suicidal for a time and I quit writing in my journal for five years. Such traumas, which are grievously common and grossly destructive of creative impulses, set a person back and poison their creative development. Eventually, though, especially given some good therapy, they simply become part of who you are. Old age (if not before) may be a prime time to confront old traumas and see their influence diminish or disappear. And art can be part of the healing. There are organizations and movements—Seattle's Path with Art is one example—designed to aid traumatized persons to heal and stabilize through art.[237]

## A New Kind of Freedom

Old creators tend to be less concerned with the opinions of others and this makes the work lighter, looser, easier. The composer Elliott Carter comes to mind. "Here was a towering contemporary composer," states an article in *The New York Times* written upon his death at age 103, "enjoying a renewed burst of creativity that started in his 90s and kept him going almost to the end." Carter composed more than sixty works after he turned 90. He composed significant works after he turned 100. His earlier works, "densely intricate and rhythmically pathbreaking pieces from the 1960s to the 1980s, the decades of his greatest influence, could confound musicians as well as audiences." But in his last fifteen years his music became "more inviting, open and lyrical." This critic notes that his new spontaneity and ease came through in every piece. "When Mr. Carter entered his 90s, he seemed to realize he had nothing more to prove. He lightened up and became emboldened to take chances."[238]

This old-age ability to lighten up, to experiment more, to work along with less anxiety about one's career or recognition, is a boon to anyone's creative work.

Miriam McKinnie Hofmeier (1906–1987) worked as a muralist during the 1930s, taught art for thirty years in St. Louis, and spent her last years in Little Rock, Arkansas. After a lifetime of making art, toward the end of her life she said, "Now I feel like I've earned the right, and this is the time to paint ridiculous things if I choose. I feel at this age I can go overboard and be as ridiculous as I want. I don't know; I want to do some big alligators. I have a sketch on my pad now of a big alligator standing with a parasol, and there's a kid sitting on top of the parasol. Just crazy, I mean, why not? I feel at this point in my life, what the hell have I got to lose?"[239]

Lynne Sharon Schwartz (b. 1939), author of some nineteen books including novels, short stories, poetry, and nonfictions, writes of the changes in her work as she moves into her 80s:

It seems a new voice has emerged...Not exactly surreal but somewhat removed from reality—an ironic, skeptical and wryly comic voice. I love this new development; it feels like a kind of freedom. As if now that I don't have to establish a reputation, I can do whatever I like, explore and experiment.[240]

The eminent visual artist Betye Saar (b. 1926), whose body of work includes mystical, political, and personal collages, assemblages, and installations, reflects on being older:

I like to think of myself as just a creative person, and in spite of being an older person, there's certain perks to being older. You can just kind of say what you want to say and do what you want to do, and I like that part of my life. And I just try to be as authentic as I can be at the moment. And make art, work in my garden, wear funny clothes or whatever. Have a little fun with it.[241]

## A Spiritual Life

In older age many persons become more spiritual. Meaning what? I see spirituality as apprehending the connections among all things and seeing oneself as part of history and as part of the larger world, part of nature. I see it as becoming more aware of the trees, the stars, flowers, ants, other people. I see it as feeling connections to one's community; in the case of artists, feeling connections to the artists of the past and to one's fellow artists.

"A significant body of literature," writes physician Christina Puchalski, director of the George Washington Institute for Spirituality and Health, "highlights the role of spirituality in aging. As we age, spirituality—broadly defined as a search for ultimate meaning and purpose and the experience of connection to the transcendent, to others, to nature and to the significant or sacred—plays a more dominant role in our lives than when we were younger."[242]

Shortly before he turned 100, the poet Stanley Kunitz wrote of his garden, "One of the satisfactions of the human spirit is to feel that one's family extends across the borders of the species and belongs to everything that lives. I feel that I'm not only sharing the planet, but also sharing my life, as one does with a domestic animal. Certainly this is one of the great joys of living in this garden."[243]

Perceiving the larger view, the view of the world beyond the self, the world that will continue to exist after one's own death—that is the perspective of age. Nearing 80, Oliver Sacks wrote of his father: "My father, who lived to 94, often said that his 80s had been one of the most enjoyable decades of his life. He felt, as I begin to feel, not a shrinking but an enlargement of mental life and perspective. One has a long experience of life, not only one's own life, but others' too. One has seen triumphs and tragedies, booms and busts, revolutions and wars, great achievements and deep ambiguities, too. One has seen grand theories rise, only to be toppled by stubborn facts. One is more conscious of transience and, perhaps, of beauty."

Sacks continues, speaking of his own old age: "I do not think of old age as an ever grimmer time that one must somehow endure and make the best of, but as a time of leisure and freedom, freed from the factitious urgencies of earlier days, free to explore whatever I wish, and to bind the thoughts and feelings of a lifetime together."[244]

Old age can be a freer time, a looser time, a more contented time. It can be a time of exploring, learning, reading, walking, thinking, conversing. It can be a time of creating—writing, painting, drawing, throwing pots, dancing, choreographing, sculpting, making collages, making video art, gardening, composing....at one's own pace, as one is given to do, as one chooses to do. Old age can be—and often is—a time of freedom, productivity, creativity—and great happiness.

## Composing Our Lives: Old Age

For each of these writing prompts, write for five or ten minutes.

1. Taking Pablo Casals's early morning piano practice as a model, is there some pleasure, some action or activity, that might become a daily practice toward amplifying the world's beauty? Sitting in the garden? Listening to a piece of music? Walking on the beach or in a park or in the woods? Write on the possibilities.

2. Write on the main traumas you have endured. What are your ideas for getting help to become more free of their influence and harm?

3. Is there a new creative endeavor you might enter into? If you are already an artist—perhaps something different? If you are a poet, might you learn to draw? If you are a master gardener, perhaps you would enjoy working in clay? Write on the possibilities.

4. What activities, or people, make you feel contented, that all is well? What activities or people make you feel anxious, uneasy, unhappy? Is there a way you can keep more of the former and lose some of the latter?

Noah Purifoy in his Workshop, Joshua Tree, 1990s, *Courtesy Noah Purifoy Foundation © 1992.*

# 4. Resource Drain or Resource?

*To be part of the community, to be part of something larger than oneself, to contribute somehow to the ongoing human enterprise, to pass on some legacy to the next generation is, it seems, a burning need of vital age....*

—Betty Friedan[245]

It is said that the burgeoning population of old people will suck up all the resources. Draw down Social Security. Bankrupt Medicare. Leave the next generation in the lurch. Terms employed are "gray tsunami," the "demographic cliff," the "demographic time bomb." We old people are going to drag the rest of you down. What's the reality?

Most of us are happy. Most of us are productive. We have our losses. We have our disabilities. But we are good parents, good grandparents, good aunts and uncles, good neighbors, good friends. Many of us are vibrant and creative and more and more of us are working.

## Working While Aging

The (paid) labor force participation of older workers is increasing, both in the United States and in Europe. In the United States, in 2010, 16 percent of people over the age of 65 were in the (paid) labor force. In 2020 that number had risen to 20 percent. The Bureau of Labor Statistics expected this trend to continue, especially for the older ages. Working in the paid labor force helps financially. But it's not only about money. Speaking of the boomer generation, Ken Dychtwald and Robert Morison write in *What Retirees Want*:

> It's not just about the money. The Boomer generation...see their later lives as active on many fronts, full of purpose, stimulation, social interaction, and fulfillment, including from work. As many of them work in later life, retirement itself is transforming.

Working at a job you like is good for your health and good for your well-being. This was the finding of a study of 83,000 older adults across fifteen years. People who worked past age 65 were three times as likely to report being in good health and about half as likely to have serious health problems.[246] Of course, dealing with a serious health issue might be a good reason to retire.

A good number of older workers work part-time or become self-employed, giving them more control over their working conditions. Nearly 17 percent of workers aged 65 and older were self-employed (in 2016) and self-employment is common among creative workers—craft workers, fine artists, photographers, and writers.[247] Self-employment also increases with age, so that, according to the Center on Aging and Work at the Boston College School of Social Work, 51 percent of all workers over the age of 80 were self-employed (2016 statistics).[248]

Older workers want more flexibility. "Most older workers," reports Laura Carstensen, director of the Stanford Center on Longevity, "say what they really want is the flexibility to work part time or take longer periods of time off, which would make older workers less expensive for employers." She described a study done in an auto plant of three teams: all young workers, all old workers, and mixed young and old workers. The mixed-aged team was the most productive. They benefitted from the experience of the older workers and the speed of the younger workers.[249]

In her book *Disrupting Aging*, Jo Ann Jenkins, CEO of the AARP, describes firms, such as the auto firm BMW, the pharmacy CVS, and Home Depot, that strive to retain and hire older workers and who reap advantages to the business of doing so. BMW retrofitted its plants to make them more ergonomic, providing for workers barbershop-like chairs and magnifying glasses, and the firm also instituted daily stretching exercises. Productivity improved and absenteeism fell. CVS has instituted a "snowbird" program in which hundreds of pharmacists and other workers are transferred to Florida and other warmer states during the winter. This helps the firm deal with the surge of business in the warmer states during the cold months and the program appeals to employees who would rather be warm in winter. Home Depot hires older workers because their preference for flexible hours helps the stores with scheduling and because, the company believes, the enormous amount of expertise contributed by these older workers gives Home Depot an advantage over competitors, both in customer service and in training younger workers.

Older workers, it turns out, learn as fast as younger workers do. And the notion that older workers are not worth the investment because "they won't be around that long" is contradicted by the fact that younger workers, especially millennials, "are known for jumping from one job to the next, not staying anywhere for more than a couple of years."[250] Older workers are in fact, more reliable; they stick around longer.

## Careers, Continuing

"What is the best time to retire?" asks neuroscientist Daniel Levitin. His answer? "Never."[251] Levitin exaggerates. True, if one loves the work and is surviving financially, why not continue? But anyone roped to a grueling or boring or unhappy job should, if possible, try to get rid of it, if not by retiring, by changing jobs. Why not move on to a more satisfying or stimulating or creative endeavor? Or maybe it's just time to turn to something different.

But many active, productive, vital old people simply do not retire. And this is particularly true of people engaged in creative work.

In older age, many artists are barely surviving financially, but they keep on making art. This according to Joan Jeffri's study of New York City aging artists carried out in 2007.[252] A few had savings or pensions, but most had not. And for most, due to having spent so many years as freelance or contract workers, holding down various jobs as well as making art, Social Security received was not much (on average $4,820 per year). Most of these artists brought in some money from their art, but again, not much. Still, they kept on making art. A 72-year-old homeless artist quoted in this report said, "Art is the only thing that's left in the world."

Many creators simply love their work. Why would they stop? Charles M. Schulz (1922–2000), creator of the *Peanuts* comic strip, produced 17,897 comic strips over a 50-year period. Each week he produced, by himself, six daily strips plus one for Sunday. He retired, ill with colon cancer, in December 1999, two months before his death at age 77. Schulz said, "I would feel just terrible if I couldn't draw comic strips. I would feel very empty if I were not allowed to do this sort of thing."[253]

In his autobiography, Quincy Jones, jazz musician; composer; arranger; and album, film, and television producer, wrote, "As far as I am concerned, retirement is like sitting around waiting to die. Staying in touch with the world is about anticipating change— cultural, spiritual, and technological—and embracing it." He goes on to speak of the technological changes he has so far witnessed and embraced in his long, multifaceted music career: the first Fender bass, the first stereo recording, the first audio cassette, the first "dime-thin video disc at Philips," the first modular Moog synthesizer, the first DVD. His book is a window into a life of growing and learning and changing.[254]

Two years before her death at age 88, the sculptor Louise Nevelson (1899–1988), said, "I still want to do my work. I still want to do my livingness. And I have lived. I have been fulfilled. I recognized what I had and I never sold it short. And I ain't through yet!" The painter Robert Motherwell (1915–1991), who at the time of this *New York Times* interview had had three surgeries on his heart (he was 71 and had five years to live), said: "For me, to retire from painting would be to retire from life."[255]

The pianist Arthur Rubinstein (1887–1982) performed for large audiences into his 90s. The year he turned 80, he gave 114 concerts and made several recordings. Far from being stuck in his musical ways, he was open to musical ideas wherever they came from. That year he recorded Brahms's *Piano Quartet in G Minor* with the Guarneri Quartet, young musicians who had formed their quartet in 1964, four years before. This report, quoted by Rubinstein's biographer, appeared in *Time:*

> The old man sat at a table in an RCA Victor recording studio in Manhattan and listened to a playback. The cello came on with a rhapsodic, throbbing solo. "Very beautiful," sighed the old man, and tapped Cellist David Soyer approvingly on the knee. Then, a gnarled passage for piano and strings. "No," said the old man, "that's not so good. Here Brahms makes a trap, and we fell in. What shall we do?"
>
> Violist Michael Tree offered a suggestion. "Maybe," he told the old man, "you could come in a little slower, maybe more quietly." Violinist John Dalley agreed with a nod. "Fine," said the old man. "Let's try it." And Arthur Rubinstein, a month short of his 81st birthday, led three members of the Guarneri Quartet, whose average age was 36, back to the microphones for another try at Brahms's *Piano Quartet in G Minor.*

The quartet's first violinist, Arnold Steinhardt (b. 1937), recalled Rubinstein's energy at a time that Steinhardt was "a guy in my early thirties." One morning in Paris, the musicians got together in the morning, played, broke for lunch during which Rubinstein had his cigar and told stories, rehearsed all afternoon, had dinner, then "*more* stories, *more* wine, *more* cigars. After dinner I was reeling, but Rubinstein said, 'Well, how about another piano quartet.'" Steinhardt, who'd been ready to drop from exhaustion, said of Rubinstein: "It was like food for him: he was living off the experience of making music. He wasn't expending energy, he was getting energy."[256]

At age 93, in 1976, Arthur Rubinstein played his last two concerts, each one to adoring audiences, one in Carnegie Hall in New York and the last one in Wigmore Hall in London.

The musician Judy Collins (b. 1939), at age 80 in 2020, has actually increased her workload. She continues to tour. Collins says, "Never stop. That's the key. Never stop. Never stop growing. Never stop being curious. Never stop thinking that there's something you want to do that you haven't done. And do it!"[257] An (unnamed) artist recipient of a grant from the Richard Florsheim Art Fund, which supported visual artists aged 60 and older, told an interviewer: "I'm not going to stop painting at 65 and take up golf, beer, and TV watching."[258]

The poet, critic, and novelist Robert Penn Warren (1905–1989) said at the age of 80: "I don't know what stopping really is."[259] In the last ten years of his life, Warren wrote about ten books (not counting selected and collected poems). He did so under conditions of ill-health, periodic hospitalization, and chronic pain.[260]

Cartoonist Jules Feiffer (b. 1929) at the age of 90, said "In my dotage everything I've been doing is more exciting than anything I've done in a very long time, and it's all very accidental. I've lived a life of entire improvisation and it's a wonderful life."[261] The author James Michener (1907–1997), who wrote more than 40 books, published 18 of them during his 80s. He died at age 90.[262]

I recently went to YouTube to watch B. B. King (1925–2015) perform, in 2010, "The Thrill Is Gone" at Chicago's Crossroads Guitar Festival—he was in his mid-80s. It is unforgettable.[263]

At age 84 Joan Semmel (b. 1932), painter of lush, gigantic, semi-abstract, semi-figurative nudes, fleshly, gorgeous, and, most recently, old, asked, "Why do I have to make more paintings? There's plenty of work. [She means that by this time she has made a large number of paintings, sufficient for one career.] Well, because that's what I do! That's just who I am and what I do. That's what makes me happy—the process of discovering things, being totally at one with myself."[264]

One non-retiring pattern is to simply keep on, to simply never quit. The work gains from the accumulation of skill, despite possible worries about repeating oneself or having nothing new to say. Late in the career there may emerge a lighter, looser feel, a greater sense of freedom, a greater capacity for innovation. What more is there to prove? Or, to put it another way, what is there to lose? We've already seen how the composer Elliott Carter's work flourished in his 90s through to his death at 103. Such innovative and transcendent work in the final years of a creative career have been termed "Late Style."

The architect Frank Gehry (b. 1929), who turned 91 in 2020, began as a designer of conventional shopping malls and office buildings. But to remodel and design his own home in Santa Monica, during the 1970s, he turned his imagination loose and followed his own predilections. The result was the original house altered and extended with multi-angled exteriors using unconventional materials such as corrugated sheet metal, plywood, and chain link. One time, when Gehry was about 50 years old, at a dinner at this Santa Monica home to celebrate the completion of a conventional shopping mall, the developer asked Gehry, "Frank, you don't like Santa Monica Place [the mall], do you?" The developer perceived that Gehry could not possibly like both the conventional shopping mall just completed and his own house. Gehry allowed that he did not like the mall. The developer said, "Why are you wasting your time and energy fighting with commercial developers when you really have a different mission in life? Why don't you just do what you are good at?"[265]

Gehry agreed. He thought about it over the weekend. He then terminated his career as a conventional architect, laying off some thirty employees of his rather successful business. He began again. The new direction began slowly and there were frugal years. But eventually Gehry's iconic buildings became destinations—the Guggenheim Museum Bilbao; Seattle's Experience Music Project (renamed Museum of Pop Culture); the Gehry Tower in Hanover, Germany; the Walt Disney Concert Hall in Los Angeles; and many others. "Why are you still doing this?" a PBS News Hour interviewer asked Frank Gehry. "You are 86..." Gehry's answer: "I don't know what else to do! I love doing it. I love working. I don't know what the word *vacation* means."[266]

In his 70s the choreographer Merce Cunningham began using computer technology to choreograph. He used a computer program called Life Forms, created at Simon Frasier University in the computer graphics research lab. The program had three-dimensional figures with moveable joints that one could manipulate on screen. Cunningham would experiment on the computer and then have his dancers try various moves no one had imagined before. Sometimes they couldn't be executed by a human body but nevertheless led to a new idea. Cunningham then joined the computer team to redesign the software, which they called Dance Forms. He also used motion-capture technology in which the dancers dance with sensors on their bodies. Their motions could then be animated into figures that made the same dance moves. In his strangely eerie dance *Biped* (1999), enormous, digitized figures dance with the dancers. (They look like chalk outlines of dancers—you can see through them and they dance in front of and behind the real dancers.) Thus were the last twenty years of Cunningham's life immersed in innovative technologies.[267]

In her last years, the sculptor and printmaker Louise Bourgeois (1911–2010), who lived until age 98, worked with almost phenomenal productivity. She continued making art up until the end. Suffering from insomnia, she would write and draw late into the night. She also had severe agoraphobia and for the last ten years of her life, did not leave her home/studio. She had a skilled, devoted assistant, Jerry Gorovoy, who worked for her for thirty years and now leads her foundation. Gorovoy would attend to gallery installations and much business, and also supported her emotionally. Bourgeois worked every day except Sunday. On Sundays she opened her home/studio to visitors to bring work, see work, and talk about work.[268]

Coming closer to home, my friend the poet, novelist, and essayist Jack Remick (b. 1941), author of (among other books) *The Weekend Novelist Writes a Mystery* (with Robert J. Ray), published, during his 70s, ten books, including nine novels, a book of poetry, and a book of essays. He just turned 80 and he is still going strong. And I myself, rather than slowing down in my 70s, have sped up. Much of my work appears in individual pieces outside of books, but of my seven books to date, five—two books of poems, a collection of memoirist essays that incorporate science, a handbook on how to carry out creative work, and this book—were published after I turned 72. At my present age I possess two things I had considerably less of in earlier days: time and confidence.

## Mandatory Retirement

The life-altering event of retirement can be involuntary. Mandatory retirement was made illegal for most occupations in the United States, but it is in full force in Europe and in other parts of the world.

And even without mandatory retirement, age discrimination is rampant when it comes to who gets a job and who gets laid off or let go. An AARP Special Report on ageism in the workplace reported that three in five workers have seen or experienced age discrimination, and of these workers, 76 percent see age discrimination as a hurdle to finding a new job. "Another report found that more than half of older workers are prematurely pushed out of jobs, and 90 percent never earn as much again." Numerous ads for jobs use discriminatory (and likely illegal) language such as "recent college graduate" or "digital native" or even "young."[269] The worldwide coronavirus pandemic in 2020 has made all of this much worse.

Before mandatory retirement was abolished, the sculptor Anne Truitt (1921–2004) was forced at the age of 70 (in 1991) to retire from her teaching job in the art department of the University of Maryland. In her memoir *Prospect* she writes how shocking and painful this was. She had worked there since 1975. She was in her prime of good teaching and she was in her prime of good artmaking. That very year she had received a "distinguished scholar-teacher" award. In a single stroke, her financial security was "annihilated." It was, she wrote, "incredible, dumbfounding, that I should be ejected from the university in the full vigor of teaching....It was as if I had been struck by lightning off a mountain, become a loose rock tumbling in space." And after she made adjustments, including a part-time teaching job (for less money) elsewhere, "I continue to feel startled that simply because I have become seventy, all other factors unchanged, I am worth so much less on the market."[270] Truitt was esteemed among museum curators, critics, and collectors, but, like most artists, she did not make enough money off her art to live on.

There are times, though, when being forced or encouraged to retire brings an unexpectedly joyful new way of life. The Arkansas painter Eva Wines (1911–1994) was a longtime elementary school teacher who loved to teach. "I did not want to retire, really; I hated to give up the children," she said. "My husband wanted me to retire....I told him if I died teaching, I'd die happy, because I was doing what I wanted to do." But she did retire and immediately found art. The first summer, she took two art courses, discovered her talent, and found a new love in life—painting. She found three friends in art class, and they met frequently to talk about art and to critique work. She said, it is "so fun—to exchange ideas—that we hate to stop and come home. We haven't finished. We just want to keep going." During her retirement Wines also jogged every morning for four miles—with friends. She said, "So many people fear retirement and say, 'Oh, I don't know what I'm going to do with myself.' And they don't know how sweet life can be after they retire. It's great."[271]

Another who felt positive joy at his mandatory retirement was the frequently performing pianist, music professor, and composer Randolph Hokanson (1915–2018). In 1984 he was required to retire from the music department at the University of Washington. In his memoir, *With Head to Music Bent*, he wrote:

> When I opened my eyes to a beautiful morning in June 1984, I felt a very special elation—I was free! From this day on I could do exactly as I wished. One of these wishes would assuredly not be the usual retiree's dream of doing nothing....In a few days I would be 70, but felt very well and in no need of relaxing in my way of life. I needed only to be invigorated by the plans that were already coursing through my head.

Hokanson's two main dreams were to stimulate the study and teaching of Bach, and to compose. On both these endeavors he went full steam ahead, along with continuing to perform ("I was busier as a performer than I had ever been"[272]), until his death at age 103. At the age of 92 he performed a series of lecture/demonstrations on Bach's "Well-Tempered Clavier" to packed audiences at the University of Washington. At age 93 he released a new recording "demonstrating his fluent technique and interpretive skills in works of considerable difficulty by Liszt, Brahms and others," according to his obituary. In celebration of his 100th birthday "he performed a remarkable solo and duo recital" with a violinist.[273]

## Shifting Priorities / Changing Strategies

In our old age, for better or worse, a lot has already been accomplished. Often, given a combination of good effort and good luck, we have more leisure, more freedom, more control over time. At age 79 I plan to never stop writing and—possibly—to never stop teaching. But at age 70 I ceased working at a major editing job that I had carried for the previous fifteen years along with teaching, coaching writers, and doing my own writing. My time has become more my own. This is happiness.

At age 84 the many-book author Penelope Lively (b. 1933) cast her eye back at what she called the "too-busy" years. During one of those years she had to be at Heathrow airport to travel on "bookish" business twelve different times. "Well," she writes, "No more of that. One of the pleasures of old age is the thought that I shall never see Heathrow again." She still writes, but now in a less driven fashion:

> In fact, I rather appreciate the old-age writing day. It is still essential to be writing something, but the pressure is off. Now that I'm done with outside commitments, pretty well, all my time is my own....If I get in two or three hours at the turquoise notebook that is great. If I decide to get out and about, or go gardening, or socialize, that is fine....[274]

At this more leisurely pace, Lively wrote a book on the history of gardening and a book of short stories.

Doris Grumbach, writer, reviewed books weekly on National Public Radio for more than five years, beginning in her 60s. Upon her move with her domestic partner from Washington, DC to Maine, at age 70, she gave up this increasingly burdensome task. She had grown weary of having to have an opinion on every book. She had grown wary of her tendency to stammer during the taping. She had grown restless in the harness of required reading for the show instead of being able to follow her own book-lover's whims.

She asked the post office to return all books sent to her. She asked the 30 or so publishers that constantly sent books to stop sending books. Now, she wrote, "my mail is reduced to human scale. I am no longer troubled by the arrival, every day, of ten and more brown-boxed books, the disposal of wrappings, the perusal, even scantily, of their contents, and the close reading of two or three for every one I had airtime to review. My sense of relief is immense." She began reading, at her leisure, *Bleak House* by Charles Dickens, "sitting in a chair on our thick, green lawn, and taking not a single note as I read."[275] Grumbach did not retire as a writer, but she set down the writing-related chore she'd come to dread.

Many artists and writers teach to earn their living, and some retire from teaching in order to focus, at last, on their own work alone. The painter Louis Freund (1905–1999) and jeweler and textile artist Elsie Freund (1912–2001), both teachers, were interviewed for a prescient 1984 book on creative elders in Arkansas, *A Fine Age: Creativity as a Key to Successful Aging*. The two were prime movers in establishing Eureka Springs, Arkansas, as a community that thrived as a destination for arts and crafts. The couple purchased a large boarding house—it was about to be razed for the lumber—and founded the summer Art School of the Ozarks. They and their students established a crafts fair and several galleries. Both Freunds taught, in Eureka Springs and elsewhere. But in their early 70s they were ready to set down teaching. Louis said:

As we got older, between teaching in winter and summer, we didn't have time to do our own work. Finally, we gave up the summer art school.

The thing is, I felt after teaching in colleges for twenty-five years, it was a good round number. But that was not my main profession….Teaching was a rewarding job [but] the painting—finally going totally to it—was a welcome relief… Now we find we are letting go, conserving our energy and time for our work. I would like to be able to paint some every day.[276]

California assemblage artist Noah Purifoy (1917–2004) profoundly altered his life and means of making art when, at the age of 72, he moved from Los Angeles to the high desert of Joshua Tree, California. Purifoy was trained as a social worker and after receiving a master's degree in social work administration and working as a social worker, he attended the Chouinard Art Institute (renamed California Institute of the Arts), the first African American to be enrolled full time at the college. He received a Bachelor of Fine Arts degree at age 39. His previous life had included teaching industrial arts and years in the navy working as a carpenter. He also worked at the Douglas Aircraft plant and as a window designer and interior designer. In 1964 he cofounded the Watts Towers Arts Center. For several years he worked with children and youth in after-school arts programs. The historic Watts Rebellion, or riot, which took place from August 11 to 16, 1965, in the Watts neighborhood of Los Angeles, changed everything for Purifoy. He wrote:

I was in the middle of the Watts Uprising but I wasn't afraid. I thought it was great because it was overdue and it turned out to be a goldmine for me. I collected three tons of debris from the riot and began making art out of it. I was searching for my own idea and had been studying the Dada movement and how it had reversed the whole concept of art, and the debris from the riot is what finally launched me on my own course.[277]

One result of this work was the pioneering exhibition *66 Years of Neon*, made by Purifoy and other artists, which used the charred debris created by the rebellion to make assemblage art.

Purifoy's next years were taken up with making art and teaching art. From 1970 to 1975 he served as the director of social services at the Central City Community Mental Health Center in Los Angeles. In 1976 California Governor Jerry Brown appointed him to the California Arts Council. He spent the next decade developing arts programs for schools and prisons. Finally in 1987 he resumed making art full time. He was then 70 years old.

But he could no longer afford to live in Los Angeles. A friend invited him to set himself up on a ten-acre piece of land she owned in the Joshua Tree high desert. At age 72, Purifoy relocated to that harsh, sparsely populated land, bringing with him a truckload of objects and debris. He took up residence in a trailer and for the next fifteen years worked on his art, getting to know other desert residents, and using their debris. Of what he created, art critic and curator Yael Lipschutz writes:

> Surrounded by trailers, busted-out homesteading shacks, and small modern abodes, over the next fifteen years Purifoy transformed the barren parcel of desert on Blair Lane into one of art history's wonders, punctuating the ten-acre site with more than 120 large-scale sculptures. Composed largely of junk, Purifoy's environmental installation in Joshua Tree is his most lasting legacy as an artist...[278]

Noah Purifoy died in a fire in his trailer on May 9, 2004. He was 87 years old. In his last fifteen years Purifoy's creative path did not so much change direction as intensify when he finally gained conditions that enabled him to build large and without interruption. (His art legacy in Joshua Tree is preserved by the Noah Purifoy Foundation and is free and open to the public.)

## Encore Careers and Encore Endeavors

There is another sort of creative path, termed an encore career. The person retires or quits to begin an entirely new life, some new work or new endeavor.

One of sociologist Sara Lawrence-Lightfoot's interviewees was an industrial chemist, age 69, whom Lawrence-Lightfoot calls "Mario Delgado." In his successful career he was often the only Latino in the room, "trying to dutifully fit in—making sure I didn't make waves." He had been "secretive" and "competitive." Late in life he turned to sculpture. He shared a studio with three other artists and had to learn to ask them for help in solving problems. He had to become more open, more vulnerable. In monitoring his own developing skills in his new art, he had to learn patience and self-compassion. He experienced the "interference of old school habits." His new work was teaching him an entirely new way of learning. But working with his hands also gave him "a new sense of connection to his father and grandfather," who had been artisans and manual laborers. He said, "I feel the imprint of my ancestors, my strong Mexican roots."[279]

Sometimes an encore career means returning to an old passion. Arkansas fiddler, woodcarver and fiddle maker Violet Hensley (b. 1916) learned to make fiddles from her father. As a child she helped her father on the farm, receiving little education. In the years to come, the work to raise her family and survive was grueling. "I married when I was eighteen to a fellow just down the road aways; we had eight children. I was busy making a home—had no time for music and carving, not much to sing about, life was hard." The couple found work where they could, picking fruit in Oregon, carrots in Arizona, then back to Oregon to pick potatoes in the fall. Finally they found a way to purchase a plot of land in Arkansas. They moved home.

Hensley began carving fiddles once again. And she kept on fiddling. Along came the folk music revival of the 1960s. She began performing at music festivals, appeared on television several times, and was featured in *National Geographic* and other magazines. With her musical family she has made three albums of old-time fiddle tunes. In 2004 Arkansas designated her a Living Treasure, and in 2018 she performed at the Grand Ole Opry. Her fiddles have become collector's items. This was not really retiring. In her late 60s she said, "I'm not prepared for any leisure home. I'm prepared to work."[280] Now a centenarian, she continues to work.

Another person who came home to art late in life was the Colorado–based painter and multimedia artist Carol Nelson (b. 1944). (Her artwork graces the cover of this book.) As a child, Nelson loved the big 64-crayon Crayola box, and she took art lessons from the seventh grade into college. But she switched majors ("Art was way too vague from an employment standpoint") and ended up as a medical technologist, one who works in a hospital lab to analyze bodily fluids such as blood and urine. In her late 50s Nelson began painting again. At age 65 she retired to become a full-time artist. Now in her late 70s, she makes art and teaches art, both in person and online.[281]

John Wright (b. 1929), Washington State–based poet, began as a physician. He practiced internal medicine and endocrinology at Seattle's Swedish Medical Center from 1964 to 1988. From 1989 to 1994 he served as the Center's Vice President for Medical Staff Affairs. He is Clinical Professor Emeritus in Medicine at the University of Washington. Now (2022) 92 years old, he has lived with his child-psychiatrist wife, Lanita, for many decades in and near Edmonds, Washington. He was effective and successful in his medical career, but suffered, over a forty-year period, four major episodes of clinical depression.

Wright came from a rural western Pennsylvania family. His father worked for Bethlehem Steel in Johnstown, Pennsylvania, beginning as a laborer and ending as a superintendent. The family and especially his father, a lay preacher, was devoutly Christian, and a central concern in Wright's original struggle for meaning took place within the Christian faith. In his mid-50s he began taking adult-education writing courses. At age 58, seven years before he retired at age 65, he arrived in the short-story-writing class of Jack Cady (1932–2004), a fantasy/horror novelist who nevertheless assigned the class: *Write a love poem, twenty-five words or less, don't use the word love, don't use the word god, and above all, make it honest.* "In doing this lesson," Wright writes in the author note to his first book of poems:

I discovered poetry, and I was, you might say, born again. For the first time, I had a tool for honestly exploring disorder, the disorder in myself and the disorder outside, and their relationship one to the other. It's a remarkable tool, providing, not only a way to say what's discovered, but the courage to say it. Looking back from this late developing vista, I'm able to give thanks for my scars and call them blessings. Blessings because they forced me to dig deeper into my own, largely inherited and culturally shaped belief system, opening me up to poetry. And a blessing because poetry, in turn, has led me to a more robust experience of grace, a grace that offsets existential angst with existential joy.[282]

John Wright, one of my longtime poetry clients, is a fine poet, actively engaged in the poetry community, author at this point of five books of poems.

What about elderly people who are in fact dependent? In the United States, the actual number of persons 65 years old and older living in institutional settings, including nursing homes, is 3.1 percent, or 1.5 million. In the population over 85, this goes up to 9 percent (2016 statistics). But consider, even after we turn 85, the majority of us *do not* require institutionalized care. As for those living at home, according to one government accounting, 22 percent of people over 85 require some help at home with personal care.[283] Do we feel this is a problem? Are we disturbed to learn that both Matisse and Renoir required extensive help with personal care at the end of their lives? How many of us have never, for one reason or another, required help with personal care?

And again, to turn the statistic around, the majority of people over 85 take care of themselves. And many of us *provide* care for younger family members, for partners, for friends. We want to contribute, and we do contribute. The "gray tsunami" claim is grounded in the notion that to be old is to be dependent, decrepit, and nonproductive. It's an ageist claim—false and insulting.

Poet John Wright, age 91, September 2021. *Photo by Terry Olmsted.*

## Redefining Productivity

Our national statistics define productivity (the Gross Domestic Product) as paid labor. John W. Rowe and Robert L. Kahn—authors of the book *Successful Aging*, which resulted from the MacArthur Foundation Study of Successful Aging—question this. So might we all. A volunteer clerk at a hospital gift shop is considered nonproductive while the person next to her getting paid for the same work is considered productive. Unpaid caregiving is nonproductive; paid caregiving is productive. A retired schoolteacher who teaches a child to read is nonproductive; a paid schoolteacher who teaches a child to read is productive. The hundreds of volunteers at COVID-19 vaccination centers are nonproductive; the paid workers there, productive. The MacArthur Foundation Study redefines productive behavior as "any activity, paid or unpaid, that generates goods or services of economic value."[284]

In the United States, one-quarter of all people over the age of 65 volunteer. In Canada one-third of all people over the age of 65 volunteer. Worldwide, volunteering contributes half a trillion dollars to local economies.[285] Volunteers are productive workers. Far from draining the economy, they contribute to it. Volunteering also contributes to the volunteer's own mental and physical well-being.

A 2018 study of people over 50 in the United States found that the majority of older adults exhibit high levels of pro-social values and behavior. They care for others and they care for the environment. They value equal treatment for all. This national study was carried out by a team at Stanford University's Graduate School of Education along with Encore.org, an organization that "taps the talent of the 50+ generation as a force for good." Nearly one-third of older adults (31 percent) exhibited a purpose beyond the self. The prevalence of this purpose to be of service to others is not affected by income levels or by health. It's true of the whole age group but higher among people of color than among whites.[286]

To name one project, Experience Corps was launched in 1996 by Encore.org, founded by Marc Freedman (b. 1958) and John W. Gardner (1912–2002), both prime movers in helping us rethink our obsolete conceptions of old age. Experience Corps is now part of the AARP Foundation. More than 2,000 volunteer mentors over age 50 work with some 31,000 urban children who are reading-challenged in 275 schools from kindergarten to the third grade. The mentors contribute fifteen hours a week for at least a year and usually two years. The program provides huge benefits to the pupils, and it also benefits the volunteer mentors, who were found to be healthier, more socially connected, happier, and physically more active since beginning their service.[287]

On a different project, another elder volunteer who changed the lives of many children was H. Eugene "Gene" Jones (1916–2013).[288] Gene Jones had been a bomber pilot during World War II and after that pursued a lucrative career bringing back companies on the brink of failure. He retired and, spurred by his love of music, became active on the board of the symphony in Tucson, Arizona. At age 84, at a conference, Jones happened upon an idea being put into practice in North Carolina—an arts program introduced into poor schools that used musicians from the local symphony. The simple program was making a radical difference in attendance, test scores, and discipline issues. Jones brought the idea back to Tucson and started Opening Minds Through the Arts, rounded up support, had the North Carolina teachers come to explain what they were doing, donated a million dollars to get the program started, and got the university involved to track progress in a statistical, non-anecdotal manner. He stayed involved until his mid-90s. What the schools did, according to a reporter:

> They played classical music in the hallways of the school—mostly major key baroque music—at moderate to low levels over the PA system. The rule became that no one could talk in the halls louder than the music was playing. Immediately the din of school hallways diminished.
>
> And funny things started happening. Sick kids started complaining to their parents that they didn't want to stay home because it was an OMA day. The music programs the teachers introduced helped them understand simple mathematical concepts—higher and lower, more and less. They started to improve their vocabulary and spelling. Their scores in standardized tests started to dramatically improve. Education was succeeding, and both the regular teachers and the OMA teachers could see it happening before their eyes.[289]

Gene Jones did not believe in retiring in order to sit around. He stated: "You sit on a shelf waiting for the billions of years that this earth has been in existence, and you have your turn on stage for a nanosecond. To waste it by doing nothing is unthinkable." His own satisfaction had to do with involvement in "a program that is changing lives." He stated: "I want to keep doing it as long as I can breathe."[290] He did just that.

To contribute, there is no need to be in perfect health. In their book *Successful Aging*, Rowe and Kahn speak of an 80-year-old actress. She continued to perform—whenever she could get work—and this put her on stage two to three months in a year. The rest of the time she volunteered at the box office and helped with theater mailings and other tasks, always keeping in her hand. This creative worker had had three heart attacks, a bad fall, and colon cancer. None of which prevented her energetic participation in life or in the theater.[291]

At age 85, my father, Winslow Long (1922–2013), who lived with congestive heart failure and was painfully (for him) hard of hearing, moved to Seattle to be near his daughters and also, I think, for the thrill of living in a city. He departed his rural community on the Eastern Shore of Maryland, where he had lived for more than sixty years. He had been a farmer, a beekeeper, and a dog trainer, and also did bookkeeping. He memorized poetry and studied Emily Dickinson. He was a gardener and a skilled amateur botanist. During his last five years (he died at age 91) he initiated and led the renovation of the grounds of Seattle's local Friends Meeting. The grounds were gradually transformed from being a mass of invasives to a native-plant garden that continues to thrive. I walk by it at least once a week and marvel at its beauty. I thank my father.

## Social Security

In the United States, Social Security is insurance that we pay for with our payroll taxes—not an entitlement. It finances the cost of retirement (or some of that cost) and provides disability and survivor benefits. Because it is not a welfare program, it's cheap to administer, since everyone who pays into it simply receives benefits. There's no need to adjudicate who qualifies and who doesn't. It's financed by its own tax fund. This is not a pension fund. All earned income under the cap of $148,800 (as of 2021) is taxed. Employers pay in the same amount as the worker pays in. Self-employed persons (such as myself) pay in for both worker and employer. No unearned income (such as stock dividends) is taxed. Your Social

Security taxes do not pay for your own benefits. They fund the benefits of those ahead of you. When you start receiving benefits, these are funded by the Social Security payroll taxes paid by those still in the workforce. The Social Security Trust Fund is where funds go that are received from taxes but not yet needed to pay benefits. Social Security benefits are also taxed (as part of federal income tax). And if you continue to work, as I do, you continue to pay the Social Security tax, even while receiving benefits.[292]

What good is Social Security? In the words of economist Paul Krugman: "Social Security is what keeps tens of millions of older Americans from being desperately poor. It's what protects your mother or grandmother against living on catfood."[293]

This is good, but is it sustainable? Will there be enough younger people in the work force paying into social security to sustain older people receiving benefits? In the United States, as we know, the birth rate is low; longevity is increasing. The big baby-boomer generation is aging into benefits. And, Krugman notes, worsening income inequality in the United States puts further pressure on Social Security funds, since wage earners are earning smaller taxable incomes and because earnings above the cap are not taxed.[294]

We're headed for a shortfall. The Social Security Administration explains, "redemption of trust fund assets will be sufficient to allow for full payment of scheduled benefits until 2035."[295] What happens then? According to the Social Security Administration, payroll taxes will continue to flow into the fund but will be sufficient to pay only about 80 percent of the costs. "The projected shortfall over the next 75 years is 2.78% of taxable payroll." "Lost in the welter of crooked statistics," notes Theodore Roszack in his book *The Making of an Elder Culture*, "is the fact that Social Security is the *only* government program that is funded 30 years into the future. In contrast, try asking where next year's Pentagon budget is coming from."[296]

The Social Security shortfall projection is in part based on the so-called "economic dependency ratio," a ratio of those in the workforce versus those "dependent," that is, not in the workforce.

This statistic obfuscates several facts. One is the above-mentioned productivity of volunteer workers, who produce goods or services of economic value. Secondly, many people who draw Social Security do not live upon it entirely; they also live on their savings or they continue to work. They are not wholly "dependent on the government." Thirdly, it was our own payroll taxes that created this fund, so we can hardly be called dependent on the government. The government is dependent on us for the fund.

Legal scholar Lincoln Caplan objects that this "dependency ratio" "bluntly separates older Americans from everyone else. It presents them as being unable to care for themselves. It puts forth an objective-seeming formula that appears to document that those who make up the 'gray tsunami' are a large and growing liability, undermining the country's assets."[297] Another phrase that drives our thinking into the dead end of our youth-obsessed culture is "prime working years." This is supposed to be age 15 to 59. "No," writes Marc Freedman. "These assumptions are extraordinarily arbitrary."[298]

Old age—is it possible to say this too often?— does not index dependency.

Still, what should be done about any forthcoming shortfall in Social Security? Cut benefits? According to an AARP survey, the great majority of Americans, both young and old, oppose such a thing.[299] I sure do. Privatize social security? Krugman argues that even supporters of privatization know it won't work; they basically oppose the program altogether and wish to get rid of it.[300] Increase the cap? Why not? Increase retirement age? This has already been done and is being done. Tax unearned income? Why not? Tax 90 percent of any given worker's income? Good idea. Have Congress direct funds into the trust fund? Again, why not?

An ameliorating factor is that immigrants joining the workforce (and paying Social Security taxes) tend to be younger. In 2017 in the United States, there were 21.2 million lawful immigrants working or looking for work. According to the Pew Research Center, "Immigrants are…projected to drive future growth in the U.S. working-age population through at least 2035.

As the Baby Boom generation heads into retirement, immigrants and their children are expected to offset a decline in the working-age population by adding about 18 million people of working age between 2015 and 2035."[301]

In short, let's keep Social Security. There are no disasters ahead, and virtually a cornucopia of solutions to the upcoming shortfall.

Another thing to consider: When old people do better, younger people do better. Older people, obviously, love and care for the younger people in their families. The MacArthur Foundation found, in a study done in South Africa, that over time, in extended families in which the older women received pensions, the granddaughters were healthier and better educated. Other studies covering the United States and 40 other countries show that financial transfers flow predominately from older generations to younger ones.[302]

## The Economic Clout of the Old

Old people nourish the economy and you could even say that old people keep the big old jalopy running. How can that be? Consider:

- Americans over the age of 50 have a combined annual personal income of more than $3.9 trillion. (However, this obscures the reality of income inequality, with the much greater wealth of the wealthiest 1 percent.)
- Americans over the age of 50 control 77 percent of the total net worth of households.
- Americans over the age of 50 account for almost half of the country's disposable income.
- Americans over the age of 50 purchase at least half of all appliances, women's apparel, housing, groceries, take-out food, entertainment, health insurance, new cars, and new trucks.
- Americans over 50 purchase one-fourth of all toys.[303]

## Aging Versus Images of Aging

These numbers are startling; at least they were to me. They challenge the pervasive youth-fixation displayed in advertising images. How rare it is to see older models modeling dresses or draping themselves over cars or trucks or driving that speedy SUV around hairpin turns. How rare it is to see anyone over 30 advertising anything (except maybe ads for prescription drugs…).

Even worse than the interminable display of youth in advertisements are those egregiously derogatory of old people. Check out "Dear Young People, Please Don't Vote," viewable on YouTube. This ad was created in 2018 with the purpose of getting out the progressive youth vote. A series of old people snarl, one by one, that they don't give a damn about school shootings—they're not in school—or climate change—"that's your problem, I'll be dead." They're against taxing the rich—"I *am* rich." And so on. The idea being that youth should vote to counter the votes of these reactionary old farts, because the reactionary old farts *will* be voting. This ad was perpetrated by the allegedly progressive organization Acronym, a Washington DC nonprofit dedicated to getting out the youth vote. And then, there is the E-Trade ad for retirement accounts, which displays incompetent, falling-down, ridiculous 85-year-olds struggling to keep up at a job because they lack sufficient retirement income. Both these ads were deplored in a recent issue of the *AARP Bulletin*.[304]

Not only ads, but photographs, portraits, and cartoons can be cruel. They can perpetrate stereotypes. This is well known in the ugly history of racism and anti-Semitism. But we are so much less conscious of this weapon as used against old people. Just Google "ugly old people" to get a nasty hit of what I mean. The portraits are mostly of people who have some sort of disfiguring ailment and most have dental issues. One man has some sort of cyst or tumor on his nose. One label reads: "Top 32 Funny Ugly People Pics." An old woman lacking teeth is labeled "Old People Are Ugly!" Another image is labeled, "How Ugly People Look When They Cry." Who is being ugly here?

Images are powerful. They are persuasive. They contribute to well-being or to unhappiness and despair. We need positive images of old people. This is why it is so deeply refreshing to spend an hour with the portraits of a painter like Alice Neel (1900–

1984). She painted—both nude and dressed—crooked people, old people, wounded people, well people, young people, children, pregnant people, people of all colors and shapes, women, men, all kinds of people. She said that when she painted, she tried for "the complete person," and "a specific person." She also puts them in their context. The sitters look like themselves. They look like individuals with lives, contexts, personalities, relationships. They do not *represent* childhood, youth, old age, or poverty or affluence or pregnancy. Of her portraits the artist said:

> A good portrait of mine has even more than just the accurate features. It has some other thing. If I have any talent in relation to people, apart from planning the whole canvas, it is my identification with them. I get so identified when I paint them, when they go home I feel frightful. I have no self—I've gone into this other person. And by doing that, there's a kind of something I get that other artists don't get.[305]

So, empathy. At the age of 80, against several centuries of tradition favoring young female nudes, Neel painted her own old body, a nude self-portrait, herself with paintbrush in hand. The picture hangs in the National Portrait Gallery in Washington, DC.

The painter Joan Semmel works against the idea that beauty inheres only to the nubile. She told an interviewer, "There's always been so much shame attached to the body....I've talked at times about working against the shame of the body, the shame of getting old, all of these shames that are laid on our heads. You should be ashamed that you're old, instead of being proud to have lived? All of these things, culturally, have really distorted what life is about....It's...about the acceptance of mortality. It's about being a body that changes, that ages, that loves, that hates, that does all of these things! It's not about being some sort of model, a perfected ideal of any kind."[306]

In her book *Ending Ageism, or How Not to Shoot Old People*, Margaret Morganroth Gullette argues that we require a turn toward age pride.[307] In our image-saturated culture we need more images of old people—old people shown within their own context, old people shown in relationship, old people shown in action, working, painting, playing music, writing.

The photographer Annie Leibovitz (b. 1949) shoots the actress Sophia Loren (b. 1934) at age 77 in a glamorous black gown standing in what must be Loren's parlor with its sofas and easychairs, artworks, framed photos, a chandelier, a piano, an elaborate tapestry hanging on one wall. She photographs Pete Seeger (1919–2014) at age 90, standing tall next to the ocean, his banjo slung over his shoulder. She photographs Gloria Steinem (b. 1934) at age 81, working on her laptop in her study crammed with books and papers. She photographs the visual artist Jasper Johns (b. 1930) at age 83, in his studio. She photographs the visual artist Susan Rothenberg (b. 1945) at age 67 in her studio. She photographs Yoko Ono (b. 1933) at age 82, seated on a high stool in full androgynous performance mode, dressed in a man's top hat, leotard, net hose, stiletto pumps, dark glasses. What do we see? What we do not see is some 82-year-old woman. What we do see is Yoko Ono herself, fully present, at the height of her creative powers. And that's how we see each of these powerful portraits.[308]

The film *Lives Well Lived* made by Sky Bergman illuminates the lives of 40 old people.[309] It's hugely inspiring to hear Wachtang "Botso" Korisheli (1921–2015) age 93, who taught music to children, who began sculpting at age 40, say, "If I sit at the piano I come alive." And, "Day by day you get up and decide what you are going to do today, and then you get up and do." Botso, as everyone called him, was a renowned music teacher: a notable number of his child pupils developed into well-known musicians.

In this film it's also inspiring to witness Emmy Cleaves, age 86, teaching the yoga she has spent her life practicing. And it is inspiring to witness the vitality and energy of dancer and quilter Blanch Brown, age 78. The 40 elders portrayed in *Lives Well Lived* are wise and they share their wisdom. They exhibit humor, courage, resilience, and striking tolerance and kindness. Their life stories, often including traumas growing out of the wars and revolutions of the twentieth century, are deeply inspiring.

We are, all of us, immersed to one extent or another in our image-saturated culture, with our phone cameras, our selfies, our posts to Instagram or Facebook, our image-heavy blogs, our texts (including photos), our various photography projects. We are amateur photographers and we are professional photographers. One project we might undertake is to challenge pervasive ageism with images of older persons relating, doing, speaking. Older persons in their work, with their people, in their own environment. This could be one way to do our part to dissipate the toxic fumes of ageism that degrade our culture and our daily lives.

## Giving Back

When it comes to philanthropic giving, elder persons are a major resource. In the United Kingdom, more than half of all charitable donations came from those over 60 years old (2012 statistics).[310] In the United States, "Older Americans have the bulk of the money and they make the bulk of philanthropic investments," writes the organization Benefactor Group, of Columbus, Ohio, which assists nonprofits with fundraising. Elder donors are not only "where the money is," states this organization. "Elders are also generous with their money."[311]

One road to generosity is through bequests. The novelist Philip Roth (1933–2018) left some two million dollars to the Newark (New Jersey) Public Library, a library that had sheltered his love of reading as a boy.[312] The painter Agnes Martin, after she became wealthy, in the words of her biographer, "sought out ways to share her bounty, from significant acts of philanthropy to taking people out to lunch. Her acts of non-material generosity were just as important in sustaining the many deeply loyal friendships she continued to have."[313] After her death in 2004 her gifts to Taos supported two parks, a public swimming pool, and a substantial gift to the Harwood Art Museum.

James Michener, toward the end of his life, donated millions of dollars to philanthropies such as the Author's League Fund, which assists authors dealing with financial emergencies, usually brought on by a health crisis.[314] Once, years ago, in the midst of just such an emergency, I received aid from the Author's League Fund; I was lifted up and hope was restored.

Giving back need have nothing to do with wealth. I like the story of New Jersey resident Bob Halberstadt, age 80, told in a recent issue of the *AARP Magazine*. He retired as a newspaper delivery truck driver for the *New York Daily News*. Since his 60s he has served as a volunteer emergency medical technician and, beginning two years ago, as a volunteer firefighter. Halberstadt said:

> I haven't had to carry anyone out of a building yet, but things can get pretty exciting. Once we were fighting a house fire from the outside. The facade fell forward toward us, and we had to rush up a hill behind us to safety. It was a little scary. But I love being a firefighter. It gives me a sense of purpose. It doesn't really matter how old I am, as long as I am able to do this.[315]

Or consider the renowned quiltmakers of Gee's Bend, Alabama. This small African American community, isolated on three sides by the Alabama River, has been making quilts for generations. According to Souls Grown Deep Foundation & Community Partnerships, an organization devoted to promoting the work of African American artists from the South, these quiltmakers:

> have produced countless patchwork masterpieces, beginning as far back as the mid-nineteenth century....Few other places can boast the extent of Gee's Bend's artistic achievement, the result of both geographical isolation and an unusual degree of cultural continuity. In few places elsewhere have works been found by three and sometimes four generations of women in the same family or works that bear witness to visual conversations among community quilting groups and lineages. Gee's Bend's art also stands out for its flair—quilts composed boldly and improvisationally, in geometries that transform recycled work clothes and dresses, feed sacks, and fabric remnants.[316]

The quilts, majestic contributions to American art, were called by *The New York Times*: "Some of the most miraculous works of modern art America has produced." The quiltmakers, particularly those of earlier generations such as Willie "Ma Willie" Abrams (1897–1987) or Plummer T. Pettway (1918–1993) or Mary Lee Bendolf (b. 1935) or Nettie Young (1916–2010) experienced difficult impoverished hardworking girlhoods. They grew up as farm workers. They had no advantages and little education. Some bore children when barely out of childhood, and raised many children. But they grew up in a culture steeped in quiltmaking, a culture that also favored individual expression within any given maker's quilt. This was a culture that originated in slavery and later sharecropping conditions, that held strong values of helping each other out, no locks on the doors.

The elderly women quiltmakers of Gee's Bend and those of younger generations continue to give back. In the midst of the worldwide coronavirus pandemic, the quiltmakers of Gee's Bend turned their sewing skills into making masks for every person in their community, and beyond.[317]

## Grandparenting

More than 90 percent of Americans over the age of 65 have grandchildren and for 80 percent of grandparents, their grandchildren are their top priority.[318] Grandparents serve as a tremendous resource to families. Often grandparents are able to relate to grandchildren with a greater sense of leisure and more patience; they're on the far side of what can be a stressful time of life managing a household and earning a living while raising small children or teenagers.

My own Pennsylvania Dutch grandmother, Olive Naomi Erisman Henry (1895–1987), was devoted to her ten grandchildren. She was a skilled seamstress and sewed all of my sister's and my school dresses, complete with piping and smocking and ruffles and puffed sleeves with cuffs. We spent two weeks of every summer at her and my grandfather's home and in the ninth grade we lived at their house to be able to attend the superior public school in their town. My grandmother was fascinated with genealogy and gave us each a written-out family tree—including both sides of the family and not just her own—going back to the 1600s. I am sure my grandparents helped my barely solvent parents financially, especially with medical insurance (my grandfather was a Traveler's insurance broker who conducted his business in Pennsylvania Dutch).

Grandparents, according to a study reported in Alan D. Castel's book *Better with Age*, are superior caregivers. Children cared for by a grandmother "have half the risk of injuries and fewer trips to the emergency room."[319] A grandparent makes a great support system and besides this, an estimated three million grandparents in the United States are doing the entire job of raising their grandkids. According to the AARP, they are doing a good job of it.[320] For grandchildren as they grow into adolescence and enter college (often partially financed by a grandparent), the caring attention and support makes a significant difference toward staying in school, staying sober, and working toward goals with self-confidence.[321]

I know my friend the writer Jack Remick to be devoted to his two grandchildren, so I asked him about it. He responded:

I see my grandkids three times a year. I have been involved with each child from birth till now. To keep in touch, I write each child a personal letter once a week and include the weekly Sunday comics. At each stage of their lives, I have overestimated how advanced they are—for example, does a four-year-old need a stereo microscope that will project onto a computer screen? Does a five-year-old know what to do with an "extract your own DNA kit"? Their closets are filled with electronic gadgetry, science kits, toys, bicycles, scooters, skates (roller and inline)—none of which they use because everything I give them is "old stuff," Grandpa stuff and they have their own ways of doing things.[322]

## We Are Old

We are old but we are not a "gray tsunami." We are old but we are not a dependency ratio or a demographic time bomb. Some of us are disabled but we nevertheless contribute. We are painters and potters and poets. We are writers and gardeners. We are caretakers, helpers, supporters of our peers and of the young. "We are not 'senior citizens' or 'golden agers,'" wrote Maggie Kuhn (1905–1995), founder of the Grey Panthers. "We are the elders, the experienced ones; we are maturing, growing adults responsible for the survival of our society. We are not wrinkled babies, succumbing to trivial, purposeless waste of our years and our time."[323]

Indeed. Let us think of the burgeoning numbers of older people, including many of us, as a tremendous resource—one that our society now has, that it did not have fifty years ago.

## Composing Our Lives: Old Age

For each of these writing prompts, write for five or ten minutes.

1. At this point in your life, what do you consider to be your life work (whether paid or unpaid)? In what ways are you doing what you want to be doing? In what ways could you move more toward doing what you want to be doing?

2. If you are at a transition point in your work life, such as retirement, job loss, or dealing with an unexpected disability, is there a way you can use your skills and experience to go in a new direction? Are there skills you would benefit from learning? If you already make art—music, poetry, sculpture, pottery, whatever—what is your next direction?

3. Does your community have an obvious need toward which you would find it meaningful to lend a hand? What are the possibilities?

4. What do you want your legacy to be? What values or artworks or experiences would you like to pass on? My friend Elana Zaiman has written a book, *The Forever Letter*, about simply (sometimes it's not exactly simple!) writing a letter addressed to those you love, articulating the values you want to pass on, as well as what you want for them.

Jack Remick, daughter Elizabeth, and grandkids Charlotte and Alexander, ca. 2011.

Violet Hensley, fiddler and violin maker, age 101, *Photo by Lydia Norvell, copyright 2018.*

# 5. Peak Ages of Creativity?

*I am not done with my changes.*
—Stanley Kunitz at age 72[324]

In her pioneering book *The Fountain of Age*, published in 1993, Betty Friedan (1921–2006) reports on the first conference on gerontology and creativity (Wisconsin, 1985). At the conference the gerontologists asked, "Why don't artists, writers, and composers consider retiring as many people do?" So bleak was their view of old age that it was difficult for them to imagine a person in old age engaging in energetic creative work. No wonder, since they had largely studied the extreme minority of old people who resided in nursing homes. These gerontologists expressed concern about promoting "the very notion of creativity in later life," since this might create a further burden on old people. As if, for the solvent and creative old person, the idea of "recreation and vegetation"—Betty Friedan's words—at some sort of retirement community would not be a devastating bore.[325]

They had not spoken to the painter Wayne Thiebaud. When asked, at age 98, whether he planned to retire from painting, he replied: "Why? Retiring means you do what you want. I love painting. It came to me. I don't know how. I'm lucky, lord yes."[326] I wonder what Thiebaud thought of what we hear *ad nauseum*: that "science" tells us that the peak ages of creativity are 39 to 42?

## Art and Age

The "peak ages of creativity" idea goes back to a book published by Princeton University Press in 1953, Harvey C. Lehman's *Age and Achievement*.[327] Lehman claimed to be presenting "factual data set

123

forth regarding age and achievement." Lehman "determined" that peak ages of creative work fell between 35 and 45 years old; within those ages he found variations among painters, poets, novelists, sculptors, and so forth. Thereafter his book was cited in support of age discriminatory policies such as mandatory retirement. His methods continue to be used by a number of present-day researchers to draw similar conclusions. In this chapter I challenge both his methods and his conclusions.

Lehman's strategy was to count mentions of artworks in art-history books such as one titled *A Composite List of Master Paintings* and two others that listed "the important paintings of the Louvre," Also, "all of the available art histories in the Ohio University library were studied." The measure of an artist's best painting was the number of times it appeared in one of these lists. The world's "40 best paintings," which are "possibly the world's greatest," are those that appeared ten or more times. As for literature, Lehman counted mentions of books in compilations of "best books," bestsellers, and "most influential" books. Lehman correlated these various artworks with the age of the artist when he or (rarely) she made it.

Thirty years later, creativity researcher and psychologist Dean Keith Simonton (b. 1948) also used popularity and recognition to index artistic greatness. He writes in his 1984 book *Genius, Creativity, and Leadership*, "My inquiry into the ages at which 696 classical composers produced the most frequently heard melodies found the decade from 33 to 43 to be the peak productive period." Simonton concludes, "the probability of conceiving notable creative products tends to diminish as the creator passes the peak productive age of around 40."[328] What artist would agree that "most frequently heard" is a good measure of good or great art? In any case, Simonton is speaking about averages and probabilities, not about fate.

Simonton himself, who in his 70s has remained a ferociously productive scholar, resists the notion of probability becoming fate. He discusses the "pervasive and overblown misconception" that older creators are "over the hill" and criticizes the use of Lehman's work to promote and justify age-discriminatory policies such as mandatory retirement.[329]

In 2016, Philip Hans Franses, of the Erasmus School of Economics located in Rotterdam, The Netherlands, counted the paintings that drew the highest prices to determine which paintings were the "best." He counted the 100 greatest hits of classical music as determined by music sales to determine "best" compositions. According to Franses, painters peak at 42, classical composers at 39.[330]

"What counts as art?" asks Nell Painter in *Old in Art School*. "Who is an artist? Who decides?"[331]

Studies of popular and commercially successful artworks conflate recognition and sales with artistic achievement. No artist would conclude that a given artwork was great based on number of mentions in art history books, much less the price it commands. No poet would determine the greatness of a poem based on how often it was anthologized. Nobody imagines a list of bestsellers to represent great literature.

"Who wants the Great American Novel anyhow?" asks Ursula K. Le Guin (1929–2018), author of twenty-two novels, eleven volumes of short stories, seven books of poetry, four collections of essays, thirteen books for children, and five works of translation. "PR people," she answers. "People who believe that bestsellers are better than other books because they sell better than other books and that the prizewinning book is the best book because it won the prize. Tired teachers, timid teachers, lazy students who'd like one text to read instead of the many many great and greatly complex books that make up literature. Art is not a horserace."[332]

## Art versus Commerce

And if art is a horserace, it's not necessarily won by aesthetic significance. Albert-László Barabási, in his book *The Formula: The Universal Laws of Success*, lays out the distinction between creative achievement and worldly success. Consider the *Mona Lisa*.[333] It was always a good painting, but it was an obscure good painting until, in 1911, it was stolen from the Louvre in broad daylight and for two years could be found nowhere except in the headlines of newspapers around the world. The thief kept it in the bottom of his trunk in a Paris boarding house, likely appalled by the publicity. He was caught two years later trying to sell it to a dealer in Florence. It was crime—not art—that made the *Mona Lisa* "one of the world's great paintings."

The composer Igor Stravinsky commented on the difference between the making of art, "which is what I do," and the *selling* of art, the art *career*—"giving interviews, newspaper reviews, lecturing to women's clubs, conducting orchestras..." In Stravinsky's view, "Making is its own end and there is no other."[334] This is the view of a composer, but it gives the social scientist nothing to count.

In fact, some creators are better at working the ropes of influence, at making themselves known to the gatekeepers, and some are more advantageously placed within a social context to receive a helping hand along the way. Barabási presents example after example of two high-level creators in the same field—their work is entirely comparable—but only one becomes eminent. The other sinks into obscurity or relative obscurity.

One case is that of two artists who as teenagers began together as a graffiti team in New York City. They signed their graffiti SAMO for "same old shit." One of the two, Jean-Michel Basquiat (1960–1988), was a master networker. Basquiat died of a heroin overdose at age 27, but while he was alive his works started selling for $25,000 each and now go for more than a million dollars. His partner in crime, who remains a working artist, was Al Diaz (b. 1959). Diaz was more reticent. Diaz, Barabási writes, "has made art in relative obscurity ever since. Basquiat, on the other hand, was a sensation as a living artist and a rampant success as a dead one."[335] The difference was Basquiat's propensity to network and his skill at it. To what extent are researchers on "peak ages of creativity" measuring an artist's skill at networking, at working the scene, at sucking up to the right folks at the right time?

And why denigrate Al Diaz? (Not that this was Barabasi's intention.) After a long struggle with drugs, Diaz is back at making art. He's also a musician. He was on a different path and he's still making art, now sober and clean, now in his 60s. And Basquiat paid a price for his ability to mesmerize the art world. Diaz told a reporter: "Some of the shit he had to do in order to be successful caused a lot of internal conflict…It made him much more angry, defensive and distrusting of others. I believe a lot of that contributed to his ruin. It manifested itself in his appetite to numb himself, to always be high."[336] Basquiat is successful but dead. Diaz is less successful but alive and still making art.

Still, for the creator, networking can be a good thing. It greatly improves the chances that an artist's work will be recognized. This striving for recognition does not have to be about celebrity. "The celebrity factor," said the sculptor Louise Bourgeois, "the work's reception, gives it a place."[337] For one's work to take its place in the world, to remain in existence, to remain a force to one degree or another after its maker's death—that is the point. To clear a space for our work in the world, we creators must work at getting our work into the world. Doing so also nurtures the *creative* process, due to the added pressure to complete work, the benefits of audience interaction, and the way recognition encourages the making of further works.

But let's be clear: In art, sales and aesthetics are two different things. Popularity and aesthetics are two different things. Even if sales can be counted whereas beauty and artistic significance can only be debated. Yet "peak ages of creativity" researchers equate sales, popularity, and recognition with greatness in art.

## The Critic Is Biased

And too, those who generate the data that creativity researchers rely on—critics, dealers, and publishers—can be (in fact, are) biased. An entire generation of critics can be biased. In 1953 Lehman valiantly defended women creators, at one point assembling a short list of significant women creators, including Louisa May Alcott, the painter Rosa Bonheur, and the writers Jane Austen, Harriet Beecher Stowe, and the Brontë sisters.[338]

But his sources failed to give him Berthe Morisot (1841–1895), the most recognized of the Impressionist painters during her lifetime. Morisot did not live to old age (she died at age 54), but she was an eminently eminent creator, as re-established by feminist art critics at the end of the twentieth century. After her death, art critics ignored her for most of a century. Anna Mary Robertson Moses, who, in 1953—the year Lehman's book came out—appeared on the cover of *Time*, was beneath their notice. Until 1987 the most widely used art-history text in the United States, H. W. Jansen's *History of Art*, omitted women artists entirely. He did not mention a single one.

In researching and writing her book *Creating Black Americans*, historian Nell Irvin Painter discovered "more good art by black artists than I could ever cram into one book..."[339] Very few appeared in the art history she had learned in school, back in the 1960s. In 2013 the artist Faith Ringgold (b. 1930) remarked that many women artists don't receive acclaim before 60, especially women of color. "There's a great deal of sexism and racism in the art world," she said. "If you're going to drop out early, you're going to miss the whole thing."[340] This sexism and racism—still ongoing—was pervasive in 1953. Harvey C. Lehman gathered statistics from authorities who utterly ignored women artists and those of color. His conclusions rest on a shaky foundation.

## Chronological Age versus Career Age

"Peak ages of creativity" studies also tend to conflate chronological age with career age (as Dean Keith Simonton noted early on). Many artists begin working in their early 20s or even in adolescence or childhood. After twenty or twenty-five years of hard work, about when they hit age 40, they are getting pretty good! Might this have nothing to do with chronological age? Might the same twenty-five years of hard work start later in life?

For some artists, chronological age and career age more or less coincide. For an eminent creator, the composer Philip Glass had a conventional career trajectory. His father ran a record shop in Baltimore, in which Philip helped out, so the future composer's childhood was saturated with music. He began music lessons at age 8; he began composing at age 15, during his freshman year at the University of Chicago. During the next twenty-five years, while also pursuing music—intensely—Glass worked at part-time day jobs from weighing nails in a steel mill to loading trucks to driving a New York City taxicab. In *Words Without Music* Glass writes:

> I actually enjoyed working at the mill. It's a good thing, too, because I would not make a living working full-time as a musician-composer until 1978 when, at the age of forty-one, I was commissioned to compose *Satyagraha* for The Netherlands Opera. Still, all the years of day jobs—twenty-four years—never bothered me.[341]

Glass began getting real recognition in the late 1970s, when he was 41, right at the supposed "peak age" of creativity. But who is to say when his creative work "peaked" or even if it has peaked yet? What does "peak age of creativity" even mean, when considering a creative worker like Philip Glass? At this writing the composer is 82 years old. The list of works he composed between the ages of 70 and 82 comprise:[342]

1 work for the Glass Ensemble
4 operas
1 chamber opera
2 piano works (different from 2 works for solo piano)
2 works for two or more pianos
3 string quartets
4 works of chamber music that are not string quartets
5 works for solo instruments
4 symphonies
4 "other works for orchestra"
1 concerto for piano
1 concerto for violin
1 concerto for cello
2 double concertos
1 vocal work

3 compositions for theater
13 film scores.

These works composed after he turned 70 add to a lifetime of work that includes twenty-seven operas, eleven symphonies, eight string quartets, twenty piano études, and fifty-odd films, "among many other works"—so far.[343]

Another artist whose chronological age more or less conflated with her career age was Georgia O'Keeffe (1887–1986). Like Philip Glass, O'Keeffe became serious about her art during childhood. When she was 11, her mother found her her first teacher. From that time on she worked assiduously on her art.

At a new and lonely teaching job at Columbia College in South Carolina, when she was age 29, O'Keeffe hung a "solo show" in her small studio for her own personal viewing. Upon seeing her work as a whole, she realized how derivative it was, how each piece reflected the view of this or that teacher.[344]

> I...had the idea that what I had been taught was of little value to me except for the use of my materials as a language––charcoal, pencil, pen and ink, watercolor, pastel, and oil. I had become fluent with them when I was so young that they were simply another language that I handled easily. But what to say with them? I had been taught to work like others and after careful thinking I decided that I wasn't going to spend my life doing what had already been done.[345]

She began to try to paint from her own feelings, to please herself. This was the moment at which she began to emerge as the Georgia O'Keeffe we know.

Her first large solo exhibition occurred in 1923 when she was 36 years old. It was held at the Anderson Galleries in New York City, ran for about ten days, and was jammed by 500 people every day. The next year she had another show, and one biographer writes: "O'Keeffe was now an established persona in the art world." In 1928, when O'Keeffe was 40, one of her works sold for the highest price of any work sold by a living American artist.[346] Like Glass, O'Keeffe's career age matched her chronological age. Still, she worked for another fifty years: it's hard to say when she "peaked."

But what if you begin at age 50? What if you begin at age 75?

Late starters include the London editor Diana Athill, who published her first book of short stories at age 45. She subsequently published a novel and collections of memoirist essays. She published her second book of short stories at the age of 94, and a final memoir, *Alive, Alive Oh!*, at age 98.[347]

Daniel Defoe (1660–1731) published his first novel, *Robinson Crusoe*, at the age of 59. He had previously worked as a journalist and a prolific writer of pamphlets. He subsequently published seven more novels, including the path-breaking *Moll Flanders*, published when he was 62, and the even more path-breaking *Roxana*, published in 1724 when he was age 64. These novels written during Defoe's last decade have caused him to be dubbed "father of the novel" and they are still being read, taught, and made the subject of critical studies relating to issues of race and gender. Defoe died at age 70.[348]

Marcel Proust (1871–1922) did not live to old age. He died at age 51. Still, he did not publish the first volume of what became that classic of Western literature, À la *Recherche du Temps Perdu* (*In Search of Lost Time*) until he had turned 43.[349]

Isak Dinesen (1885–1962), the nom de plume of Danish writer Baroness Karen Blixen, published her first book, *Seven Gothic Tales* (1934), when she was 48 years old. Her nonfiction *Out of Africa* (1937) came out when she was 52. Her other collections, *Winter's Tales* (1942), and *Last Tales* (1957), came out when she was 57 and 72.[350] She became a renowned writer, one who is still being read, but she was never a young writer.

The novelist Raymond Chandler (1888–1959) published his first novel, *The Big Sleep*, at the age of 44. He subsequently published six novels and five film scripts. His many short stories were collected into twelve volumes. Chandler died at age 71.[351]

Harriet Doerr (1910–2002) published her debut novel, *Stones for Ibarra*, at age 74. It received the National Book Award for debut fiction. She subsequently published another novel and a book of short stories and essays.[352]

Annie Proulx (b. 1935) began as a journalist. She published her first book of short stories at age 53, and her first novel, *Postcards*, at age 57. *Postcards* won the PEN/Faulkner award and her next novel, *The Shipping News*, published when she was 58, won both the Pulitzer and the National Book Award. She has written, to date, five novels and four collections of short stories.[353]

The painter Peter M. Sacks (b. 1950) began as a poet. He painted his first painting at age 49. According to his *New Yorker* profile, he spends fourteen hours a day alone, painting. Some of his paintings take years to complete. He has made more than a thousand artworks and mounted ten solo shows. His work, called "ravishingly beautiful" by the director of the Museum of Modern Art, has been collected by museums and is offered by prestigious galleries.[354] As he moves into his 70s, he continues to paint.

Bill Traylor (1853–1949)[355] was poor and old and lived on the street, and he also made great art. He began drawing around age 85 and left more than a thousand images. Traylor was born into slavery in Alabama. After Emancipation he and his family continued as agrarian laborers, remaining with their former owners. He married three times and had fourteen or fifteen children. At some point, he and his family became tenant farmers outside of Montgomery, Alabama. About 1927, after the death of his third wife, Traylor moved alone to the African American section of Montgomery, eventually began living on the street and making his powerful images with pencil, charcoal, and colored pencils. He became a street artist, selling his work for a dime or a quarter.

Artists within a white artists' coalition calling itself the New South began collecting and saving Traylor's work, preserving it for decades. In 1940 they mounted a small show of his work in Montgomery. During World War II, Traylor lost contact with these supporters and died in poverty. Only after his death did his work became well known.

Traylor lived during bitter years in the South, years fraught with lynching and which included the Birmingham, Alabama, police murder of his son Will. Traylor's fluid, expressive images can be angry and fearful (such as "Dog on Red Background" or "Possum Hunt," in which men with rifles have treed several possums and two men). They can be strange or humorous (such as "Man Sprouting Leaves"). His art, now widely shown, published in several books, and well-recognized, transcends the labels "folk" or "outsider." Art is art.

These and other late starters were hardly going to experience their "peak age of creativity" at age 39.

## Transcendent Late Work

And let's also consider artists who were not only productive in their last decade, but who in that decade achieved transcendent work—sometimes breaking with what went before, a phenomenon referred to as Late Style. These artists incinerate the notion of 39 as the peak age of creativity.

Frank Lloyd Wright (1867–1959) designed the Solomon R. Guggenheim Museum, on Fifth Avenue in New York City, between the ages of 89 and 91, the year he died. His objective, he explained, was to make "the building and the painting an uninterrupted, beautiful symphony such as never existed in the World of Art before."[356] This he did.

Leonard Cohen, between the age of 72 and his death at 82, created eight new albums.[357] His last, *You Want it Darker*, released on October 21, 2016, a couple of weeks before his death, is one of the masterworks of his oeuvre.

The painter Vija Celmins (b. 1938) had a major retrospective of her work at the San Francisco Museum of Modern Art in 2019, when she turned 81. She is a slow-working, obsessive artist—successful. Each painting brings in between three and five million dollars. Her works have gone through various stages: images of skies and seas, spiderwebs, "stones" and real stones, exhibited together. "She has erased the line," writes art critic Calvin Tomkins, "between figuration and abstraction. Composition, bright color, narrative, and the human figure have no place in her work, which, at its best, conveys a timeless, impersonal, and rather cold beauty that can be inexplicably moving." Of her life at 81 Celmins says, "I'm lucky to be alive, and to still make work....And I have a lot of energy."[358]

## Age and Productivity

"Peak ages of creativity" studies tend to confound quantity with quality. Not that quantity is unimportant. As Dean Keith Simonton found, a correlation exists between a creator's productivity and their production of masterworks: The more an artist produces, the more likely it is that this artist will produce a masterwork.[359] And too, the more the artist produces, the more likely he or she is to produce a dud. Thus, the greatest creative geniuses produce both more masterworks and more duds. So perhaps creativity studies are measuring not age but productivity. Some artists were more productive in their middle years. (Others are extremely productive—I think of the composer Elliott Carter—in their later years.) Productivity matters, but productivity is not age.

There's also another point of view about productivity. One of Sara Lawrence-Lightfoot's interviews with an (unnamed) older person who had changed careers late in life, said, "I'm interested in going slower and deeper, not faster and farther....I want to become wise, not just smart."[360]

The composer Randolph Hokanson also spoke of the value of slowing down. Following a series of lectures and performances, he got back to composing a group of Inventions. "I found with dismay that many things in them did not seem right, and I realized that I had failed to follow my often repeated warning to my students: 'Never be in a hurry!' Due to my advancing age, perhaps....I had been too anxious to get them down, and too readily satisfied with things that I now find unsatisfactory." The composer resolved to not make this mistake again. He now composed "as if he had all the time in the world, even though I have little: if nine bars emerge satisfactorily in a day now, I feel it was a good day's effort. I may have spent several hours weighing and considering those few notes."[361]

Hokanson's reflection points to the question: Is the most productive artist always going to produce the greatest art? The French novelist Georges Simenon (1903–1989)[362] published 475 novels in his lifetime. He made a pot of money. He wrote some very good novels. He would write a novel in less than two weeks. But, the critic Joan Acocella writes:

> This method damaged his work terribly. Halfway through some books, subplots get dropped, characters change weirdly. If Simenon had cared about revising, he would have seen the problems and either fixed the book or given up on it. Surely he noticed that the few novels for which he violated the schedule and took more time—notably "Pedigree," which contains the most beautiful writing he ever did—were among his finest. But, again, this wasn't just a case of not knowing. He didn't want to bother. Once more, we should not forget about the money.[363]

Sometimes working slower works better than working faster. Sometimes an older artist will slow down to do his or her last works because this artist is working out a totally new thing. Giuseppe Verdi (1813-1901), the Italian composer of operas such as *Rigoletto* and *La Traviata*, was one of these.[364] By the time Verdi turned 50 he had composed two dozen operas; he was considered the most important Italian composer of his time. Like Philip Glass and Georgia O'Keeffe, he started early, and his career was in full bloom in his 40s. At age 58, after having composed *Aida*, after having achieved a brilliant career, after having attained financial security, Verdi retired from composing and purchased a working farm near where he had grown up. Sixteen years passed.

To return to composing, Verdi received a little help from his friends. According to Linda Hutcheon and Michael Hutcheon's account of the composer's late work, "What in fact brought Verdi back to composing for the theater was an elaborate plot instigated by his publisher, [Giulio] Ricordi, and his friend (and now favorite conductor) [Franco] Faccio…" Verdi's "final tragic masterpiece,"

*Otello*, premiered in 1887 when the composer was 74 years old. Everyone, the Hutcheons write, "including Verdi, assumed this would be his last opera." Verdi's great worry was that his last work would not come up to what he had previously achieved. This was a huge incentive to stop. "Had this indeed been Verdi's last opera," the Hutcheons continue, "then everyone would have seen *Otello* as the crowning achievement of a master of tragic opera."

But no. Then Verdi's librettist, Arrigo Boito (1842–1918), urged him to compose yet another opera, this one a comedy, which would be a first for Verdi. Boito played on Verdi's lifelong rivalry with the German composer Richard Wagner (1813–1883), who was born the same year (Wagner died at age 69), and whose theories and music were sweeping Europe, and, most distressing to Verdi, enthralling the young art and music bohemians of Italy. Verdi felt this was fine for Germany but a travesty for Italy and Italian music and culture. Boito argued that a new Verdi opera, a comedy, would hold up the Italian end of things.

So not to stir up speculation and anticipation, Boito and Verdi began working on *Falstaff* in secret. Verdi took a rather long time to compose *Falstaff*: It premiered six years after *Otello*. He took longer because he was feeling his way into new musical territory. *Falstaff* incorporates elements of melody, duets, and arias Verdi was known for, as well as quotes from other musicians, but the action is constantly interrupting everything so the opera became weirdly fragmented—prescient of post-Verdi, postmodern aesthetics. *Falstaff* is about old age and its sensual pleasures. It's full of jokes and hilarity. It premiered when Verdi was 80 years old, and quintessentially illustrates Late Style. It is considered a masterpiece.

The last works of the Impressionist painter Claude Monet (1840–1926)—the massive water lily canvases now on display at Musée de l'Orangerie in Paris—also represent a spectacular last work done in old age. The painter executed them during unhappy last years that included the death of his wife Alice (in 1911) followed by the death of his son Jean (1914), followed by battles of World War I near his home at Giverney that were close enough to hear gunfire and that included the constant passing traffic of ambulance carts. Monet suffered deteriorating eyesight and his family suffered his rages. To dispose of slashed up paintings became one of the duties of the servants. According to biographer Ross King, Monet "was volatile, insecure, and prone to petulance, frustration, and despair." (Happiness in old age? Not Monet.) The last waterlilies were bequeathed to the French nation in 1922 but the painter refused to part with them and not until his death in 1926 were they removed to the museum. There they remained, vastly under-appreciated, until, after World War II, American painters in Paris recognized in them a break from all that had gone before, a foreshadowing of the abstract expressionism to come.[365]

Of course, some creators peter out or quit. There's the famous case of Philip Roth, who, after writing twenty-seven novels or novellas and many short stories, quit writing fiction eight years before his death at age 85. Roth explained to an *LA Times* reporter: "I have no desire to write fiction. I did what I did and it's done. There's more to life than writing and publishing fiction." Yet it's hard to say whether or when Roth "peaked"—only when he received his biggest honors. He continued to write like a steam engine until he was done, about age 76. His first novel, *Goodbye Columbus*, received the National Book Award when he was 27. *American Pastoral* received the Pulitzer when he was 64. *The Human Stain* received the UK's prestigious W.H. Smith Literary Award when he was 67. (Later awards such as the Man Booker and the National Humanities Medal were lifetime achievement awards rather than honoring specific books.)[366]

## Recalibrating the Direction of Work

Looking back is one of the privileges of old age and added to this many artists look back over their work as it presently stands as an aid to mapping their forthcoming directions. In her dazzling book of portraits, the photographer Annie Leibovitz recalled the advice of one of her mentors:

Bea [Feitler, art director of *Ms.* magazine and later of *Harper's Bazaar*] had been very generous in sharing her finely honed understanding of the process of making art. She was particularly firm about stopping from time to time and looking back at your work. She said that you will learn the most from your own work, and by looking back you will find how you need to go forward.[367]

Changing direction from time to time is what artists do; they are not a manufacturing enterprise. And old age may bring its own pressures and constraints, resulting in a change of direction. We've seen how the sculptor Sarah Yerkes turned to writing poetry in her 90s after sculpting became too physically challenging. And how the sculptor Marilee Shapiro Asher turned to making digital images for the same reason.

Also, one direction may feel used up. Finished. Time to move on. The poet Donald Hall ceased writing poetry in his early 80s. In *A Carnival of Losses: Notes Nearing Ninety* he wrote: "It was a relief. Quality had diminished along with testosterone. How many good poems are written by people in their eighties? I hoped that prose might continue." Prose did continue. Hall writes:

These days I start writing prose first thing in the morning, as I used to do with poems. After "Out the Window," I worked on further essays with passion and concentration. Some pieces took as many as eighty drafts. Rewriting, I turned an adjective into a particular, more appropriate noun. I removed an adverb and tried twenty verbs before I found an exact and witty one. New topics kept arriving.[368]

Hall's engaging pieces in *Essays After Eighty* and *A Carnival of Losses: Notes Nearing Ninety* show him to be in fine and witty form as he approaches the end.

Ursula K. Le Guin, born in 1929 a few months after Donald Hall and who also died in 2018 at age 89, found late in life that it was poetry that came most easily. A central question confronting any old, quite accomplished artist may be: Can I do it again? Certainly, this was Le Guin's anxiety. She told an interviewer, "Every time I finished a novel I thought, *That's it, I'm done, I'm all washed up.* [But then] something would come along." Her last book, published in her last year, was a book of poems, *So Far, So Good.* It helped, no doubt, that she had companions in the work. "I'm in a little group," she said, "eight of us, that write for each other and read to each other."[369]

Each creator is different. Each old age is different.

## Ageism and Creativity

Finally, it's worth asking to what extent the motivation and energy of any given creator was affected by the acid rain of ageism and by the creator's own negative age stereotypes. The pathbreaking research of Becca Levy at the Yale School of Public Health shows that "Positive age beliefs protect against dementia even among elders with high-risk gene" and that "Negative age stereotypes predict Alzheimer's disease biomarkers" and that "Age stereotypes held earlier in life predict cardiovascular events in later life" and that "Memory [is] shaped by age stereotypes over time," to quote the titles of some of her research papers.[370]

Internalized ageism has a biological consequence. Levy and her team have found that "positive self-perceptions of aging" are associated with greater longevity. Those with negative self-perceptions of aging have a protein bio-maker that indexes "cumulative stress-related inflammation," which is bad news for both sharp wittedness and longevity. Aged creators of the past could not have been immune. Canadian researchers Michael Hutcheon and Linda Hutcheon emphasize the damage ageism does to creative workers:

The internalization of societal attitudes toward aging presents challenges to artists, as it does to everyone who ages. The theory, propagated by the gerontological thinking of the 1950s, of social disengagement, passivity, and lack of agency as the fate of the elderly has continuing power to this day. The crisis of confidence that aging artists might experience is likely related to the internalization of this stigmatizing "script of decline," inactivity, and helplessness.[371]

The current push against ageism and for "successful" and "optimal" aging will no doubt help more people to live healthier, longer, and more creative lives.

Dean Keith Simonton concludes that whereas age decrement (decrease in quality or quantity) is highly predictable at the aggregate level, it's *unpredictable* at the individual level. In part this is due to Simonton's notion of "initial creative potential," whatever that is. For those who have a lot of it, it doesn't run out so fast. But also, any given work has an equal or random chance of being a "hit," so that the connection between productivity and "hits" matters more than any connection between age and "hits." Finally, there is the "swan song phenomenon," in which the creator, seeing death on the horizon, rises to the occasion with new works, sometimes innovative new works, to complete the body of work being offered to the world.[372]

This does not prevent Simonton from being cited in a 2019 article in *The Atlantic* titled "Your Professional Decline Is Coming (Much) Sooner Than You Think" in support of the ludicrous suggestion that we should cease creative work at some point—the author of this opinion piece, Arthur C. Brooks, keeps mentioning the age of 50—after which we surely will have "peaked." We should turn to teaching instead![373]

No thank you. Probability is not fate. Averages do not predict individual outcomes. Thus may we, each and every one, take heart. May we keep on creating.

## Composing Our Lives: Old Age

For each of these writing prompts, write for five or ten minutes.

1.  If you have been making work for some time, do you have it organized in such a way that you can look back on it in a coherent way? Can you see where you have been? Georgia O'Keefe made a page for each painting, date of completion, its size and what it was made of, where it was located. I keep my poems in a three-ring binder, organized in chronological order (latest version only) with its date of composition, and where published if published. How do you inventory your work? If you don't, how might you begin? Are there ways to improve this aspect of creating your body of work?

2.  What is your dream of a work or works to be achieved in the remainder of your life? What would you do if you could do anything at all you wanted to do?

3.  What are the steps toward this goal? Remember to take small steps. Remember to work every day. Begin.

4.  What is to be done with works still in your possession upon your death? Artists with resources may form a trust, or may have a gallery or estate to take care of their work, but what if you don't have resources? I have two charcoal drawings, which I treasure, that I purchased from the visual artist Eugene "Gene" Olson (1927–2009) about twenty years ago. For his own reasons, he wanted to clean the slate and his house of all his current work, so invited a group of poets to read their poems and to buy a piece or two for a very low price. One way, following Olson's example, is to open your house to friends, family, and neighbors and to invite them to choose a favorite piece. What will be your way?

Kay WalkingStick, age 85, in Studio, 2020. *Photo by Rick Schultz for* The Boston Globe.

## 6. Advantages of Being an *Old* Creator

*You know what I think prolongs life? Art and Music. Beyond that, it's to have a heart full of love.*

—Harry Shapiro, painter, age 100[374]

Going forward, growing into old age, we may develop a disability that requires us to change our life to accommodate the disability. We may get physically weaker, have trouble walking, or be confined to a wheelchair. We may be dealing with chronic pain. We worry about dementia, that it may happen to us. And yes, it may happen to us. Or it may happen to our beloved partner. What could be more painful? We may—more minor but no one's idea of fun—experience the frequent need to urinate. Or worse, incontinence. We may have to scrimp along, financially. We are losing people, our parents, our siblings, our best friend, our oldest friend, then another friend, then another. Our world may appear to be falling apart or falling away. We face the ageism that can corrode an older person's self-esteem and creative practice. For example, how many grants and fellowships exist for end-career artists versus emerging or mid-career artists? Very few.

And there are other challenges. As I write this at age 79, I worry about repeating myself. I worry: Will I run out of anything to say? I worry that my best work is in the past. I worry: Will any publisher take any interest whatsoever in my next book of poems? I worry: Will I become an "old fart," stuck in past practices, unable to innovate? And I am writing this during the years of the coronavirus pandemic. Will I even survive to finish *this* book, not to mention all the other works I have in progress? These are a few of the challenges that come up.

So what could possibly be an advantage?

## Experience

Skills honed over years of learning, practicing, and experimenting are worth growing old for. What skills? Technical craft skills—that is one type. Another type is what I call meta-skills.

Technical craft skills matter, and they are common to old-age creators. The potter for whom glazes and kiln temperatures are second nature. The painter whose instincts regarding composition and color are highly developed. The poet who knows what a line in a poem is good for and how to recognize a weak one. This doesn't make making new works easy. But such skills serve as a tremendous resource base that the creative worker can transfer to new works and new directions.

Meta-skills have to do with attitudes and ways of working. In my own case I would say that I have learned how to learn. I have learned how to focus, how to break a problem down into its component parts, how to encourage myself, how to take my time when venturing into new territory. In my younger days I would at times go awash with feelings of inferiority. Nothing is worse for learning. And I could be terribly impatient and distractible. I now know how to finish a piece or a poem or a book. Finishing is a skill. I am deeply familiar with the pit in the middle of a big project where the whole thing looks like a bad joke. I know there are times of muddling about, of not knowing what you are doing, of seeking…. all necessary phases of making new work.

Seasoned artists use both types of skills. After Alex Katz turned 90, his dealer, Gavin Brown, said: "Alex is in top mental and physical condition, and he's applying seventy-five years of eye, hand, and brain experience to this craft….He is also making astounding paintings—paintings that astound him. I think my job is to push him up in people's eyes to the premier league."[375]

Another artist whose decades of experience served him well was one who often signed his work "Old Man Crazy to Paint."

This was the renowned Japanese artist Katsushika Hokusai (1760–1849). Hokusai lived to be 89 years old (90 in the Japanese manner of starting age 1 at birth). His body of work includes 3,000 color prints, more than a thousand paintings, hundreds of drawings, and illustrations for more than 200 books. For much of his younger life he was a "busy commercial artist," according to art historian Timothy Clark. His commercial work involved producing "detailed block-ready drawings for colour woodblock print and book illustrations, at the employ of competing publishers." In his later years he increasingly turned to what was for him more personal—painting. "The formats," writes Clark, "—fans, handscrolls, albums, hanging scrolls, folding screens and even ceiling panels…were generally larger, too, giving greater scope to Hokusai's constantly evolving explorations of form. Technically, some of the late paintings are staggeringly complex, mobilizing a facility born of decades of praxis."

The artist worked to the end. He did not retire. He did not slow down. He did accept the assistance of his daughter, the artist Eijo (art name Oi), for some years after he became partially disabled from a stroke. "Day by day in my old age," he wrote in response to someone who had complained that his pictures were too detailed, "I am developing my technique by building on my past failures. Even though I am nearly eighty, my eyesight and the strength of my brush are no different from when I was young. Let me live to one hundred and I will be without equal!" Actually, Hokusai was already without equal. I think of him as the Picasso of nineteenth-century Japan. So passionate was his desire to make great art that he longed for more time. At age 89 (or 90), doctors told him there was nothing more they could do for him. Close to death, he famously said: "'If heaven will extend my life by ten more years…', then, after a pause, 'If heaven will afford me five more years of life, then I'll manage to become a true artist.'" These were his last words.[376]

A 1997 study interviewed eighty-eight older, well-recognized visual artists who were fully engaged in making art. Martin S. Lindauer and team asked the artists about the effects of aging on their work. The artists, who were unnamed in the published study, were in their 60s, 70s, and 80s. Both men and women artists in all three age groups felt that aging had a strong positive effect on both the quantity and quality of their work. Why? They had more skill. They had more knowledge. They accepted themselves more. They were less concerned with the opinions and evaluations of others. A 63-year-old woman artist reported, "I now feel free to do what I want in painting. After many years of trying to do salable, 'relevant,' or so-called important work, I feel free to be myself and not concern myself with how others judge me or my work."[377]

They had more time. A 79-year-old male artist said, "The more time available for creativity, the more artistic productivity." A 71-year-old woman artist said, "I have never really had time to work until now. In the past I worked at night or at any odd time I had; there was no real development of a theme or a series of works." An 80-year-old artist, also a woman, said, "In my teens I had studies other than my art. In my twenties I was at art school and teaching. In my thirties and forties, I did full-time teaching. In my fifties, sixties, and seventies, I did full-time painting."[378]

Finally, their work was in greater demand and received greater recognition. Many artists in the study found that they were more open to new ideas, new materials. A 67-year-old woman artist stated that since becoming a grandmother at age 58, "my personality changed and I became happier. My production, in size and amount, skyrocketed."[379]

The experienced artist has learned how to work. In his early 80s, Philip Glass works ten to twelve hours per day. He taught himself to work at composing a long time ago, while he was studying at the Julliard School. His technique was to place a clock on the piano beginning at 8 a.m. and to sit there until 11 a.m. He could just sit there or he could compose. At first it was very boring. He began to compose. As an old artist he said, "After a while, I just wrote [composed] because I had nothing else to do." "Ever since," according to a 2018 article about Glass that appeared in *The Washington Post*, "he's put a premium on showing up every day. 'It's not about writing fast,' he says. 'It's about being able to spend hours. If you can solve the stamina problem it helps a lot.'"[380]

There is also social intelligence and emotional intelligence—an asset of older people who continue to grow and develop. Beginning with self-compassion, self-acceptance, self-esteem. The painter Joan Semmel said, "In the work itself you know who you are as an artist. You're not struggling with finding your voice and doubting everything you do in quite the same way as when you're younger. It's all part of self acceptance."[381] A 70-year-old male artist, another (unnamed) subject in Martin S. Lindauer's study of accomplished older artists, said, "I used to look for inspiration in the work of others. Now I have no patience for that. I want to enjoy and appreciate the work of others, but for my own work, I listen to my inner voice."[382]

At the age of 80, the artist Michelle Stuart (b. 1933) said, "Experience certainly gives you insights into things you didn't have in your earlier years. You've made more things, you've honed your craft, you've experienced more books, you've experienced more criticism or praise. You don't need to worry about what people think. There's that kind of freedom."[383]

A 65-year-old male artist, another Lindauer subject, said, "There have been various stages in my work. My best works have been the last ones. Maturity, time to concentrate, and a peaceful way of life have all contributed to my growth and progress." An artist in his 60s felt that "older is better," at least in the arts:

> Greater depth of understanding—of nature, society, and of oneself—comes with age. An age that is alive and alert can't help but make for greater art. The older artist is also less likely to be seduced by the tricks of the marketplace.[384]

In old age, craft skills, social intelligence, emotional intelligence, learning how to learn, how to connect with others—all support the artist who continues to work or even one who is just starting out on a path of creative work.

## Discovering Beauty, Articulating Meanings

"Creativity doesn't protect us from life," wrote Gene D. Cohen, "it helps us engage more fully in it and helps us develop the opportunities inherent in life's challenges."[385] The novelist and translator Jhumpa Lahiri (b. 1967) wrote, "Writing is a way to salvage life, to give it form and meaning. It exposes what we have hidden, unearths what we have neglected, misremembered, denied. It is a method of capturing, of pinning down, but it is also a form of truth, of liberation."[386]

At age 80, the painter Kay WalkingStick (b. 1935), in a video produced by the National Museum of the American Indian, states: "I think artmaking is the visual history of our experience on earth and this is a fuller way to talk about our lives here, our humanity, our existence, our planet."[387] Her paintings of a lifetime inscribe personal and cultural history in a way that crosses back and forth between representation and abstraction. There is the apron series, the apron streaked, abstractly, with paint and hanging on a drawn triangle, the apron evoking her years as a mom and housewife (while she also painted). Or—or *and*—it is a painter's apron. This dynamic evolved into diptychs, one side abstract, the other representational. There is the Chief Joseph series; there is the tepee-like construction titled *Messages to Papa*; there is a painting titled *For John Ridge*, an elegy for a prominent Cherokee statesman killed in 1839.[388] Her paintings are, dare I say, beautiful, and also hold both her own personal life and our American life in visible form. To look at them is to realize how meaningful a life in art can be.

The visual artist Marilee Shapiro Asher, writing at age 102, reflected:

> While I am very familiar with the frustrations of the creative process, a successful result gives me pure joy. The dialogue that occurs between me and the piece I am working on does not always go my way. The material can say "no" to me and then I must listen and find another way to reach my goal. This is the creative process....The making of an object of art, the creative process, is a struggle. It involves all of one's attention and intuitive powers. For me, it has been fascinating, joyful and totally life-enhancing.[389]

Toward the end of her life, the painter Alice Neel wrote:

I do not know if the truth I have told will benefit the world in any way. I managed to do it at great cost to myself and perhaps to others. It is hard to go against one's time, milieu, and position. But at least I tried to reflect innocently the twentieth century and my feelings and perceptions as a girl and a woman. Not that I felt they were all that different from men's.

I did this at the expense of untold humiliations, but at least after my fashion I told the truth as I perceived it, and, considering the way one is bombarded by reality, did the best and most honest art of which I was capable.[390]

Alice Neel's gallery of portraits, still lifes, and cityscapes amounted to some 3,000 works, not including the 60 paintings and 300 drawings cut up by a drug-crazed lover in the winter of 1934.[391] They add to the world's beauty and the portraits exhibit the empathy through which Neel saw the people who sat for her—who they were, what they suffered, what their times were.

## Time to Experiment, Fail, Begin Again, Start Late

For the late starter, the slow-to-develop, the late to be recognized, more time—longevity—is more than an advantage. It is both a blessing and a necessity. Alice Neel, in a lifetime of making art, did not sell her first painting until after she had turned 70.[392]

If Paul Cézanne (1839–1906), considered the father of modern art, had died at age 50, would we have even heard of him? He received his first solo exhibit in 1895 at the age of 56. He lived to age 67, long enough for his work to enter the world and stay there. He painted during his entire adult life, but in the first decades no one was lining up to exhibit his works, much less buy one.[393]

Some artists—we've mentioned the painter Anna Mary Robertson Moses and the poet Sara Yerkes—begin in old age. Sally Gabori (1924–2015) was an Australian Aboriginal artist early skilled in traditional crafts and weaving, who lived her life deeply immersed in her Aboriginal culture, who raised eleven children, and who began painting at the age of 80. At that time, at an art center, she encountered art materials. In her eleven remaining years her vibrant, brilliantly colored abstractions—vivid expressions of her culture and her country—became renowned, exhibited throughout Australia and around the world. In 2013 her work was chosen to represent Australia at the internationally important Venice Biennale. Gabori died at age 91.[394]

Beloved couples never want to lose one another. They dread the life-altering moment of losing their spouse. Yet it is largely inevitable that one will predecease the other. And it has sometimes happened that, even if not wished for, the survivor is thereby liberated to do creative work. Gertrude Stein (1874–1946) died of stomach cancer at age 72, leaving her life partner, Alice B. Toklas (1877–1967), to live for another twenty years. During their four-decade life as a couple, Janet Malcolm writes in *Two Lives*, "The division of household labor between the two women, with one doing nothing and the other doing everything, was the precondition for the flowering of Stein's genius."[395]

Toklas's labors went beyond housekeeping and monitoring their busy social life to typing every word Stein wrote. Who could even imagine Toklas also being a writer while Gertrude Stein was alive? After Stein's death, though, things changed. The tragedy was that Stein's family manipulated Gertrude's will to take funds meant for Alice and they also stole the great paintings that remained in Toklas's possession, leaving Alice to a penniless old age, with friends taking up collections to keep her in tea.

Meanwhile, she became her own kind of writer, beginning with letter writing. "Toklas called letter-writing her 'work,' and she did it extremely well," writes Malcolm. "She had a kind of genius for it. The epistolary art is the art of favorable self-representation; Toklas emerges from her letters as a great lady, witty, self-deprecating, attentive, cultivated." She also wrote newspaper and magazine articles, a memoir titled *What Is Remembered* and two cookbooks, including the famous and witty *Alice B. Toklas Cook Book*, which contains as much reminiscence as recipe.

## Art and Elegy

To elegize is one of the jobs of art. Elegy remembers and honors the deceased. It means the beloved will not disappear into nothingness, will not be utterly forgotten. Their existence and who they were will remain in the world somehow, in some form.

Elegy honors the dead but also recognizes grief and gives it a visible place in the world. An artwork transcends the grief of one individual survivor; it has the ability to connect with that of the viewer or the reader or the listener. And the old are survivors. Is there any person past middle age who has *not* lost some vital, essential, beloved person?

Art can provide a shelter, a kind of home, a means of sustenance, for a person in the midst of the shock and sorrow of grief. At the age of 90, the pianist/composer Randolph Hokanson said, "I continue to play because I love music so. It has been the sustaining force in my life. I'd just go down the drain without it. It was such a savior after my wife died."[396]

Is it too obvious to say that one advantage of growing old is to remain alive to the beauty and suffering of the world? To make an elegy is to express that beauty and that suffering.

That I have been able to elegize my younger sister Susanne gives me great satisfaction. Does that sound odd? She was a stunning beauty with a funny sense of humor, and she was very creative. Her drawings and watercolors still hang on my walls (and the walls of other family members). In her early 30s she developed paranoid schizophrenia. At the age of 40 she disappeared from a mental-health facility; we conducted a nationwide search. A few months later she was found dead, a likely suicide. During the thirty years since we lost Susanne, I have written poems about her and to her. I have written the story of what happened to her. I have written a piece that includes her story as well as the current science on schizophrenia. I have dedicated a book of poems to her memory. All this makes her memory more than a newspaper story, more than a case number at the sheriff's department, more than one more sad story forgotten among all the other sad stories. Art helps to make us part of a world larger than just ourselves and our own circles and family members. What transpires and who we are is not merely private or shameful or secret or just plain lost, as if it had never happened.

Michael Echols, husband of the artist Kay WalkingStick, died suddenly in 1989 when the artist was 54 years old. They had been a close family and had elaborately and joyfully planned for his retirement years. His death was a shock, totally unexpected. Her grief and emotional turmoil is expressed in a series of diptychs with titles like *The Abyss* (1989), *Is That You?* (1989), *I Can't Make It Without You* (1989), *Loss* (1989), and *Letting Go from Calm to Chaos* (1990). On the representational side, her emotional turmoil is often expressed in the depiction of a nearby violent white-water creek.[397] The grief and pain depicted is personal and specific to WalkingStick, but in externalizing it and shaping it into art she makes it stand for human grief and human loss.

An elegy can lament catastrophic events larger than one person, as important as one person may be. Robert Motherwell's more than two hundred abstract paintings variously titled Elegy to the Spanish Republic occupied him for forty years, the last one completed shortly before his death in 1991. The painter was coming of age during the 1930s when the Spanish Civil war occurred. This conflict between democracy and fascism, with fascism under Franco victorious in 1939, profoundly affected Motherwell and many of his generation. The atrocities of the war included more than 700,000 dead and the first aerial bombing of civilians in history (at Guernica).[398] But the artworks such as *Elegy to the Spanish Republic No. 172 (with blood)* (1989–1990) and *Lament for Lorca* (1981–1982)—the great Spanish poet murdered by the fascists in 1936—also transcend this one bitter episode. Motherwell stated that the elegies represent the Internationalist in him, his interest in "the historical forces of the twentieth century." He stated: "Making an Elegy is like building a temple, an altar, a ritual place." For him they represented "a universal lament on people struggling everywhere to gain freedom and independence."[399]

## Recognition at Last

If the work matters, then recognition matters. It's not about celebrity, that shallow media adulation that results in movie stars' makeovers, sexual affairs, and gaudy mansions being exhibited on endless slideshows as clickbait on the internet. It's about the work reaching an audience out there in the world, adding meaning to other lives besides that of the creator. For some artists, an advantage of longevity is that after a lifetime of diligent labor, their work finally receives the recognition it deserves.

An article on ArtNet titled "These 8 Female Artists Only Saw Their Careers Catch Fire Well into Their 80s" showcases artists like Carmen Herrera and Etel Adnan, who persisted doing their art for decades before they were recognized late in life.[400] Finally.

Françoise Gilot is a prolific and significant painter. As a young woman she had celebrity of the media variety, whether or not she wanted it, as mistress of Picasso for a decade and mother of two of his children, Paloma and Claude. After Gilot left Picasso, she co-wrote *Life with Picasso*, an insightful book on the world's most famous artist and her life as a young artist living with him. Picasso despised the book—though it was written in English and he was unable to read it—and made every attempt to destroy Gilot's career. He failed. Gilot had begun to paint before falling in love with Picasso, she continued to paint while she lived with him, and she kept on painting after she left him. She married two more times and had a third child. By age 90, she'd made 5,000 drawings and 1,600 paintings. Her work is now well recognized in its own right, no longer overshadowed by her association with Picasso. At age 97, despite a heart condition and near-blindness in her left eye, François Gilot paints every day.[401]

Painter Luchita Hurtado (1920–2020) had worked on her art for her entire life. She was born in Venezuela, immigrated to New York with her family at the age of 8, and from the 1950s, lived in Los Angeles. She worked on her art privately, on the kitchen table, after the children had been put to bed, making hundreds of works. Later she just continued working on her art. She lived immersed in the art world (two of her three marriages were to painters and she befriended artists such as Rufino Tamayo and Marcel Duchamp), but she remained private as a painter. She worked steadily, but without seeking recognition.

Luchita Hurtado began exhibiting in 2016. She was then 95 years old. In 2020 she received a major career survey at the Los Angeles County Museum of Art. The show opened six months before her death at age 99. "She was greeted as an overnight success in the art world. An overnight success that was eight decades in the making," reported the *LA Times*. "She was a very original artist," said the curator of the exhibition. "She was a formal innovator. She was an incredible colorist."[402] Fortunately she lived long enough to experience recognition that was, to put it mildly, long overdue. In turn, this assured that her work would be preserved, would remain in the world.

The London editor and writer Diana Athill describes another case of exceedingly late recognition. Athill was introduced to a woman in her 80s named Marie-Louise von Motesiczky (1906–1996). This former lover of the Nobel-prize-winning writer Elias Canetti (1905–1994) was "funny, warm, charming, and indiscreet." This despite a difficult life begun as a Jew in Vienna during the Nazi era. In London, Athill got to know her a bit, and heard rumors that this charming old person painted. But there was no evidence of it in her richly appointed, art-filled (other people's art) house. On one visit Athill asked Motesiczky if she could see some of her paintings. She asked a bit nervously, since "nothing is more embarrassing than being shown paintings that turn out to be dreadful." Motesiczky led Athill up to her bedroom. Not a good sign. The painter went over to "an enormous built-in cupboard. This she opened, to reveal racks crammed with paintings, two of which she pulled out. And I was stunned. This sweet, funny, frail old woman was indeed a painter, right up there with Max Beckmann and Kokoschka."[403]

Before she died, Motesiczky had a retrospective exhibition

at London's Goethe Institute. The exhibition was raved in both London and European newspapers as a major discovery, a "blinding revelation." One reviewer described her as "a dazzling talent." Her paintings and drawings began to be shown in other exhibitions and her paintings are now represented in major galleries and museums such as the Tate. The monograph and Catalogue Raisonné of her work, published after she died, describes her intense pleasure and satisfaction at the recognition of her work.[404] Her art was recognized in time for it to be saved for the world. As for Motesiczky's life, Athill comments, "She was an object lesson on the essential luck, whatever hardships may come their way, of those born able to make things."[405]

Recognition does not have to denote world fame. To me it means that the work has taken its place in the world, at least to the extent that, when I have to leave this world, it will not disappear with me. It will remain, or some part of it will remain, perhaps adding meaning or grist to someone else's life, someone I've never met and will never meet. That is my dream.

The potter and teacher Paulus Berensohn, in his Archives of American Art (Smithsonian) interview, told how every year he made an image for the winter solstice, hand-produced it, and mailed it to 300 friends. Then, on Valentine's Day, he made a second image, wondering "what image of the heart will speak for itself." He sent a hundred of these. He reflected:

> Yes, those two mailings. That's my gallery. When I travel and visit friends, they'll say, oh, look, and they'll show me a folder in which they've collected every card I've sent them. I visited a friend a couple of years ago in Amsterdam and he had framed 30 of the cards.
>
> This satisfies my need to exhibit. It's more intimate than in a museum space. I seem to need intimacy, to thrive on it.[406]

The Irish-born interior designer and architect Eileen Gray (1878–1976) worked (in France) up until the week before she died at age 98. She designed chairs, beds, tables, screens, rugs, rooms, apartments, and most famously a small villa, called E-1027, built on the Cote D'Azur. "She was a pioneer," stated one art critic, "who carved out her space in the hostile, male-centric world of Modernism. After finding success as a furniture designer, she turned to architecture and with no formal training created an iconic building that reinstated comfort and warmth as principal tenets of Modernist design."[407]

Eileen Gray worked against the ideas of the famed Modernist architect Le Corbusier (1887–1965), who proposed that a building should be "a machine for dwelling in." She instead felt that a house was an "extension of the inhabitant," a home for "actual people," involving furniture, textures, and lighting—this according to an insightful graphic biography.[408] Le Corbusier later lived in Gray's architectural masterpiece and desecrated its meticulously designed interior by painting garish Picasso-esque murals on the walls. He failed to deny claims and the increasingly common perception that it was he who had designed the house. It has since been returned to Gray's original design and to her credit and is open to the public.[409]

Gray was a shy, non-pushy type, which contributed to how long it took for recognition to shine a light on her work. But she was industrious and intensely original. She was known and admired in avant-garde circles but not until she was in her 90s did her work begin to be recognized in a wider world. At age 98, in the midst of designing a new table, after sending her housekeeper out to obtain the correct wood, she fell into a coma. She never woke from it. Six days later, she died. More than forty years after her death, her reputation continues to grow.

## Paying It Forward

Older, experienced people have riches to offer the community in terms of sharing knowledge, experiences, practices, and methods, and of course, in the case of artists, artworks. The visual artist Betye Saar has created a body of work that includes the mystical, the political, and the personal. She writes, "My art becomes an explorer, a tracer of forgotten tribes, a seeker of sanctified visions. These works are what I leave behind." She also says:

I do it [make art] because I think I have a message. I think there's something that I have to say that I have to give back. When you get over 80 years old, you want to find out what the payback is, what you could give to share with the planet. And I like to think that my art does it.[410]

Another way to pay it forward is to teach and mentor beginners in the arts, whether young or old, and to do one's part to uphold the infrastructure of whatever domain the artist works in. Clark Terry blew off the first adolescent who asked to be mentored in playing trumpet. This was a skinny high-school student named Dewey Davis. A few years later, at some sort of gig, Terry heard—in amazement—a young trumpet player. He went up to talk to the lad and it was this same Dewey Davis, *Miles* Dewey Davis. He resolved never again to blow off another request for help from a young musician. The next request came from Quincy Jones, a Garfield High School student who approached Terry when his band was playing in Seattle. Quincy Jones became Terry's first mentee.

In his 50s and 60s, after he was known as a jazz legend, Clark Terry made a major turn toward spreading the gospel of jazz and teaching and mentoring high-school and college-age musicians. As he put it, "I'd always thought that the most important thing was to play my horn—to get into this band or that band or Duke's band [Terry played in Duke Ellington's band for nine years], to have my own band, to perform, to record....But later on I had a new dream: helping young musicians to make their dreams come true. That became my supreme joy."

Clark Terry ended up mentoring dozens of young musicians through jazz camps and clinics. He articulated what he wanted for them:

I wanted them to know how to play from their hearts, how to play it *right*. I wanted them to find *ten thousand ways* to do things with their instruments. Determination. That's what I wanted them to have. How to make it out there on the road, no matter what....how to pay dues by sticking to a dream no matter what obstacles come around. How to learn *from* obstacles....[411]

At age 93 he coached and encouraged his last mentee. The film *Keep on Keepin' on* tells their moving story. Ill with diabetes, with both feet amputated, Clark Terry's mastery of his music and his love for the young, blind pianist Justin Kauflin (b. 1986) permeates the film.[412]

The sculptor Anne Truitt felt great satisfaction in being an elder (as I would put it) in the arts community. Speaking of sitting on a panel that selected artists for grants, she wrote:

> I enjoy such meetings. The company of other artists is a pleasure and it is a privilege to serve one's peers by helping to support them. I have been looking at art for almost fifty years....Years of service on panels, on advisory boards, boards of directors and for the National Endowment of the Arts, plus visits to universities and art schools around the country have revealed to me a responsive network offering opportunities to talented artists.[413]

Truitt's memoirs, *Daybook*, *Turn*, and *Prospect*, offer insight into working as an artist, into living a life in art.

After she retired from her teaching job at age 67, the painter Alma Thomas's care for children continued: "Even after I retired in 1960, I devoted my time to the children who lived nearby. Rounding my neighborhood were the slums of the world. On Sundays these children would be running up and down the alley. So I got them to clean up and come to my house and we made marionettes and put on plays."[414]

## Passing the Torch

What we know is mostly going to die with us. But not all of it. Not if we articulate our knowledge and pass it on through an instruction book or a video or some other media.

After he turned 50, Hokusai published several brush-stroke manuals and in 1847, two years before his death, created a painting manual titled *Picture Book: Essence of Colouring*.[415] In his 50s, Clark Terry put together three jazz instruction books. It was at the beginning of the era when the jazz trumpeter began to modify his frenetic performing schedule to devote time to teaching and mentoring high school jazz hopefuls in Harlem and elsewhere.[416]

I was age 67 when I published my own how-to-write book, *The Writer's Portable Mentor*.[417] To write it, I drew upon twenty years of teaching and many more decades of honing my writing skills. It is an offering that at a younger age I simply would not have had the knowledge or experience to create.

Certain books can aid the process of navigating one's way forward in any realm of creative work. After I turned 73, I wrote: *Minding the Muse: A Handbook for Painters, Composers, Writers, and Other Creators*. It presents the insights of many different artists on their creative practices and takes the reader-creator through every aspect of the process of making art.

Another book that speaks profoundly to creators in all fields is the architect Kyna Leski's *The Storm of Creativity*. Just reading it gives ideas on how to negotiate the creative process, such as beginning by stepping away from what one "knows" or thinks they know, to open the space of ambiguity, of *not* knowing.

Yet another book is Twyla Tharp's *The Creative Habit*. In it, Tharp articulated everything she had so far learned about making creative work. So many paths and directions here, such as "you don't really have a good idea until you combine two little ideas," or "A story told backwards is just as interesting as a story told in the traditional way" or the chapter on finding the spine of a piece, that which runs through it and holds it up.[418]

My friend Jack Remick, poet and novelist, published *What Do I Know? Wisdom Essays* the year he turned 80. These essays do not instruct. They do not advise. They ask. They probe. They explore far-reaching questions that pertain to all our lives. "Wisdom, it seems," writes Remick, "isn't something you wait for, it is something you have to search for. But how do you do that?" A question we each might ask for ourselves. And since Jack is a writer, many of his essays alight on questions of art. In "The Wisdom of Finishing," he writes, "Finishing to me implies a process. How do you begin in such a way that the ending is implied in the beginning?"[419] Jack's search for wisdom does not provide answers but rather stirs up the reader's own questions. Thus does he pass on what he knows.

## As Death Draws Near

Death can come at any age but at the conclusion of old age it will come. What's the good in that? Well, death is our deadline. Approaching death, you realize the time remaining is not forever. This tends to focus the mind. You ask: What do I need to finish, what work is most important for me to do in whatever time I have left? What do I want to leave behind?

"We are all candidates for composting," observed Stanley Kunitz in his final book, *The Wild Braid*, a book that weaves together his two passions, poetry and gardening.[420] At age 99, with a year left to live, Kunitz wrote about death with apparent equanimity, knowing, obviously, that his own remaining time was short. He asks us to consider the disaster that immortality would be. If no one died we'd be overcrowded on Earth, squashed, standing room only. But, Kunitz wrote, "When an individual dies, the web connecting all life remains. The whole construct is renewed; the individual creatures who inhabit the web keep changing."[421] The way Kunitz honors the interconnectedness of life—when his own life was close to its end—that is spirituality.

The painter Henri Matisse, after becoming disabled and wheelchair-bound, told an interviewer: "More than ten years ago I underwent a serious operation—so grave that the doctors gave up on me. *Il est foutu!* [he is fucked!] they said to each other." The lesson he learned from his illness, the painter went on:

has been shaping my life ever since. The doctors gave up on you, I told myself, because they were convinced that you were going to die soon. Therefore, the time that you live from now on is a gift from life itself—each year, each month, each day. So from now on, you will do only what pleases you, without thinking about what others expect and want from you. Everything that I did before this illness, before this operation, gives the feeling of too much effort; before this, I always lived with my belt buckled. Only what I created after the illness constitutes my real self: free, liberated.[422]

The awareness of how little time remains can act as a force to shape last works. The painter Robert Motherwell, who for his whole life was intensely involved with literature, undertook a project in 1985 (completed in 1988) to make images for James Joyce's novel *Ulysses*. It was a daunting project for him, in part because the novel had had an overwhelming importance for him since his youth and in part because he wanted to make images that complemented the text but did not illustrate it. Motherwell made 450 images for the project and chose forty for the book. He would have liked to go on endlessly. But, "at seventy-three," he said, "one has to make choices. I am not in particularly good health and there are so many things I want to do. I have to limit myself."[423] Motherwell died in 1991 at the age of 76.

Time running out can spur intense artmaking. Yayoi Kusama (b. 1929) is a prolific, obsessive Japanese artist who lived in New York from 1957 to 1973. In New York she participated in the art world and in anti-war and anti-establishment events and "happenings," many including nudity. She and her work received a lot of press. Her work features obsessive repetitiveness such as a room covered in polka dots, including floor, furniture, and ceiling, amplified to infinity with mirrors. Her life has been marked with severe depressions and other psychological troubles and, in contrast to Agnes Martin, whose works screened her mental illness, Kusama uses her mental disturbances in her work and her work displays them. In 1973 she returned to Japan, and since 1977 has lived voluntarily in a mental hospital, continuing as a working artist with a growing international reputation, including major retrospectives at the Los Angeles County Museum of Art and the Museum of Modern Art (MoMA), and later at the Whitney Museum of Art in New York. She has represented Japan at the Venice Biennial. In 2017 she opened a museum dedicated to her work, in Tokyo, near the hospital where she lives. Of her fast-paced, nearly continuous work, she wrote while in her 70s:

> New ideas naturally come welling up every day. I always keep a sketchbook and colored pencils at my side. Even in the middle of the night, if an idea comes to me I grab my sketchbook and draw. And each day I do a tremendous amount of work. New ideas and new visions of things I want to create are always percolating and swirling around in my head, in no particular order. All I can do in the limited time left to me, is to turn these visions, one by one, into concrete forms.[424]

Since she is "no longer young," Kusama "has come to regard each day as precious." Comparing her life now to when she was a restless teen, she wrote, "I am more keenly aware of the time that remains and more in awe of the vast scope of art. Oh, time, hold still a while. I have so much more work to do. There are so many things I want to express." Finally Kusama states, "Nowadays, the main theme of my work is death."[425]

## Modeling How to Grow Old

As we who are now growing old shape a new sort of old age—one full of flourishing well-being, social connection, learning, moving our bodies to the extent we are able, and engaging in creative work—we are at the same time helping to reshape the future of everyone else, the middle aged, the young, the generations to come. Just so, all the old, uber-creative, extremely productive artists who appear in this book—and so many more who do not—have lighted the way forward for me and for us all.

How great it would be, I can't help but think, to live to a great old age. It is something to wish for, to hope for, and to work toward by caring for our bodies, our minds, our friends and loved ones, and by caring for, nurturing, and continuing our creative work. Old age, here I come!

## Composing Our Lives: Old Age

The visual artist Faith Ringgold was asked by an interviewer, "Can you tell me what's happening in your studio in 2019? What are you working on now?" Her answer: "I am working on a series about aging. I want to show how it is changing and will continue to change. I am 88 and 89 is coming up in October. I think there's going to be a change in the way we think about aging in another 10, 20 years."[426] Next, the interviewer changed the topic: What is your advice for young people? I hereby change the topic back: What is your advice for old people? We will have to answer that question for ourselves.

Write for five or ten minutes on each of the following questions.

1. Given your current experience, wisdom, challenges, successes, failures, what is your advice for those who are growing old? What would you advise yourself?

2. What are you working on now? What do you hope to achieve in the coming period of time?

3. What are your goals? For the next five years? For this week? For today?

# Acknowledgments

I thank my friend Libby Brydolf for her meticulous read of an early draft and insightful suggestions. I also thank my friend Rabbi Elana Zaiman, who brought to a discerning read her long experience as a chaplain to elders. I am utterly dependent on my sister Pamela O. Long and brother-in-law Bob Korn for their perceptive attention to my prose works, including this one. The poet Bethany Reid cannot be thanked enough for her friendship over the decades and for sage advice concerning these pages. My third-Sunday workshop—Jack Remick, Geri Gale, M. Anne Sweet, Frank Araujo, Jasante Howard, and Meredith Bricken Mills—is quintessential to my own creative process. I would not know what to do without you.

My dear friend Thomas Hubbard combed this work with his fine-toothed mind and saved me a few embarrassments. Thank you.

I worked out much of *Dancing with the Muse* during "writing practice," a biweekly gathering (on Zoom during the pandemic) to do "discovery writing," during which we write, usually by hand without stopping, for forty-five minutes to find out what it is we want to say. Then we read to each other what we have written—no critiquing. I am grateful to my fellow writers Jerry Jaz, Nancy-Lou Polk, Melanie Grimes, Heide Darchuk, Susan Knox, Trudy Cusella, Catherine DeNardo, Betsy Bell, Karen Rolls, and Kira Shipley. Thank you for being part of my community and for inspiring me with your words.

Seattle and the Pacific Northwest is where I love to live, and not only because of the mountains, lakes, rivers, forests, and the Salish Sea—a land inhabited and sustained for centuries by Indigenous peoples including the Duwamish—but also because of our communities of poets, writers, book people, booksellers, bookstores, libraries, and coffeehouses. To mention a few prime movers is to skim the surface but here goes: our very own national treasure Nancy Pearl, Carla Shafer, Michael Daley, Claudia Castro Luna, Rena Priest, Gary Lilley, Paul Nelson, Sam and Sally Green, Kathleen Flenniken, Tod Marshall, Holly Hughes, Sheila Bender, Nick O'Connell, Scott Driscoll, Phoebe Bosché of Raven Chronicles, Anna Bálint and the Recovery Café, Cami Ostman, Elizabeth Austin, Koon Woon, Brendan McBreen of Striped Water Poets, Leopoldo Seguel of Poetry Bridge, Lillian Dabney of Folio Library, and Peggy Sturdivant of the It's About Time reading series. I also thank Richard Hugo House, Magus Books, The Elliott Bay Book Co., Third Place Books, Village Books in Bellingham, Chris Jarmick of BookTree in Kirkland, Imprint Bookstore in Port Townsend, Edmonds Bookshop, Eagle Harbor Books and BARN (Bainbridge Artisan Resource Network) on Bainbridge Island, and Seattle's Café Allegro, which, we mostly agree, roasts the nation's best coffee.

For all kinds of reasons, I am lucky in my niece Joanna Long and also thank her for her perspicacious read of this manuscript. As well I am grateful to our friend Marigrace Becker for helping me to a greater comprehension of issues around memory loss.

HistoryLink.org, the free online encyclopedia of Washington state history, is the pride of our state and I am ever-proud to be part of its convivial and erudite team.

My partner Jay Schlechter and the rest of my long-term pod seem intent on making my forthcoming old age a rather jolly prospect. Thanks to Liz Long and David Messerschmidt, Joanna Long and Mike Becker, Eric Messerschmidt and Maddy Rock, Dan Long and Kyla (and, in memory, our beloved Michele Cooper-Long), Allison Korn, Marco Yunga Tacuri and Lucas and Asha, and Pamela O. Long and Bob Korn.

I am indebted to those old salts of the book trade, Phil Garrett and Jennifer McCord of Epicenter Press. Due to their dedication and skill, this little book is in your hands. Thank you.

# Notes

## Introduction

1    "Participating in the Arts Creates Paths to Healthy Aging," National Institute on Aging, February 15, 2019, https://www.nia.nih.gov/news/participating-arts-creates-paths-healthy-aging.

2    Rebecca Perron, "The Value of Experience: AARP Multicultural Work and Jobs Study," Washington, DC: AARP Research, July 2018, https://doi.org/10.26419/res.00177.000.

3    "O Is for Old," *Post Road* No. 24 (2013), 84–91.

4    Gene D. Cohen, *The Creative Age: Awakening Human Potential in the Second Half of Life*, 22.

5    Fenn's career is described in Albert-László Barabási's *The Formula: The Universal Laws of Success*, 230–231.

6    "Barbara McClintock: American Scientist," *Encyclopedia Britannica*, August 29, 2019; "Barbara McClintock (1902–1992)" Cold Spring Harbor Laboratory, and "Barbara McClintock" archives, Cold Spring Harbor Laboratory, https://www.cshl.edu.

7    Oliver Sacks, "The Joy of Old Age (No Kidding)," *The New York Times*, July 6, 2013, SR12.

8    "Sam Gilliam," Pace Gallery website accessed October 6, 2021, https://www.pacegallery.com/exhibitions/sam-gilliam/.

9    Peter Schjeldahl, "Off the Wall," *The New Yorker*, November 16, 2020, 62.

10   Ted Loos, "Sam Gilliam Fires Up His Competitive Spirit," *The New York Times*, June 13, 2018, S5.

11   Alexandra Alter, "At 99, Ferlinghetti Has a New Novel," *The New York Times*, June 6, 2018, C3.

12   Margaret Atwood's interview appears in the AARP magazine: Hugh Delehanty, "Margaret Atwood: Q and A," *AARP.org Bulletin*, December 2020, 39, 41.

13   Paulus Berensohn, *Finding One's Way with Clay*, 21.

14   Marvin Bell, "Thirty-two Statements about Writing Poetry," in *When the Rewards Can Be So Great*, 36.

15   Shaun McNiff, *Art Heals*, xii–xiii.

16   Mary Catherine Bateson, *Composing a Further Life*, 209.

**Chapter 1: Creating While Aging**

17    Faith Ringgold quoted in Hilarie M. Sheets, "You Become Better with Age," *ARTnews* May 20, 1913, http://www.artnews.com/2013/05/20/making-art-after-8/.

18    World Bank, Population ages 65 and above for the United States, retrieved from FRED, Federal Reserve Bank of St. Louis, https://fred.stlouisfed.org/series/SPPOP65UPTOZSUSA, October 29, 2021.

19    Projected Age Groups and Sex Composition of the Population: Main Projections Series for the United States, 2017–2060. U.S. Census Bureau, Population Division, Washington DC. Revised Release Date: September 2018, 8.

20    The drop in life expectancy is mentioned in Atul Gawande, "Inside the Worst-Hit County in the Worst-Hit State in the Worst-Hit Country," *The New Yorker*, February 8, 2021; Jessica Wolf, "Tracking How COVID-19 is Changing Life Expectancy," April 1, 2021, UCLA Newsroom, https://newsroom.ucla.edu/releases/covid19-changed-life-expectancy.

21    "World Population Prospects, 2019—Highlights," United Nations, Department of Economic and Social Affairs, Population Division, https://population.un.org/wpp/Publications/Files/WPP2019_10KeyFindings.pdf.

22    Projected Age Groups and Sex Composition of the Population: Main Projections Series for the United States, 2017–2060. U.S. Census Bureau, Population Division, Washington DC. Revised Release Date: September 2018, 8, https://www.cdc.gov/nchs/data/nvsr/nvsr67/nvsr67_05.pdf.

23    "World Population Prospects, 2019—Highlights," United Nations, Department of Economic and Social Affairs, Population Division, https://population.un.org/wpp/Publications/Files/WPP2019_10KeyFindings.pdf.

24    Laura Carstensen discusses maternal and infant deaths in 1900 in *A Long Bright Future*, 43.

25    Steven Johnson, *Extra Life*, 57.

26    Kevin M. White and Samuel H. Preston, "How Many Americans Are Alive Because of Twentieth-Century Improvements in Mortality?" *Population and Development Review*, Vol. 22, No. 3 (September 1996), 415–429; Gina Kolata, "Model Shows How Improved Medical Care Allowed Population Surge," *The New York Times*, January 7, 1997, 3.

27    For the numbers of Americans over age 90 see Eric B. Larson and Joan DeClaire, *Enlightened Aging*, 4; Marissa Fessenden, "There Are Now More Americans Over Age 100 and They're Living Longer Than Ever," Smithsonian.com, January 22, 2016.

28   Christie Aschwanden, "The Longevity Files: A Strong Grip? Pushups? What actually Can Help You Live to a Ripe Old Age?" *The Washington Post*, September 28, 2019.

29   Oliver Sacks, "The Aging Brain," in *Everything in its Place: First Loves and Last Tales*, 152.

30   "Profile: Warren MacKenzie: A Self-Confessed Man of Mud," June 1, 2018, Goldmark Gallery, Rutland, UK, https://discover.goldmarkart.com/warren-mackenzie-american-ceramics/; Mary Divine, "Warren MacKenzie, World-Renowned Potter, Dies at 98," TwinCities.com Pioneer Press, January 2, 2019.

31   Calvin Baker, "Derek Walcott," *The New York Times Magazine*, December 31, 2017, 50–51.

32   Diana Athill, *Somewhere Towards the End*, 145.

33   Roy Hoffman, "Alive Alive Oh! by Diana Athill," *New York Times Book Review* February 12, 2016; Polly Pattullo, "Diana Athill Obituary," *The Guardian*, January 24, 2019.

34   Nicole Rudnick, "The Shape of the Mountain: Etel Adnan," *The Paris Review*, Spring 2018, 64–87.

35   "Etel Adnan: Light's New Measure," October 8, 2021–January 10, 2022, Solomon R. Guggenheim Museum, https://www.guggenheim.org/exhibition/etel-adnan-lights-new-measure.

36   Otto Kallir, *Grandma Moses* Abridged Version; *Time* cover: December 28, 1953; Peter Schjeldahl, "The Original," *The New Yorker*, May 20, 2001.

37   Alma Thomas is interviewed in Eleanor Munro, "Alma W. Thomas," *Originals: American Women Artists*, 189–197; Paul Richard, "Alma Thomas, 86, Dies," *The Washington Post*, February 25, 1978.

38   Richard Pallardy, "Richard Adams," *Encyclopaedia Britannica*, May 5, 2020.

39   Tara Bahrampour, "At Age 101, This Woman Released her First Collection of Poems," *The Washington Post*, July 28, 2019; Dan Sheehan, "Is this the Oldest Debut Author in History?," *Literary Hub*, July 29, 2019, https://lithub.com/is-this-the-oldest-debut-author-in-history/.

40   That the majority of adults over age 85 need no assistance is noted in Marisha Pasopathi and Corinna E. Lockenhoff, "Ageist Behavior" in *Ageism* ed. by Todd E. Nelson, 202–203.

41   The increasing cohort of very well very old people is discussed in J. W. Rowe, et al., "Facts and Fictions about an Aging America," Fall 2009. Macarthur Foundation Research Network on an Aging Society, https://www.macfound.org/media/files/AGING-CONTEXTS-FACTFICTION.PDF; Ashton Applewhite, *This Chair Rocks: A Manifesto Against Ageism*, 29.

42    World Health Organization, "World Report on Disability" (2011), https://www.who.int/disabilities/world_report/2011/report.pdf.

43    These creatures are described in Daniel J. Levitin, *Successful Aging*, 314–317. See also, Stephanie Pappas, "Hail the Hydra, an Animal That May Be Immortal," *Live Science*, December 22, 2015, https://www.livescience.com/53178-hydra-may-live-forever.html.

44    Daniel J. Levitin, *Successful Aging*, 87.

45    For risks of dementia and improving health of 90-year-olds, see Laura L. Carstensen, "Our Aging Population—It May Just Save Us All," in *The Upside of Aging* ed. by Paul H. Irving, 7, 9.

46    Dementia statistics are taken from "Global Health and Aging," National Institute on Aging National Institutes of Health, NIH Publication no. 11-7737, October 2011, https://www.who.int/ageing/publications/global_health.pdf; "A Profile of Older Adults with Dementia and their Caregivers," *ASPE Issue Brief*, (US Dept. of Health and Human Services) September 2018, https://aspe.hhs.gov/system/files/pdf/260391/DemChartIB.pdf; World Health Organization, "Dementia," September 21, 2020, https://www.who.int/news-room/fact-sheets/detail/dementia.

47    Thanks to Marigrace Becker, Program Manager of the University of Washington Memory and Brain Wellness Center, for further educating me on the issue of memory loss. Matt M. McKnight, "As Memory Fades, An Artist Emerges," *Crosscut*, January 15, 2019; Marigrace Becker email to Priscilla Long, October 10, 2021, in possession of Priscilla Long, Seattle.

48    Dementia rates falling, from 2000 to 2012: Gina Kolata, "U.S. Dementia Rates Are Dropping Even as Population Ages," *The New York Times*, November 21, 2016; Laura L. Carstensen, "Our Aging Population—It May Just Save Us All," in *The Upside of Aging* ed. by Paul H. Irving, 7, 9.

49    "Baby Boomers Face Greater Cognitive Decline than Previous Generations," *Medical News Today Newsletter*, n.d. accessed October 27, 2020, https://www.medicalnewstoday.com/articles/baby-boomers-face-greater-cognitive-decline-than-previous-generations.

50    Lifestyle factors are discussed in Daniel J. Levitin, *Successful Aging*, 83.

51    For an analysis of this economic crisis in the United States see Helen Epstein, "Left Behind," *The New York Review of Books*, March 26, 2020, 28–30; Atul Gawande, "The Blight," *The New Yorker*, March 23, 2020, 59–61; Steven H. Woolf et al., "Changes in midlife death rates across racial and ethnic groups in the United States: systematic analysis of vital statistics," PubMed, August 15, 2018, https://pubmed.ncbi.nlm.nih.gov/30111554/.

52    Hui Zheng, "A New Look at Cohort Trend and Underlying Mechanisms in Cognitive Functioning," *The Journals of Gerontology: Series B*, gbaa107, https://doi.org/10.1093/geronb/gbaa107.

53    Zheng is quoted in "Baby Boomers Face Greater Cognitive Decline than Previous Generations," *Medical News Today Newsletter*, n.d. accessed October 6, 2021, https://www.medicalnewstoday.com/articles/baby-boomers-face-greater-cognitive-decline-than-previous-generations.

54    Zheng quoted in "Faster Mental Decline for Boomers?" *AARP Bulletin*, October 2020.

55    Dialynn Dwyer, "Katherine Beiers is 85 years old. She finished the 2018 Boston Marathon," *The Boston Globe* April 17, 2018.

56    For Betty Jean McHugh see "90 'just a number' for marathon record-setting B.C. senior," CTV news, March 22, 2018, https://www.ctvnews.ca/canada/90-just-a-number-for-marathon-record-setting-b-c-senior-1.3853762).

57    Scott Purks, "The Iron Nun Still Going Strong at Age 88," *Tampa Bay Times*, April 26, 2018; Madonna Buder, "What Running Taught the Iron Nun about Aging," *America: The Jesuit Review*, March 18, 2019.

58    Michael Segalov, "It's Never Too Late: Elderly High-Achievers," *The Guardian*, February 21, 2021.

59    J. V. Herod, "Series Solutions for Nonlinear Boltzmann Equations," *Journal Nonlinear Analysis*, Vol. 7, No. 12 (1983), 1373–1387; Herod's nonmathematical writings can be found at https://sites.google.com/site/jimherodtales/home; Jim Herod emails to Priscilla Long, July 6 and July 9, 2020, in possession of Priscilla Long, Seattle.

60    Chris van Leuven, "Robert Kelman, 87, Becomes Oldest Person to Climb Devils Tower," *Climber*, September 14, 2017, https://www.climbing.com/news/robert-kelman-87-becomes-oldest-person-to-climb-devils-tower/.

61    Stimson Bullitt, *Illusion Dweller: The Climbing Life of Stimson Bullitt*, throughout.

62    Mary Kay Ash is quoted in Gene D. Cohen, *The Creative Age: Awakening Human Potential in the Second Half of Life*, 257.

63    Anders Ericsson and Robert Pool, *Peak*, 195.

64    Stanley Kunitz quoted in Wendy Lustbader, *Life Gets Better: The Unexpected Pleasures of Growing Older*, 174.

65    Russell Freedman, *Martha Graham*, 144–147.

66    "Wayne Thiebaud," Napa Valley Art Camp blog, March 29, 2010, http://napavalleyartcamp.blogspot.com/2010/03/wayne-thiebaud.html accessed July 2, 2020.

67    Ashton Applewhite, *This Chair Rocks*, 77.

68 Chronological age no longer a proper metric: David J. Lowsky, S. Jay Olshansky, Jay Bhattacharya, and Dana P. Goldman, "Heterogeneity in Healthy Aging," *Journal of Gerontology Biological Sciences Medical Sciences* Vol. 69, No. 6 (June 2014), 648.

69 Seth Feman and Jonathan Frederick Walz, "Then the Light Would Come Around" in *Alma W. Thomas: Everything Is Beautiful*, 21.

70 Zeisel quoted in Ashton Applewhite, *This Chair Rocks*, 108; William L. Hamilton, "Eva Zeisel, Ceramic Artist and Designer, Dies at 105," *The New York Times*, December 31, 2011, B7.

71 Johnny Cash quoted by producer Rick Rubin in "Johnny Cash Biography," April 2, 2014, The Biography.com website accessed May 2, 2020, https://www.biography.com/musician/johnny-cash; Robert Hilburn, *Johnny Cash: The Life*.

72 "John Huston," *Encyclopaedia Britannica*, August 24, 2020; Christine Smallwood, "What Do Artist's Final Works Say About their Lives," *The New York Times*, September 19, 2017.

73 Pauline Kael's December 14, 1987 *New Yorker* review is reprinted in "The Dead (1987)—Review by Pauline Kael," *Scraps from the Loft*, July 5, 2020.

74 Jean Renoir, *Renoir, My Father*, 25, 426, and 431.

75 Riva Castleman, "Introduction," *Jazz* by Henri Matisse, vii.

76 Matisse discusses the chapel in *Matisse on Art* ed. by Jack Flam, 191–192, 197–199.

77 Francois Gilot's passage from *Life with Picasso* is quoted in *Matisse: A Retrospective* ed. by Jack Flam, 371.

78 "Most dancers today..." (and following): Roundtable discussion with Patricia Bloom, Carmen De Lavallade, Audrey Flack, Elinor Fuchs, and Gordon Rogoff, YouTube Philocetes Center Discussion on Aging and Creativity, published December 30, 2009, https://www.youtube.com/watch?v=NhjCvilYq5w&t=1030s.

79 Brian Doyle, "How Many of You Are There in the Quartet," in *Spirited Men*, 90.

80 The story of Dave Brubeck is told in Alan D. Castel, *Better with Age*, 149.

81 Joan Jeffri, *Above Ground: Information on Artists III: Special Focus New York City Aging Artists*, 40.

82 All Sonny Rollins quotes and that of his biographer are from Eric Nisenson, *Open Sky: Sonny Rollins and his World of Improvisation*, 211 and 221.

83 Martha Graham quotes are from Russell Freedman, *Martha Graham*, 137, 140.

84    "Chance Conversations: An Interview with Merce Cunningham and John Cage," Walker Art Center, Minneapolis, Minnesota, Spring 1981, posted on YouTube, July 27, 2009, https://www.youtube.com/watch?v=ZNGpjXZovgk.

85    *Merce Cunningham: A Lifetime of Dance* directed by Charles Atlas, DVD, 1999, Merce Cunningham Trust.

86    Sarit A. Golub, Allan Filipowicz, and Ellen J. Langer, "Acting Your Age," in *Ageism: Stereotyping and Prejudice against Older Persons* ed. by Todd D. Nelson, 292.

87    Jonathan Rauch, *The Happiness Curve*, 226.

88    Becca R. Levy and Mahzarin R. Banaji, "Implicit Ageism," in *Ageism: Stereotyping and Prejudice Against Older Persons* ed. by Todd D. Nelson, 60.

89    Susan Krauss Whitbourne and Joel R. Sneed, "Paradox of Well-Being, Identity Processes, and Stereotype Threat: Ageism and Its Potential Relationships to the Self in Later Life," in *Ageism: Stereotyping and Prejudice Against Older Persons* ed. by Todd D. Nelson, 265.

90    Becca R. Levy and Mahzarin R. Banaji, "Implicit Ageism," in *Ageism: Stereotyping and Prejudice Against Older Persons* ed. by Todd D. Nelson, 58.

91    Mainland China and deaf community: Susan Krauss Whitbourne and Joel R. Sneed, "Paradox of Well-Being, Identity Processes, and Stereotype Threat: Ageism and Its Potential Relationships to the Self in Later Life," in *Ageism: Stereotyping and Prejudice Against Older Persons* ed. by Todd D. Nelson, 266.

92    Zuckerberg is quoted in Steven Kotler, "Is Silicon Valley Ageist or Just Smart?" *Forbes*, February 14, 2015.

93    Vivek Wadwha, "Innovation without Age Limits," *MIT Technology Review*, February 1, 2012, https://www.technologyreview.com/s/426760/innovation-without-age-limits/.

94    Bess Levin, "Texas Lt. Governor: Old People Should Volunteer to Die to Save the Economy," *Vanity Fair*, March 24, 2020.

95    Laura Newberry, "The pandemic has amplified ageism. 'It's open season for discrimination' against older adults," *The Los Angeles Times,* May 1, 2020.

96    Ashton Applewhite, *This Chair Rocks*, 20.

97    Twyla Tharp, *Keep It Moving*, 6.

98    These Becca Levy quotes are from Becca R. Levy et al., "Ageism Amplifies Cost and Prevalence of Health Conditions," *The Gerontologist*, 2018, 2.

99    Jonathan Rauch, *The Happiness Curve*, 227.

100   Gene D. Cohen, *The Creative Age*, 5.

## Chapter 2: Brilliant Old Brains

101    Calvin Tomkins, "Painterly Virtues: Alex Katz's Life in Art," *The New Yorker*, August 27, 2018, 56.

102    Michael Ramscar et al., "The Myth of Cognitive Decline: Non-Linear Dynamics of Lifelong Learning," in *Topics in Cognitive Science* Vol. 6, No. 1, January 2014; Bill Myers, "Provider Exclusive: Michael Ramscar on the 'Myth of Cognitive Decline,'" *Provider*, February 19, 2014; Benedict Carey, "Older Really Can Mean Wiser," *The New York Times*, March 16, 2015, D3.

103    Ramscar quoted in Ashton Applewhite, *This Chair Rocks*, 82.

104    Roberto Cabeza's work is reported in Gene Cohen, *The Mature Mind*, 20–21. See Roberto Cabeza, Center for Neuroscience, Duke University, https://dibs.duke.edu/scholars/roberto-cabeza.

105    John Medina, *Brain Rules for Aging Well*, 103.

106    Oliver Sacks, "The Aging Brain" in *Everything in its Place*, 153.

107    Rachel Wu, George W. Rebok, and Feng Vankee Lin, "A Novel Theoretical Life Course Framework for Triggering Cognitive Development Across the Lifespan," *Human Development*, Vol. 59, No. 6 (2016), 342–365.

108    Paterno's graduation was reported widely, including in Michael Segalov, "It's Never Too Late: Elderly High Achievers," *The Guardian*, February 21, 2021.

109    Michael Segalov, "It's Never Too Late: Elderly High Achievers," *The Guardian*, February 21, 2021.

110    Alison Starling, "Working Woman: 106 Years Old, A Sculptor Turned Photographer and Still Going Strong," video broadcast WJVA, April 12, 2019, https://wjla.com/features/working-women/working-woman-106-years-old-a-sculptor-turned-photographer-and-still-going-strong; Marilee Shapiro Asher on Ralph Nader Radio Hour, March 23, 2019, https://ralphnaderradiohour.com/dancing-in-the-wonder/; Petula Dvorak, "Meet Two Amazing Women Who Are Still Working at Age 102," *The Washington Post*, November 16, 2015; Petula Dvorak, "At 107, She's a Force Who's Conquered 2 Pandemics," *The Washington Post*, May 8, 2020, B1; For Asher's home page see Marileeshapiroasher.com.

111    David Hockney: "Sometime Make the Time: Yorkshire Watercolors" in *True to Life* by Lawrence Weschler, 197–198.

112    David Hockney on iPad: Francoise Mouly, "David Hockney's 'Hearth,'" *The New Yorker*, December 14, 2020.

113    On Moses: Peter Schjeldahl, "The Original," *The New Yorker*, May 20, 2001.

114    Otto Kallir, *Grandma Moses* Abridged version, 133.

115    Daniel J. Levitin, *Successful Aging*, 93, 115.

116   Daniel J. Levitin, *Successful Aging*, 25.

117   Nell Painter, *Old in Art School*, 70.

118   "Josh Carter's" story is told in Sara Lawrence-Lightfoot, *The Third Chapter: Passion, Risk, and Adventure in the 25 Years After* 50, 178–187.

119   Neenah Ellis, "Harry Shapiro," *If I live to be 100*, 95.

120   Interview of Harry Shapiro by Marjory Silver (New England Centenarian Study) in *Cognitive Functioning in Old Age* (video), nd, accessed December 2019 (no longer available).

121   Daniel J. Levitin, *Successful Aging*, 85–86.

122   Eric B. Larson and Joan DeClaire, *Enlightened Aging*, 124.

123   ohn Medina, *Brain Rules for Aging Well*, 160.

124   Nicholas Delbanco, *Lastingness*, 37.

125   Calvin Tomkins, "Painterly Virtues: Alex Katz's Life in Art," *The New Yorker*, August 27, 2018, 65.

126   Twyla Tharp, *Keeping It Moving*, 33.

127   Lauren Valenti, "At 75, Mick Jagger Shares His Incredible Post–Heart Surgery Dance Moves," *Vogue*, May 15, 2019.

128   "Hearne Pardee in Conversation with Wayne Thiebaud," *Catamaran*, 113; Charles Desmarais, "Artist Wayne Thiebaud, at 99, Decides to Play the Clown," *San Francisco Chronicle*, January 2, 2020; Sam Whiting, "Wayne Thiebaud, Approaching 98, Takes Stock of the Big Picture," *San Francisco Chronicle*, September 26, 2018.

129   Patti Smith is quoted in Rebecca Solnit, *Wanderlust: A History of Walking*, 186.

130   Marily Oppezzo and Daniel L. Schwartz, "Give Your Ideas Some Legs: The Positive Effect of Walking on Creative Thinking," *Journal of Experimental Psychology* Vol. 40, No. 4 (2014), 1142-1152.

131   Twyla Tharp, *Keep It Moving*, 176.

132   Joshua Rothman, "What Lies Beneath," *The New Yorker*, March 25, 2019, 44.

133   Amy Gorman, *Aging Artfully*, 18–30.

134   Frank Lipman and Danielle Claro, *The New Rules of Aging Well*, 185–186.

135   "Physical Activity Guidelines for Americans," 2nd edition, 2018, https://health.gov/sites/default/files/2019-09/Physical_Activity_Guidelines_2nd_edition.pdf.

136   George Burns is quoted in Gene D. Cohen, *The Mature Mind*, 83–84.

137   Donald Hall, "No Smoking," in *Essays After Eighty*.

138   Tom Bryant, "Keith Richards Stops Smoking at 75—But Says Cigarettes Harder to Quit than Heroin," *Mirror*, February 14, 2019.

139     Sarah L. Delany and A. Elizabeth Delany with Amy Hill Hearth, *Having Our Say*, 230–231.

140     Anthony J. Lin, et al., "Body Weight Changes During Pandemic-Related Shelter-in-Place in a Longitudinal Cohort Study," JAMA Open Network, March 22, 2021; Karia Walsh, "Americans Gained 12.5 Pounds on Average During the Pandemic—Here's Why That's OK, According to an R.D." EatingWell.com, June 30, 2020.

141     Data on food-insecure households is taken from Alisha Coleman-Jensen et al., "Household Food Security in the United States in 2020," September 2021, Economic Research Service, US Dept. of Agriculture, https://www.ers.usda.gov/webdocs/publications/102076/err-298.pdf?v=2213.6; Number of food-insecure elders: Kenneth Terrell, "Food Insecurity Leaves People Over 60 Hungry," May 16, 2019, AARP, https://www.aarp.org/politics-society/advocacy/info-2019/older-americans-food-insecure.html.

142     Stephen M. Stahl, *Stahl's Essential Psychopharmacology* 3rd ed. 748–749, 752–754.

143     Anders Ericsson and Robert Pool, *Peak*, 174–176.

144     Sarah Yerkes, "Sarah Yerkes, author of *Days of Blue and Flame*, discusses what led her to poetry at age 96," (video) Passager Books website accessed December 27, 2020, http://www.passagerbooks.com/days-of-blue-and-flame-by-sarah-yerkes/; Tara Bahrampour, "At Age 101, This Women Released Her First Collection of Poems," *The Washington Post*, July 28, 2019.

145     Philip Glass, *Words Without Music*, 242–243.

146     Sarah L. Delany with Amy Hill Hearth, *On My Own*, 134.

147     Patti Smith, *Year of the Monkey*, 78–79.

148     Roger Angell, "This Old Man," in *This Old Man*, 271–272.

149     Patti Smith, *Year of the Monkey*, 79–80.

150     Wayne Thiebaud speaking in "Hearne Pardee Conversation with Wayne Thiebaud," *Catamaran* Vol. 7, Issue 3 (Fall 2019), 124.

151     Philip Clark, *Dave Brubeck: A Life in Time*, x, 362.

152     *Visages/Villages (Faces/Places)* by Agnès Varda and JR DVD, Cohen Media Group, 2017.

153     Nicholas Delbanco, *Lastingness*, 13.

154     Imogen Cunningham, *After Ninety*, 10, 17.

155     Allan Kozinn, "Elliott Carter, Composer Who Decisively Snapped Tradition, Dies at 103," *The New York Times*, November 5, 2012, A27.

156     Also on Elliott Carter: Tim Page, "Late Bloomer," *The New York Review of Books*, April 28, 2019, pp. 30, 32.

157   Deborah Sontag, "At 94, She's the Hot New Thing in Painting, and Enjoying It," *The New York Times,* December 20, 2009, A1.

158   Adam D. Weinberg, "Foreword," in Dana Miller, *Carmen Herrera: Lines of Sight,* 7, 13.

159   Andrew Russeth, "'Don't Be Intimidated by Anything': Carmen Herrera at 100," *ARTnews,* June 5, 2015, https://www.artnews.com/art-news/news/dont-be-intimidated-about-anything-carmen-herrera-at-100-4281/.

160   Carmen Herrera is quoted in Adam D. Weinberg, "Foreword," in Dana Miller, *Carmen Herrera: Lines of Sight,* 6.

161   *W. B. Yeats: The Poems: A New Edition* ed. by Richard J. Finneran, 346–348; Brenda Maddox, *Yeats's Ghosts: The Secret Life of W. B. Yeats.*

162   Angela Glendenning, "Self, Civic Engagement and Late Life Creativity," in *Creativity in Later Life* ed. by David Amigoni and Gordon McMullan, 162–163.

163   Igor Stravinsky, "Perspectives of an Octogenarian" in *Memories and Commentaries,* 263.

164   Eric Walter White, *Stravinsky: The Composer and His Works* 2nd ed., 155–156.

165   Otto Kallir, *Grandma Moses* (abridged version), 101–102.

166   Fred H. Gage, "Adult Neurogenesis in Mammals," *Science,* May 31, 2019, Vol. 364, No. 6443, 827–828; Norman Doidge, *The Brain That Changes Itself.*

167   The work on our number of neurons done by Suzana Herculano-Houzel is reported by James Randerson, "How Many Neurons Make a Human Brain: Billions Fewer Than We Thought," *The Guardian,* February 28, 2012.

168   That each of our neurons has 7,000 or more connections is noted by John Medina, *Brain Rules for Aging Well,* 9.

169   Kirk I. Erickson et al., "Exercise training increases size of hippocampus and improves memory," PNAS, Vol. 108, No. 7, (February 15, 2011), 3017–3022.

170   "State Variation in Meeting the 2008 Federal Guidelines for Both Aerobic and Muscle-strengthening Activities Through Leisure-time Physical Activity Among Adults Aged 18–64: United States, 2010–2015," *National Health Statistics Reports* (U.S. Department of Health and Human Services) No. 112 (June 28, 2018), 1.

171   "Adults Need More Physical Activity," Digital Press Kit, Centers for Disease Control and Prevention, November 9, 2018.

172   Jialu Streeter, Megan Roche, and Anne Friedlander, "From Bad to Worse: The Impact of Work-From-Home on Sedentary Behaviors and Exercising," Sightlines 2021 Survey, Stanford Center on Longevity, https://longevity.stanford.edu/wp-content/uploads/2021/05/Sedentary-Brief.pdf.

173   Daniel J. Levitin reports the statistic on silent strokes in Daniel J. Levitin, *Successful Aging*, 96.

174   Sarah H. Delany with Amy Hill Hearth, *On My Own*, 95.

175   Sadie speaking in Sarah L. Delany and A. Elizabeth Delany with Amy Hill Hearth, *Having Our Say*, 288.

176   Stephen M. Stahl, *Stahl's Essential Psychopharmacology* 3rd ed., 912.

177   Lawrence R. Samuel, "Creative Aging," *Psychology Today*, September 29, 2017; Lifetime Arts, www.lifetimearts.org.

178   Ina Bray emails to Priscilla Long, April 29 and 30, May 6, 12, 2020, in possession of Priscilla Long, Seattle; Elderwise website accessed October 6, 2021, www.elderwise.org.

179   Aaron Copland is quoted in Michael Hutcheon and Linda Hutcheon, "Late Style(s): The Ageism of the Singular," 6.

180   Steve Chawkins, "Miriam Schapiro dies at 91; pioneer of feminist art movement," *Los Angeles Times*, July 2, 2015.

181   Michael Kimmelman, "Willem de Kooning Dies at 92; Reshaped U.S. Art," *The New York Times*, March 20, 1997, 1.

182   Marigrace Becker is quoted in "Alzheimer's Art Exhibit Takes Away Fear, Sows Hope," *The Seattle Times*, February 15, 2016.

183   Jamie Landers, "Laura L. Carstensen Explores Opportunities Facing an Aging World," *The Chautauquan Daily*, July 15, 2019.

184   *2021 Alzheimer's Disease Facts and Figures*, 19, Alzheimer's Association, https://dshs.texas.gov/alzheimers/pdf/2021-Facts-and-Figures.pdf.

185   We are reminded to consider the sometimes overwhelming influences outside of individual effort by James D. Stowe and Teresa M. Cooney, "Examining Rowe and Kahn's Concept of Successful Aging: Importance of Taking a Life Course Perspective," *Gerontologist*, Vol. 55, No. 1 (February 2015), 43–50.

## Chapter 3: The Happiness of the Old

186   Pablo Casals, *Joys and Sorrows*, 15.

187   Alan D. Castel, *Better with Age*, 26.

188   Marcia Muth is quoted in Ashton Applewhite, *This Chair Rocks*, 82.

189    Robert Nott, "Marcia Muth, 1919–2014: Living Treasure Launched Art Career Late in Life," *The New Mexican*, April 30, 2014; Nott, "Jody Ellis, 1925–2018: Cellist Who Co-Founded Santa Fe Community Orchestra Dies at 92," *The New Mexican*, February 18, 2018.

190    Jonathan Rauch, *The Happiness Curve,* 51–54.

191    The Brookings Institute study is reported in Carol Graham and Julia Ruiz Posuelo, "Happiness, Stress, and Age: How the U-Curve Varies Across People and Places," *Journal of Population Economics,* Vol. 30, Issue 1 (January 2017), 225–264.

192    Daniel J. Levitin, *Successful Aging*, 372.

193    Quotes about and by Sonny Rollins are from David Marchese, "Sonny Rollins," *New York Times Magazine*, March 1, 2020, 11.

194    Jonathan Rauch details various happiness studies in *The Happiness Curve*, 64, 68, 117.

195    Randy Lilleston, "How Much Do You Know About Senior Poverty?," May 14, 2018, AARP website accessed December 4, 2019, https://www.aarp.org/politics-society/advocacy/info-2018/senior-poverty-quiz.html#triviaresults; Randy Lilleston, "AARP Foundation Fights Senior Poverty," May 14, 2018, website accessed October 6, 2021, https://www.aarp.org/politics-society/advocacy/info-2018/aarp-foundation-senior-poverty.html; Ellen O'Brien, Ke Bin Wu, and David Baer, "Older Americans in Poverty: A Snapshot," April 2010, AARP Public Policy Institute https://assets.aarp.org/rgcenter/ppi/econ-sec/2010-03-poverty.pdf.

196    Laura Carstensen discusses the chronic stress that accompanies poverty in *A Long Bright Future*, 247.

197    National Council on Aging, "Economic Security for Seniors Facts," accessed October 6, 2021, https://www.ncoa.org/news/resources-for-reporters/get-the-facts/economic-security-facts/; "Federal Poverty Level Guidelines and Chart," accessed October 7, 2021, https://www.thebalance.com/federal-poverty-level-definition-guidelines-chart-3305843.

198    The statistic on patrons of food banks is given in Helen Epstein, "Left Behind," *The New York Review of Books*, March 26, 2020, 28–30.

199    "Depression on Rise," *AARP Bulletin* November 2019, 40; Randy Lilleston, "How Much Do You Know About Senior Poverty?" May 14, 2018, AARP website accessed October 7, 2021, https://www.aarp.org/politics-society/advocacy/info-2018/senior-poverty-quiz.html#triviaresults.

200    Ken Dychtwald, "A Longevity Market Emerges," in *The Upside of Aging* ed. by Paul H. Irving, 65.

201    Jonathan Rauch is quoting and citing research done by David Branchflower and Andrew Oswald, *The Happiness Curve*, 51–52.

202    Laura Carstensen is reporting on the work of Steve Cole, of UCLA and John Cacioppo, of the University of Chicago. Laura Carstensen, *A Long Bright Future*, 104–105.

203    National Council on Aging, "American Perceptions of Aging in the 21st Century," 2002 update, Washington DC: National Council on Aging, 2002, 2–5.

204    "Average number of people per household in the United States from 1960 to 2019," Statista website accessed October 8, 2021, https://www.statista.com/statistics/183648/average-size-of-households-in-the-us/.

205    "Social Isolation, Loneliness in Older People Pose Health Risks," April 23, 2019, National Institute on Aging, https://www.nia.nih.gov/news/social-isolation-loneliness-older-people-pose-health-risks.

206    Laura Carstensen, *A Long Bright Future*, 111, 115.

207    Social relationships were studied and are discussed in Joan Jeffri, *Above Ground*, 8.

208    Imogen Cunningham, *After Ninety*, 22–23.

209    Laura L. Carstensen, "Our Aging Population: It May Just Save Us All," in *The Upside of Aging* ed. by Paul H. Irving, 15.

210    Daniel Levitin, *Successful Aging*, 144.

211    Twyla Tharp, *Keep It Moving*, 159 and 162.

212    Pablo Casals, *Joys and Sorrows*, 17.

213    Asher mentions the thrill of clay in the video, Alison Starling, "Working Woman: 106 Years Old, A Sculptor Turned Photographer and Still Going Strong," video broadcast WJVA, April 12, 2019, https://wjla.com/features/working-women/working-woman-106-years-old-a-sculptor-turned-photographer-and-still-going-strong; Marilee Shapiro Asher on Ralph Nader Radio Hour, March 23, 2019, https://ralphnaderradiohour.com/dancing-in-the-wonder/; Petula Dvorak, "Meet Two Amazing Women Who Are Still Working At Age 102," *The Washington Post*, November 16, 2015; Petula Dvorak, "At 107, She's a Force Who's Conquered 2 Pandemics," *The Washington Post*, May 8, 2020, B1.

214    Marilee Shapiro Asher, *Dancing in the Wonder for 102 Years*, 105.

215    Diana Athill, "The Decision," in *Alive, Alive Oh!*, 97–118.

216    Agnes Martin, *Beauty Is in Your Mind*, Tateshots video, https://www.youtube.com/watch?v=902YXjchQsk

217    Arne Glimcher in Conversation with Frances Morris, September 25, 2015, video, Tate Modern, https://www.youtube.com/watch?v=jAdCqj-wuww.

218  Glimcher discusses Martin's mental illness in Arne Glimcher in Conversation with Frances Morris, September 25, 2015, video, Tate Modern  https://www.youtube.com/watch?v=jAdCqj-wuww;  Nancy Princenthal, *Agnes Martin*, 9, 34, 151,152.

219  "Beauty is the Mystery of Life," in *Agnes Martin* ed. by Barbara Haskell, 17.

220  Arne Glimcher in Conversation with Frances Morris, September 25, 2015, video, Tate Modern, https://www.youtube.com/watch?v=jAdCqj-wuww.

221  Wayne Thiebaud is quoted in Hilarie M. Sheets, "You Become Better with Age," *ARTnews*, May 20, 2013.

222  "Alma W. Thomas" in *Originals: American Women Artists* by Eleanor Munro, 197 and 194.

223  May Sarton, *At Eighty-Two*, 128 (Saturday, November 6, 1993); "May Sarton," Poetry Foundation website accessed December 12, 2019, https://www.poetryfoundation.org/poets/may-sarton.

224  Doris Grumbach, *Coming into the End Zone*, 23, 43. 52. 58, 81.

225  Jimmy Carter, *The Virtues of* Aging, 87; "Jimmy Carter," The Carter Center website accessed February 11, 2020, https://www.cartercenter. org/about/experts/jimmy_carter.html.

226  George E. Valliant, *Triumphs of Experience: The Men of the Harvard Grant Study*, 157.

227  Gene D. Cohen, "Creativity with Aging: Four Phases of Potential in the Second Half of Life," *Geriatrics*, Vol. 56, No. 4, 54.

228  Clark Terry with Gwen Terry, *Clark: The Autobiography of Clark Terry*, 4 and throughout.

229  Johann Wolfgang von Goethe, *Maxims and Reflections*, 7.

230  Leonard Woolf, "Virginia's Death," in *The Journey Not the Arrival Matters*, 9–96.

231  Henry Roth's story is told in Jonathan Rosen, "Writer, Interrupted," *The New Yorker*, August 1, 2005. I have also consulted Charles McGrath, "Breathing Life into Henry Roth," *The New York Times*, May 23, 2010; Morris Dickstein, "Memory Unbound," *The Threepenny Review*, Summer 2007; Richard E. Nicholis, "Henry Roth, 89, Who Wrote of an Immigrant Child's Life in *Call It Sleep*, Is Dead," *The New York Times*, October 15, 1995, and Steven G. Kellman, *Redemption: The Life of Henry Roth*.

232  Becca Levy on Henry Roth is quoted in Mary Kent and Rose Maria, *The Arts and Aging: Building the Science*, 24.

233  Also on Henry Roth, Jonathan Rosen, "Writer, Interrupted," *The New Yorker,* August 1, 2005.

234  Maya Angelou, *Mom & Me & Mom*. I take the number of Angelou's books, which are given differently in different sources, from the list in front of this her last book.

235  Sara Lawrence-Lightfoot, *The Third Chapter*, 80.

236  The names used for these interviewees are "Steven Fox," "Jasmine Jones," and "Flora Featherstone." Sara Lawrence-Lightfoot, *The Third Chapter*, 81–83, 176–177.

237  Path with Art can be found at https://www.pathwithart.org/.

238  Anthony Tommasini, "Elliott Carter: Master of Complexity," *The New York Times*, November 6, 2012; Tim Page, "Late Bloomer," *The New York Review of Books*, April 18, 2019, 30, 32.

239  "Miriam McKinnie Hofmeier" in *A Fine Age: Creativity as a Key to Successful Aging*, ed. by Dana Steward, 97.

240  Schwartz is quoted in Barbara DeMarco-Barrett, "11 Over 70: Writers Who Persevere," *Authors Guild Bulletin*, Fall 2018–Winter 2019, 21.

241  Betye Saar, *Still Tickin'*, 28.

242  Christina M. Puchalski of George Washington Institute for Spirituality and Health, quoted in Steven Knapp, "Aging and Learning: The Future University," in *The Upside of Aging* ed. by Paul H. Irving, 168.

243  Stanley Kunitz with Genine Lentine, *The Wild Braid*, 54.

244  Oliver Sacks, "The Joy of Old Age (No Kidding)," *The New York Times*, July 6, 2013, SR12.

**Chapter 4: Resource Drain or Resource?**

245  Betty Friedan, *The Fountain of Age*, 612.

246  The preceding quote and this information are from Ken Dychtwald and Robert Morison, *What Retirees Want*, 67, 69.

247  Mitra Toossi and Elka Torpey, "Older workers: Labor force trends and career options," United States Bureau of Labor Statistics, May 2017, https://www.bls.gov/careeroutlook/2017/article/older-workers.htm.

248  Cal J. Halversen and Jacquelyn B. James, "3 Fast Facts: Self-Employment Trends Among Older Americans," July 2020, https://www.bc.edu/content/dam/files/research_sites/agingandwork/pdf/publications/FS40-Trendsinself-employment.pdf.

249  "Q&A: Laura Carstensen," *AARP Bulletin*, May 2018, 30.

250  This and the preceding quote are from Jo Ann Jenkins, *Disrupting Aging*, 166, 168–169

251  Daniel Levitin, *Successful Aging*, 378.

252  Joan Jeffri, "Executive Summary," *Above Ground: Information on Artists III: Special Focus New York City Aging Artists*.

253    Mason Currey, "Charles M. Schulz" in *Daily Rituals*, 217–218; "Biography," Charles M. Shulz Museum website accessed April 22, 2020, https://schulzmuseum.org/about-schulz/schulz-biography/.

254    Quincy Jones, *The Autobiography of Quincy Jones*, 300.

255    Louise Nevelson and Robert Motherwell are quoted in N. Robertson, "Artists in Old Age: The Fires of Creativity Burn Undiminished," *The New York Times*, January 22, 1986, C1.

256    All quotes referring to Arthur Rubinstein are from Harvey Sachs, *Rubinstein: A Life*, 345–346, 337, 343, 359–361.

257    Judy Collins is quoted in Daniel J. Levitin, *Successful Aging*, 80, 379; Judy Collins website, www.judycollins.com.

258    The person who is "not going to stop painting" is quoted in August L. Freundlich and John A. Shively, "Creativity and the Exceptional Aging Artist," *Clinical Interventions in Aging*, Vol 1, No. 2 (2006), 200.

259    Robert Penn Warren quoted in N. Robertson, "Artists in Old Age: The Fires of Creativity Burn Undiminished," *The New York Times*, January 22, 1986, C1.

260    Joseph Blotner, *Robert Penn Warren*, 482–499.

261    Jules Feiffer is quoted in Barbara DeMarco-Barrett, "11 Over 70: Writers Who Persevere," *Authors Guild Bulletin*, Fall 2018–Winter 2019, 21.

262    James Michener is discussed in Martin S. Lindauer, *Aging, Creativity, and Art*, 59–60; A chronological list of Michener's books is presented in the website Book Series in Order, https://www.bookseriesinorder.com/james-a-michener/.

263    B. B. King can be seen performing at the 2010 Crossroads Guitar Festival, Chicago, YouTube, Rhino channel, accessed December 27, 2020, https://www.youtube.com/watch?v=SgXSomPE_FY.

264    Clarity Haynes, "'You Have to Get Past the Fear': Joan Semmel on Painting her Aging, Nude Body," *Hyperallergic*, September 9, 2016, https://hyperallergic.com/321781/you-have-to-get-past-the-fear-joan-semmel-on-painting-her-aging-nude-body/.

265    Paul Goldberger, *Building Art: The Life and Work of Frank Gehry*, 208–209; Rowan Moore, "Frank Gehry at 90: I Love Working. I Love Working Things Out," *The Guardian*, February 24, 2019.

266    "Looking Back at Frank Gehry's Building-Bending Feats," PBS News Hour, September 11, 2015.

267  Matthew Shaer, "Remembering Merce Cunningham, Technology Pioneer," *The Christian Science Monitor*, July 27, 2009; "Merce Cunningham + Biped," The Kennedy Center website accessed October 8, 2021, https://www.kennedy-center.org/education/resources-for-educators/classroom-resources/media-and-interactives/media/dance/merce-cunningham--biped/; "Biped" The Merce Cunningham Trust website accessed April 11, 2020, https://www.mercecunningham.org/the-work/choreography/biped/.

268  Holland Carter, "Louise Bourgeois, Sculptor of Psychologically Powerful Works, Dies at 98," *The New York Times*, June 1, 2010, B14; Jerry Gorovoy, "The Louise Bourgeois I knew, by her Assistant Jerry Gorovoy," *The Guardian*, December 11, 2010; Email, Maggie Wright (The Easton Foundation) to Priscilla Long, April 10, 2020, in possession of Priscilla Long, Seattle; "Louise Bourgeois: Complete Prints and Books," Museum of Modern Art (MoMA).

269  Joe Kita, "Special Report on Ageism in the Workplace," AARP.org Bulletin, January/February 2020, 13–22.

270  Anne Truitt, *Prospect*, 33–34.

271  Eva Wines was interviewed in *A Fine Age: Creativity as a Key to Successful Ageing* ed. by Dana Steward, 71–72.

272  This and the preceding quote is from Randolph Hokanson, *With Head to Music Bent*, 189, 191.

273  Melinda Bargreen, "Randolph Hokanson, pianist and UW Professor Emeritus, Dies at 103," *The Seattle Times*, October 20, 2018.

274  Penelope Lively, "My Writing Day," *The Guardian*, September 23, 2017.

275  Doris Grumbach, *Coming into the End Zone*, 225–226.

276  "Louis and Elsie Freund" in *A Fine Age: Creativity as a Key to Successful Ageing*, ed. by Dana Steward, 24; Alan Du Bois, "Harry Louis Freund (1905–1999)," *Encyclopedia of Arkansas*, September 16, 2011; Alan Du Bois, "Elsie Mar Bates Frend (1912–2001)," *Encyclopedia of Arkansas*, November 3, 2006.

277  "Noah-isms: More Thoughts from Noah Purifoy" in *Noah Purifoy: High Desert*, 16.

278  Yael Lipschutz, "A NeoHooDoo Western" in *Noah Purifoy: Junk Dada*, 42.

279  Sara Lawrence-Lightfoot, *The Third Chapter*, 176 and 219.

280  Violet Hensley is interviewed in *A Fine Age: Creativity as a Key to Successful Ageing* edited by Dana Steward, 98–101; Ann Phillips Worster, "Violet Brumley Hensley (1916–)," *Encyclopedia of Arkansas*, May 16, 2018; Violet Hensley website accessed May 23, 2020, http://www.violethensley.com.

281   Carol Nelson emails to Priscilla Long, October 24 and 30, 2021, and November 1 and 4, 2021, in possession of Priscilla Long, Seattle.

282   John L. Wright, "Biography," *The Beginning of Love*, 63; Personal email communication, John L. Wright to Priscilla Long, April 2020, and April 27, 2020, in possession of Priscilla Long, Seattle.

283   Percentages of persons over 65 living in institutional care and over 85 requiring help at home are given in "2017 Profile of Older Americans," Administration for Community Living and Administration on Aging, an operating division of U.S. Department of Health and Human Services, 2018, 1, 5.

284   John W. Rowe and Robert L. Kahn, *Successful Aging*, 169.

285   Daniel J. Levitin, *Successful Aging*, 202–203; Alan D. Castel, *Better with Age*, 99–100.

286   The purpose to be of service to others was exhibited by 43 percent of African Americans, 46 percent of multiracial, 46 percent of Hispanic, 33 percent of Asians, and 27 percent of whites. "Purpose in the Encore Years: Shaping Lives of Meaning and Contribution," Stanford Graduate School of Education and encore.org, 2018, https://encore.org/wp-content/uploads/2018/03/PEP-Full-Report.pdf.

287   "Experience Corps," Encore.org, https://encore.org/experience-corps/; Nancy Morrow-Howell and Erwin Tan, "Researchers Find Sustained Improvement in Health in Experience Corps Tutors Over 55," *The Source*, March 12, 2009; Allan Porowski, et al. (Abt Associates), "Experience Corps Social-Emotional Learning Evaluation," August 30, 2019, AARP Foundation; Marc Freedman, *How to Live Forever: The Enduring Power of Connecting the Generations*, 68–78.

288   Gene Jones is discussed at length in Marc Freedman, *The Big Shift*, 96–97.

289   Daniel Buckley, "Gene Jones—An Appreciation," January 11, 2013 Daniel Buckley Arts website accessed May 28, 2020, http://www.danielbuckleyarts.com/2013/01/gene-jones-an-appreciation/.

290   "H. Eugene Jones (1916–2013)," Video, Encore.org, https://encore.org/purpose-prize/h-eugene-jones/.

291   John W. Rowe and Robert L. Kahn describe this actress in *Successful Ageing*, 173.

292   "Fast Facts and Figures About Social Security, 2019," Social Security Administration, https://www.ssa.gov/policy/docs/chartbooks/fast_facts/2019/fast_facts19.pdf.

293   Paul Krugman, "The Future of Social Security," talk given at the Woodrow Wilson School, Princeton University, available on Paul Krugman website accessed March 30, 2020, http://www.krugmanonline.com.

294    Paul Krugman, "Social Security: The Non-Sequitor Wars," *The New York Times*, January 21, 2020.

295    "Fast Facts and Figures About Social Security, 2019," Social Security Administration, https://www.ssa.gov/policy/docs/chartbooks/fast_facts/2019/fast_facts19.pdf.

296    Theodore Roszack, *The Making of an Elder Culture*, 66.

297    The "old age dependency ratio" is critiqued in Lincoln Caplan, "The Fear Factor," *The American Scholar*, June 9, 2014.

298    Marc Freedman, *The Big Shift*, 47.

299    James Palmieri, "Do Views on Social Security Spending Differ by Age?" AARP blogs accessed December 27, 2020, https://blog.aarp.org/thinking-policy/do-views-on-social-security-spending-differ-by-age.

300    Paul Krugman, "The Future of Social Security," talk given at the Woodrow Wilson School, Princeton University, available on Paul Krugman website accessed March 30, 2020, http://www.krugmanonline.com.

301    Jynnah Radford, "Key Findings about U.S. Immigrants," June 17, 2019, Pew Research Center, accessed December 27, 2020, https://www.pewresearch.org/fact-tank/2019/06/17/key-findings-about-u-s-immigrants/.

302    Jody Heymann, "The Mature Workforce: Profiting from All Abilities," in *The Upside of Aging* ed. by Paul H. Irving, 124.

303    Paul H. Irving and Anusuya Chatterjee, "Introduction," (xxxi); A. Barry Rand, "Life Reimagined: The Second Aging Revolution" (244); Ken Dychtwald, "A Longevity Market Emerges," (65) in *The Upside of Aging* ed. by Paul H. Irving.

304    Ken Dychtwald, "Ageism: Alive and Well in Advertising," *AARP Bulletin*, September 2021, 6.

305    Patricia Hills, *Alice Neel*, 183.

306    "'You Have to Get Past the Fear': Joan Semmel on Painting her Aging, Nude Body," *Hyperallergic*, September 9, 2016, https://hyperallergic.com/321781/you-have-to-get-past-the-fear-joan-semmel-on-painting-her-aging-nude-body/.

307    Margaret Morganroth Gullette, *Ending Ageism*, 22–53.

308    Leibovitz dates the photographs and from photo date and birth date I extrapolated the ages of the sitters. Annie Leibovitz, *Portraits 2005–2017*.

309    *Lives Well Lived* a feature documentary film by Sky Bergman, https://www.lives-well-lived.com. Botso Korisheli had a documentary made of his life (*Botso,* a film by Tom Walters, 2014), and was recognized in a number of press notices during his life and upon his death.

310 "Mind the Gap: The Growing Generation Divide in Charitable Giving," September 2012, Charities Aid Foundation, https://www.cafonline.org/docs/default-source/about-us-policy-and-campaigns/mind-the-gap-reportddffcb334cae616587efff3200698116.pdf.

311 "Sixty and Over: Elders and Philanthropic Investment," Benefactor Group (Columbus, Ohio), blog accessed April 23, 2020, https://benefactorgroup.com/sixty-and-over-elders-and-philanthropic-investments/. See also: Susan Raymond, "Boomer Philanthropists: A Golden Age of Civil Society," in *The Upside of Aging* ed. by Paul H. Irving, 134.

312 Candace Taylor, "Philip Roth Left More than $2 Million to his hometown Library in Newark, NJ," *The Wall Street Journal,* October 30, 2019.

313 Nancy Princenthal, *Agnes Martin: Her Life and Art,* 235, 242.

314 "James Michener," *Encyclopaedia Britannica,* November 11, 2019; Author's League Fund website accessed July 14, 2020, https://authorsleaguefund.org.

315 "'Hey, Chief, Sign Me Up'," *AARP Magazine,* April/May 2021, 69.

316 "Gee's Bend Quilters," Souls Grown Deep website accessed April 25, 2020, https://www.soulsgrowndeep.org/gees-bend-quiltmakers.

317 "Gee's Bend Quilters," Souls Grown Deep website accessed April 25, 2020, https://www.soulsgrowndeep.org/gees-bend-quiltmakers; Taylor Dafoe, "The Famed Quilters of Gee's Bend Are Using Their Sewing Skills to Make a Face Mask for Every Citizen in Their Small Alabama Town," *ArtNet News,* April 13, 2020, https://news.artnet.com/art-world/gees-bend-masks-1831854; *The Quiltmakers of Gees Bend* PBS film by Celia Carey, 2004, https://www.pbs.org/video/alabama-public-television-documentaries-quiltmakers-of-gees-bend/.

318 Ken Dychtwald and Robert Morison, *What Retirees Want,* 147, 148.

319 Alan D. Castel, *Better with Age,* 77.

320 Kent Allen, "Grandparents Report Success in Raising Grandchildren," AARP November 6, 2018, https://www.aarp.org/home-family/friends-family/info-2018/grandparents-raising-kids.html.

321 Ken Dychtwald and Robert Morison, *What Retirees Want,* 148.

322 Jack Remick email to Priscilla Long, September 14, 2021, in possession of Priscilla Long, Seattle.

323 Maggie Kuhn quoted in Theodore Roszack, *The Making of an Elder Culture,* 12.

**Chapter 5: Peak Ages of Creativity?**

324 This is the last line of Stanley Kunitz's poem "The Layers," composed in 1977. Reprinted in *The Wild Braid,* 82–83.

325    Betty Friedan, *The Fountain of Age*, 607.

326    Sam Whiting, "Wayne Thiebaud, Approaching 98, Takes Stock of the Big Picture," *San Francisco Chronicle*, September 26, 2018.

327    Harvey C. Lehman, *Age and Achievement*, vii, 12, 73, 74, 75, 77, 80–81, 86–87.

328    Dean Keith Simonton, *Genius, Creativity, and Leadership: Historiometric Inquiries*, 95. A good introduction to Simonton's thought is the YouTube talk: Dean Keith Simonton, "Diversifying Experiences & Creative Development: Historiometric, Psychometric, and Experimental Findings," The University of Georgia College of Education, November 11, 2014, https://www.youtube.com/watch?v=t2WqOaIKPoc.

329    Dean Keith Simonton, "Age and Creative Productivity," *International Journal of Aging and Human Development*, Vol. 29, No. 1 (1989), 32.

330    Philip Hans Franses: P. H., "When Do Painters Make Their Best Work"" *Creativity Research Journal*, Vol. 25, Issue 4, 2013; Christopher Ingraham, "When Will You most likely Hit Your Creative Peak, According to Science," *The Washington Post*, June 23, 2016; Megan Willett, "Study Suggests Artists Don't Reach Peak Creativity Until Age 42," *Business Insider*, December 4, 2013; Drew Boyd, "Have You Reached Your Creative Peak?" *Psychology Today*, February 3, 2014.

331    Nell Painter, *Old in Art School*, 32.

332    Ursula K. Le Guin, "TGAN Again," in Ursula K. Le Guin, *No Time to Spare*, 72–73. Publishing details are taken from "Ursula K. Le Guin," National Book Foundation website accessed November 27, 2019, https://www.nationalbook.org/people/ursula-k-le-guin/#fullBio.

333    Albert-László Barabási, *The Formula: The Universal Laws of Success*, 61–62; "The Theft that Made the 'Mona Lisa' a Masterpiece," NPR, All Things Considered, July 30, 2011, https://www.npr.org/2011/07/30/138800110/the-theft-that-made-the-mona-lisa-a-masterpiece.

334    Igor Stravinsky and Robert Craft, "Perspectives of an Octogenarian," in *Memories and Commentaries*, 259.

335    Albert-László Barabási, *The Formula: The Universal Laws of Success*, 55–56.

336    Diaz is quoted in Cian Traynor, "The Wild Story of Basquiat's Original Partner in Crime," *Huck* 61 accessed November 4, 2019, https://www.huckmag.com/art-and-culture/art-2/al-diaz-bomb-one-graffiti-pioneer/; Al Diaz's website may be reached at https://al-diaz.com.

337    Donald Kuspit, *An Interview with Louise Bourgeois*, 51.

338    H. C. Lehman's defense of women creators can be found in *Age and Achievement*, 90-91.

339    Nell Painter, *Old in Art School*, 25.

340   Faith Ringgold is quoted in Hilarie M. Sheets, "'You Become Better with Age,'" *ARTnews*, May 20, 3013.

341   Philip Glass, *Words Without Music*, 61.

342   "List of Compositions by Philip Glass" (organized by date), Wikipedia, https://en.wikipedia.org/wiki/List_of_compositions_by_Philip_Glass accessed October 4, 2019; Based on Philip Glass, "Compositions." alphabetical list on philipglass.com, https://philipglass.com/compositions/all/, accessed October 4, 2019.

343   Anne Midgette, "If You Think You Know Who Philip Glass Is, You Probably Don't," *The Washington Post*, November 29, 2018.

344   Sarah Whitaker Peters, *Becoming O'Keeffe: The Early Years*, 31.

345   Georgia O'Keeffe, *Some Memories of Drawings*, 11

346   Roxana Robinson discusses O'Keeffe's stature in the art world in *Georgia O'Keeffe*, 304.

347   Harrison Smith, "Diana Athill, 101," *The Washington Post*, January 25, 2019, B1; Polly Pattullo, "Diana Athill Obituary," *The Guardian*, January 24, 2019.

348   Reginald P. C. Mutter, "Daniel Defoe," *Encyclopaedia Britannica*, May 4, 1999, last updated January 11, 2020. The critical studies of Defoe's novels are voluminous. See for example Julie Crane, "Defoe's *Roxana*: The Making and Unmaking of a Heroine," *The Modern Language Review* Vol. 102, No. 1 (January 2007), 11–25.

349   George Duncan Painter, "Marcel Proust," *Encyclopaedia Britannica*, July 6, 2020.

350   "Isak Dinesen," *Encyclopaedia Britannica*, April 13, 2020.

351   "Raymond Chandler," *Encyclopaedia Britannica*, July 20, 1998, last updated March 22, 2020.

352   Douglas Martin, "Harriet Doerr Is Dead at 92; Writer of Searing, Sparse Prose," *The New York Times*, November 27, 2002, B9.

353   "E. Annie Proulx Biography," *Encyclopedia of World Bio*graphy, https://www.notablebiographies.com/Pe-Pu/Proulx-E-Annie.html; "Annie Proulx, The Art of Fiction No. 199," interviewed by Christopher Cox, *Paris Review*, Issue 188 (Spring 2009).

354   Peter Sacks is profiled in Joshua Rothman, "What Lies Beneath," *The New Yorker*, March 25, 2019.

355   "Bill Traylor," Smithsonian American Art Museum, website accessed October 6, 2021, https://americanart.si.edu/artist/bill-traylor-4852; Leslie Umberger, *Between Worlds: The Art of Bill Traylor*, 11–88; Frank Maresca and Roger Ricco, *Bill Traylor: His Art and Life*, 87, 54, 87, 174; Mechal Sobel, *Painting a Hidden Life: The Art of Bill Traylor*, 72–76.

356   Ian Volner, *This Is Frank Lloyd Wright*, 74.

357 Leonard Cohen's oeuvre is listed on his website: www.leonardcohen. com/albums.

358 Calvin Tomkins, "Surface Matters: The Timeless Work of Vija Celmins," *The New Yorker*, September 2, 2019, 18–24; Peter Schjeldahl, "The Beautiful and the Unexpected," *The New Yorker*, February 19, 2017.

359 Dean Keith Simonton, "Creative Productivity: A Predictive and Explanatory Model of Career Trajectories and Landmarks," *Psychological Review* Vol. 104, No. 1 (1997), 66–89.

360 Sara Lawrence-Lightfoot, *The Third Chapter*, 44.

361 Randolph Hokanson, *With Head to Music Bent*, 194.

362 "Georges Simenon," *Encyclopaedia Britannica*, February 9, 2020.

363 Joan Acocella, "Crime Pays," *The New Yorker*, October 3, 2011.

364 All quotes and information on Verdi are from Linda Hutcheon and Michael Hutcheon, *Four Last Songs: Aging and Creativity in Verdi, Strauss, Messiaen, and Britten*, 23–41.

365 Ross King, *Mad Enchantment*, 11; Adrien Goetz, *Monet at Giverney*; Thomas Dormandy, *Old Masters: Great Artists in Old Age*, 222–230.

366 Charles McGrath, "Philip Roth, Towering Novelist Who Explored Lust, Jewish Life and America, Dies at 85," *The New York Times*, May 22, 2018; Carolyn Kellogg, "Philip Roth Has Quit Writing Fiction. He Means it. Really," *Los Angeles Times*, February 5, 2014.

367 Annie Leibovitz, *Portraits 2005–2016*, 303.

368 Donald Hall, "In Praise of Paragraphs," in *A Carnival of Losses*, 10–11.

369 Ursula K. Le Guin is quoted in John Freeman, "My Last Conversation with Ursula K. Le Guin," *Literary Hub*, January 24, 2018, https://lithub. com/my-last-conversation-with-ursula-k-le-guin/; Ursula K. Le Guin, *So Far, So Good: Final Poems, 2014–2018* (Port Townsend: Copper Canyon Press, 2018).

370 Becca R. Levy et al., "Positive Age Beliefs Protect Against Dementia Even Among Elders with High-risk Gene," *PLoS One*, 2018, Vol. 13, No. 2; Becca R. Levy et al., "Survival Advantage Mechanism: Inflammation as a Mediator of Positive Self-Perceptions of Aging on Longevity," *J Gerontol B Psychol Sci Soc Sci*, Vol. 73, No. 3 (March 2018), 409–412; Becca R. Levy et al., "A Culture-Brain Link: Negative Age Stereotypes Predict Alzheimer's-disease Biomarkers," *Psychological Aging*, February 31, 2016, Vol. 31, No. 1, 82–88; Becca R. Levy et al., "Memory Shaped by Age Stereotypes Over Time," *J Gerontol B Psychol Sci Soc Sci* Vol 67, No. 4 (July 2012), 432–436; Becca R. Levy et al., "Age Stereotypes Held Earlier in Life Predict Cardiovascular Events in Later Life," *Psychol Sci* Vol. 20, No. 3 (March 2009), 296–298.

371   Michael Hutcheon and Linda Hutcheon, "Late Style(s): The Ageism of the Singular," *Occasion: Interdisciplinary Studies in the Humanities* Vol. 4 (May 31, 2012), 7.

372   Dean Keith Simonton, "Aging and Creative Productivity: Is there an Age Decrement or Not?" PowerPoint presentation listed under "Research" on Simonton's Homepage: https://simonton.faculty. ucdavis.edu/wp-content/uploads/sites/243/2015/08/MxAgCrProd-1. pdf; Simonton, "Age and Creative Productivity: Nonlinear Estimation of an Information-Processing Model," *International Journal of Aging and Human Development*, Vol. 29, No. 1 (1989), 23–37; Simonton, "The Swan-Song Phenomenon: Last-Works Effects for 172 Classical Composers" in *Genius and Creativity*, 217–230.

373   Arthur C. Brooks, "Your Professional Decline Is Coming (Much) Sooner Than You Think," *The Atlantic*, July 2019, 66–74.

## Chapter 6: Advantages of Being an *Old* Creator

374   Harry Shapiro quoted in Neenah Ellis, *If I Live to Be 100*, 100.

375   Calvin Tomkins, "Painterly Virtues: Alex Katz's Life in Art," *The New Yorker*, August 27, 2018, 58.

376   Timothy Clark, "Late Hokusai, Backwards," (p. 12) and Matsuba Ryoko, "The Power of Hokusai's Line" (p. 37) in *Hokusai: Beyond the Great Wave*; Thomas Dormandy, *Old Masters*, 95–106.

377   Martin S. Lindauer, *Aging, Creativity, and Art*, 129.

378   The quotes in this paragraph are all from Martin S. Lindauer, *Aging, Creativity, and Art*, 131.

379   Martin S. Lindauer et al., "Aging Artists on the Creativity of Their Old Age," *Creativity Research Journal*, Vol. 10, No. 2–3 (1997), 141.

380   Anne Midgette, "If You Think You Know Who Philip Glass Is, You Probably Don't," *The Washington Post*, November 29, 2018.

381   Joan Semmel quoted in Hilarie M. Sheets, "You Become Better with Age," *ARTnews*, May 20, 2013, http://www.artnews.com/2013/05/20/ making-art-after-8/.

382   Martin S. Lindauer, *Aging, Creativity, and Art*, 135.

383   Michelle Stuart quoted Hilarie M. Sheets, "You Become Better with Age," *ARTnews* May 20, 1913, http://www.artnews.com/2013/05/20/ making-art-after-8/.

384   Both quotes are from Martin S. Lindauer, *Aging, Creativity, and Art*, 139 and 187.

385   Gene D. Cohen, *The Creative Age*, 19.

386    Jhumpa Lahiri, "Jhumpa Lahiri on the Compulsion to Translate Domenico Starnone," *Literary Hub*, March 7, 2017, https://lithub.com/jhumpa-lahiri-on-the-compulsion-to-translate-domenico-starnone/.

387    *Kay WalkingStick: An American Artist* November 25, 2015, video produced by the Museum of the American Indian (Smithsonian).

388    Kathleen Ash-Milby and David W. Penney, eds., *Kay WalkingStick: An American Artist*, 43, 58, 63.

389    Marilee Shapiro Asher, *Dancing in the Wonder*, 104–105.

390    Patricia Hills, *Alice Neel*, 185.

391    Pamela Allara, *Pictures of People: Alice Neel's American Portrait Gallery*, xvi; Cindy Nemser, *Art Talk*, 123.

392    Pamela Allara, *Pictures of People: Alice Neel's American Portrait Gallery*, xv.

393    John Rewald, "Cézanne and his Father," in *Studies in Impressionism*, 69–102; White, *The Impressionists Side by Side*, 109–110.

394    On Sally Gabori: Katie White, "These 8 Female Artists Only Saw Their Careers Catch Fire Well into Their 80s," *Artnet.com*, November 27, 2019, https://news.artnet.com/art-world/8-women-artists-over-80-1710444.

395    Janet Malcolm, *Two Lives: Gertrude and Alice*, 40.

396    Hokanson is quoted in his obituary. Melinda Bargreen, "Randolph Hokanson, Pianist and UW Professor Emeritus, Dies at 103," *The Seattle Times*, October 20, 2018.

397    *Kay WalkingStick: An American Artist*, ed. by Kathleen Ash-Milby and David W. Penney, 34, 90–91, 93, 94.

398    Mary Ann Caws, *Robert Motherwell: What Art Holds,* 15, 46–47, 118.

399    *Elegy to the Spanish Republic No. 172 (with Blood)* (1989–1990) Denver Art Museum. (https://www.denverartmuseum.org/object/1994.1134).

400    Katie White, "These 8 Female Artists Only Saw Their Careers Catch Fire Well into Their 80s," *Artnet.com*, November 27, 2019, https://news.artnet.com/art-world/8-women-artists-over-80-1710444.

401    Malte Herwig, *The Woman Who Says No: François Gilot on her Life with and Without Picasso,* 12–13.

402    Carolina A. Miranda, "Painter Luchita Hurtado, Who Became at Art Star in her Late 90s, Has Died at 99," *Los Angeles Times,* August 14, 2020.

403    Diana Athill, *Somewhere Towards the End*, 6–8.

404    Ines Schlenker, *Marie-Louise von Motesiczky: A Catalogue Raisonné of the Paintings*, 50–51; Peter Black, "Obituary: Marie-Louise von Motesiczky," *Independent*, June 15, 1996.

405    Diana Athill, *Somewhere Towards the End*, 8.

406    Mark Shapiro interview with Paulus Berensohn, "Oral History Interview with Paulus Berensohn, 2009 March 20–21," Archives of American Art, Smithsonian.

407    Michelle Doyle, "Eileen Gray: An Architect and Designer You Should Know," March 2, 2020, Royal Academy of Arts website accessed October 9, 2021, https://www.royalacademy.org.uk/article/eileen-gray-architect-designer.

408    Charlotte Malterre-Barthes and Sosia Dzierzawska, *Eileen Gray: A House Under the Sun*, 49–52. See also *Eileen Gray* ed. by Cloe Pitiot and Nina Stritzler.

409    *Eileen Gray*, ed. by Cloe Pitiot and Nina Stritzler, 374.

410    Betye Saar, *Still Tickin'*, 33 and 29.

411    This and the preceding quote are from Clark Terry and Gwen Terry, *Clark: The Autobiography of Clark Terry*, 214.

412    *Keep on Keepin' on*, film directed by Al Hicks, 2014.

413    Anne Truitt, *Prospect*, 176.

414    Eleanor Munro, "Alma W. Thomas," *Originals: American Women Artists*, 193.

415    Timothy Clark, "Late Hokusai, Backwards" in *Hokusai: Beyond the Great Wave*, 14–15.

416    Clark Terry with Gwen Terry, *Clark: The Autobiography of Clark Terry*, 198.

417    The first edition of Priscilla Long, *The Writer's Portable Mentor: A Guide to Art, Craft, and the Writing Life* was published in 2010.

418    Twyla Tharp, *The Creative Habit*, 97, 111, 140.

419    Jack Remick, *What Do I Know? Wisdom Essays*, 102, 178.

420    Stanley Kunitz, *The Wild Braid*, 65.

421    Stanley Kunitz, *The Wild Braid*, 100.

422    Henri Matisse quoted by Gotthard Jedlicka, "Encounter with Henri Matisse," (1955) in *Matisse: A Retrospective* edited by Jack Flam, 378.

423    Robert Motherwell "Interview with David Hayman," July 12 and 13, 1988, in *The Collected Writings of Robert Motherwell*, 289.

424    Yayoi Kusama, *Infinity Net: The Autobiography of Yayoi Kusama* translated by Ralph McCarthy (London: Tate Publishing, 2011), 227.

425    "Yayoi Kusama," *Encyclopaedia Britannica*, June 21, 2019; Yayoi Kusama website accessed September 17, 2019, http://yayoi-kusama.jp/e/information/index.html.

426    Faith Ringgold, *Faith Ringgold*, 39.

# Bibliography

Adams-Price, Carol E., ed. *Creativity and Successful Aging*. New York: Springer Publishing Company, Inc., 1998.

Allara, Pamela. *Pictures of People: Alice Neel's American Portrait Gallery*. Hanover: University Press of New England, Brandeis University Press, 1998.

Amigoni, David and Gordon McMullan, eds. *Creativity in Later Life: Beyond Late Style*. London and New York: Routledge, 2019.

Angell, Roger. "This Old Man," (pp. 266–282) in *This Old Man*. New York: Doubleday, 2015.

Applewhite, Ashton. *This Chair Rocks: A Manifesto Against Ageism*. Networked Books, 2006.

Asher, Marilee Shapiro with Linda Hansell. *Dancing in the Wonder for 102 Years*. CreateSpace.com, 2015.

Ash-Milby and David W. Penney. *Kay WalkingStick: An American Artist*. Washington, DC: National Museum of the American Indian, Smithsonian, 2015.

Athill, Diana. *Somewhere Towards the End*. New York: W. W. Norton & Company, 2008.

Athill, Diana. *Alive, Alive, Oh!*. London: Granta Publications, 2015.

Aubrecht, Katie and Christine Kelly and Carla Rice, eds. *The Aging-Disability Nexus*. Vancouver, BC and Toronto: UBC Press, 2020.

Barabási, Albert-László. *The Formula: The Universal Laws of Success*. Boston: Little, Brown and Co., 2018.

Bateson, Mary Catherine. *Composing a Further Life: The Age of Active Wisdom*. New York: Vintage Books, Random House, Inc., 2010.

Bayley, John. *Iris: A Memoir*. London: Gerald Duckworth & Co., Ltd. 1998.

Berensohn, Paulus. *Finding One's Way with Clay*. New York: Simon and Schuster, 1972.

Blotner, Joseph. *Robert Penn Warren*. New York. Random House, 1997.

Brooks, Arthur C. "Your Professional Decline Is Coming (Much) Sooner Than You Think." *The Atlantic*, July 2019, 66–74.

Bullitt, Simson. *Illusion Dweller: The Climbing Life of Stimson Bullitt*. Seattle: Mountaineers Books, 2013.

Carstensen, Laura. *Long Bright Future: The Very Good News About Living Longer*. New York: Broadway Books, 2009.

Carter, Jimmy. *The Virtues of Aging*. New York: The Ballantine Publishing Group, 1998.

Casals, Pablo. *Joys and Sorrows: Reflections by Pablo Casals as told to Albert E. Kahn*. New York: Simon and Schuster, 1970.

Castel, Alan D. *Better with Age: The Psychology of Successful Aging*. New York: Oxford University Press, 2019.

Clark, Philip. *Dave Brubeck: A Life in Time*. New York: Hachette Books, 2020.

Clark, Timothy, ed. *Hokusai: Beyond the Great Wave*. London: Thames & Hudson and The British Museum, 2017.

Cohen, Gene D. *The Creative Age: Awakening Human Potential in the Second Half of Life*. New York: HarperCollins Publisher, 2000.

Cohen, Gene D. *The Mature Mind: The Positive Power of the Aging Brain*. New York: Basic Books, [2005] 2006.

Constable, Joseph, et al. *Luchita Hurtado: I Live, I Die, I Will Be Reborn*. Cologne: Walther König, 2019.

Cowart, Jack and Juan Hamilton. *Georgia O'Keeffe: Art and Letters*. Washington, DC: National Gallery of Art; Boston: New York Graphic Society Books, 1987.

Cunningham, Imogen. *After Ninety*. Seattle: University of Washington Press, 1977.

Currey, Mason. *Daily Rituals*. New York: Alfred A. Knopf, 2013.

David Kordansky Gallery, "Sam Gilliam," David Kordansky Gallery website accessed March 22, 2021, http://origin.www.davidkordanskygallery.com/artist/sam-gilliam.

Dawes, Kwame, ed. *When the Rewards Can Be So Great*. Forest Grove, Oregon: Pacific University Press, 2016.

DeBaggio, Thomas. *Losing My Mind: An Intimate Look at Life with Alzheimer's*. New York: The Free Press, 2002.

DeBaggio. Thomas. *When It Gets Dark*. New York: The Free Press, 2003.

Delany, Sarah L. and A. Elizabeth Delany with Amy Hill Hearth. *Having Our Say: The Delany Sisters' First 100 Years*. New York: Dell Publishing, 1993.

Delany, Sarah L. with Amy Hill Hearth. *On My Own: Reflections on Life without Bessie*. New York: HarperCollins Publishers, 1997.

Delbanco, Nicholas. *Lastingness: The Art of Old Age*. New York: Grand Central Publishing, 2011.

Doidge, Norman. *The Brain That Changes Itself*. Viking/Penguin, 2007.

Doidge, Norman. *The Brain's Way of Healing*. New York: Penguin Books, 2016.

Dormandy, Thomas. *Old Masters: Great Artists in Old Age*. London: Hambledon and London, 2001.

Doyle, Brian. *Spirited Men.* Cambridge, MA: Cowley Publications, 2004.

Dychtwald, Ken and Robert Morison. *What Retirees Want: A Holistic View of Life's Third Age.* Hoboken, New Jersey: John Wiley & Sons, Inc. 2020.

Ellis, Neenah. *If I Live to Be 100.* New York: Crown Publishers, 2002.

Ericsson, Anders, and Robert Pool. *Peak: Secrets from the New Science of Expertise.* Boston: Houghton Mifflin Harcourt, 2016.

Feman, Seth, and Jonathan Frederick Walz. *Alma W. Thomas: Everything Is Beautiful.* New Haven: Yale University Press, 2021.

Finley, Cheryl, et al. *My Soul Has Grown Deep: Black Art from the New South.* New York: The Metropolitan Museum of Art, 2018.

Finneran, Richard J., ed. *W. B. Yeats: The Poems: A New Edition.* New York: Macmillan Publishing Company, 1983.

Flam, Jack, ed. *Matisse: A Retrospective.* New York: Hugh Lauter Levin Associates, Inc., 1988.

Flam, Jack, ed. *Matisse on Art.* Revised Edition. Berkeley: University of California Press, 1995.

Freedman, Russell. *Martha Graham: A Dancer's Life.* New York: Clarion Books, Houghton Mifflin, 1998.

Freedman, Marc. *Encore: Finding Work That Matters in the Second Half of Life.* New York: Public Affairs, 2007.

Freedman, Marc. *The Big Shift: Navigating the New Stage Beyond Midlife.* New York: Public Affairs, 2011.

Freedman, Marc. *How to Live Forever: The Enduring Power of Connecting the Generations.* New York: Public Affairs, 2018.

Friedan, Betty. *The Fountain of Age.* New York: Simon and Schuster, 1993.

Gilliam, Sam. *Sam Gilliam: Existed Existing.* New York: Pace, 2020.

Glass, Philip. *Words Without Music.* New York: Liveright Publishing Company, a division of W.W. Norton, 2015.

Goethe, Johann Wolfgang von. *Maxims and Reflections.* London and New York: The Penguin Group, 1988.

Goetz, Adrien. *Monet at Giverny.* Giverny: Foundation Claude Monet-Giverny, 2015.

Goldberger, Paul. *Building Art: The Life and Work of Frank Gehry.* New York: Vintage, Penquin Random House LLC (2015) 2017.

Golub, Sarit A., Allan Filipowicz, and Ellen J. Langer. "Acting Your Age," in *Ageism: Stereotyping and Prejudice against Older Persons* ed. by Todd D. Nelson, 277–294.

Gorman, Amy. *Aging Artfully: 12 Profiles: Visual and Performing Women Artists, Aged 85–105.* Berkeley, CA: PAL Publishing, 2006.

Graham, Martha. *Blood Memory: An Autobiography.* New York: Doubleday, 1991.

Grumbach, Doris. *Coming into the End Zone.* New York: W. W. Norton & Company, 1991.

Gullette, Margaret Morganroth. *Ending Ageism, Or How Not to Shoot Old People.* New Brunswick: Rutgers University Press, 2017.

Hall, Donald. *Essays After Eighty.* Boston: Houghton Mifflin Harcourt, 2014.

Hall, Donald. *A Carnival of Losses: Notes Nearing Ninety.* Boston: Houghton Mifflin Harcourt, 2018.

Haskell, Barbara, ed. *Agnes Martin.* New York: Whitney Museum of American Art, 1992.

Hensley, Violet, with Randall Franks. *Wittlin' and Fiddlin' My Own Way: The Violet Hensley Story.* Tunnel Hill, Georgia: Peach Picked Publishing, 2014.

Herwig, Malte. *The Woman Who Says No: François Gilot on her Life With and Without Picasso* trans. by Jane Billinghurst. Vancouver: Graystone Books, 2016.

Hilburn, Robert. *Johnny Cash: The Life.* New York: Little, Brown and Company, 2013.

Hills, Patricia. *Alice Neel.* New York: Harry N. Abrams, Inc. Publishers, (1983) 1995.

Hokanson, Randolph. *With Head to Music Bent: A Musician's Story.* Seattle: Third Place Press, 2011.

Hutcheon, Michael, and Linda Hutcheon. "Late Style (s): The Ageism of the Singular," *Occasion: Interdisciplinary studies in the Humanities,* Vol. 4 (May 31, 2012), http://occasion.standford.edu/node/93.

Hutcheon, Linda and Michael Hutcheon. *Four Last Songs: Aging and Creativity in Verdi, Strauss, Messiaen, and Britten.* Chicago: University of Chicago Press, 2015.

Irving, Paul H., ed. *The Upside of Aging.* Hoboken, NJ: John Wiley and Sons, 2014.

Jabr, Ferris. "Why Walking Helps Us Think," *The New Yorker,* September 3, 2014.

Jeffri, Joan. *Above Ground: Information on Artists III: Special Focus on New York City Aging Artists.* New York: Columbia University Research Center for Arts and Culture, 2007. https://artsandcultureresearch.org/portfolio/above-ground

Jeffri, Joan. *Still Kicking: Aging Performing Artists in New York City and Los Angeles Metro Areas.* Information on Artists IV. New York: Columbia University Research Center for Arts and Culture, 2011.

Jenkins, Jo Ann. *Disrupt Aging.* New York: Public Affairs, 2016.

Jenkins, Jo Ann. "The Keys to Healthy Living: Friendship and Purpose," *AARP Bulletin,* June 2018, 42.

Johnson, Steven. *Extra Life: A Short History of Living Longer*. New York: Riverhead Books, 2021.

Jones, Quincy. *Q: The Autobiography of Quincy Jones*. New York: Doubleday, 2001.

Kabat-Zinn, Jon. *Mindfulness for Beginners*. Boulder: Sounds True, 2012, 2016.

Kallir, Otto. *Grandma Moses* Abridged Version. New York: Harry N. Abrams Inc., 1973.

Katz, Alex. Homepage, https://www.alexkatz.com.

Kellman, Steven G. *Redemption: The Life of Henry Roth*. New York: W. W. Norton, 2005.

Kent, Mary and Rose Maria. *The Arts and Aging: Building the Science*. Washington D.C.: National Endowment for the Arts, February 2013.

King, Ross. *Mad Enchantment: Claude Monet and the Painting of the Water Lilies*. New York: Boomsbury, 2016.

Kunitz, Stanley, with Genine Lentine. *The Wild Braid: A Poet Reflects on a Century in the Garden*. New York: W.W. Norton & Company, 2005.

Kusama, Yayoi. *Infinity Net: The Autobiography of Yayoi Kusama* trans. by Ralph McCarthy. London: Tate Publishing, 2011.

Kuspit, Donald. *An Interview with Louise Bourgeois*. New York: Vintage Books, 1988.

Lamb, Sarah, ed. *Successful Aging? Global Perspectives on a Contemporary Obsession*. New Brunswick: Rutgers University Press, 2017.

Larson, Eric B., and Joan DeClaire. *Enlightened Aging*. Lanham, MD: Rowman & Littlefield, 2017.

Lawrence-Lightfoot, Sara. *The Third Chapter: Passion, Risk, and Adventure in the 25 Years After 50*. New York: Farrar, Straus and Giroux, 2009.

Lehman, Harvey C. *Age and Achievement*. Princeton: Princeton University Press, 1953.

Leibovitz, Annie. *Portraits 2005–2016*. New York: Phaidon Press Inc., 2017.

Leski, Kyna. *The Storm of Creativity*. Cambridge MA: The MIT Press, 2015.

Levitin, Daniel. *Successful Aging: A Neuroscientist Explores the Power and Potential of Our Lives*. New York: Dutton, 2020.

Levy, Becca R., et al., "Ageism Amplifies Cost and Prevalence of Health Conditions," *The Gerontologist*, 2018, Vol. XX, No. XX, 1–8.

Levy, Becca R., and Mahzarin R. Banaji. "Implicit Ageism," in *Ageism: Stereotyping and Prejudice Against Older Persons* ed. by Todd D. Nelson, p. 52–57.

Lindauer, Martin S. et al. "Aging Artists on the Creativity of Their Old Age." *Creativity Research Journal*. Vol. 10, No. 2–3 (1997), 133–152.

Lindauer, Martin S. *Aging, Creativity, and Art: A Positive Perspective on Late-Life Development*. New York: Kluwer Academic/Plenum Publishers, 2003.

Lipschutz, Yael, et al. *Noah Purifoy: Junk Dada*. Los Angeles and Munich: Los Angeles County Museum of Art and Prestel Verlag, 2015.

Long, Priscilla. *The Writer's Portable Mentor: A Guide to Art, Craft, and the Writing Life*, second edition. Albuquerque: University of New Mexico Press, 2018.

Long, Priscilla. *Minding the Muse: A Handbook for Painters, Composers, Writers, and Other Creators*. Seattle: Epicenter/Coffeetown, 2016.

Lustbader, Wendy. *Life Gets Better: The Unexpected Pleasures of Growing Older*. New York: Jeremy P. Tarcher/Penguin, 2011.

Maddox, Brenda. *Yeats's Ghosts: The Secret Life of W. B. Yeats*. New York: HarperCollins Publishers, 1999.

Malcolm, Janet. *Two Lives: Gertrude and Alice*. New Haven: Yale University Press, 2007.

Malterre-Barthes, Charlotte, and Zosia Dzierzawska. *Eileen Gray: A House Under the Sun*. London: Nobrow Ltd., 2019.

Maresca, Frank, and Roger Ricco. *Bill Traylor: His Art and Life*. New York: Alfred A. Knopf, 1991.

Martin, Agnes. *Beauty Is in Your Mind*. Tateshots video https://www.youtube.com/watch?v=902YXjchQsk

Matisse, Henri. *Jazz*. New York: George Braziller, Inc., 1985.

McNiff, Shaun. *Art Heals*. Boston: Shambhala, 2004.

Medina, John. *Brain Rules for Aging Well*. Seattle: Pear Press, 2011.

Miller, Dana. *Carmen Herrera: Lines of Sight*. New York: Whitney Museum of American Art, 2017.

Munro, Eleanor. "Alma W. Thomas" in *Originals: American Women Artists*. New York: Simon and Schuster, 1979.

Nelson, Todd D., ed. *Ageism: Stereotyping and Prejudice against Older Persons*. Cambridge, MA: MIT Press, 2002.

Nisenson, Eric. *Open Sky: Sonny Rollins and his World of Improvisation*. Da Capo Press, 2000.

Nordstrand, Dorothea. *Pork Neckbones, Sauerkraut & Rutabagas: Memories of My Green Lake Girlhood*. Seattle: HistoryLink/History Ink in association with History House, 2011.

Nussbaum, Martha C., and Saul Levmore. *Aging Thoughtfully: Conversations about Retirement, Romance, Wrinkles, and Regret*. New York: Oxford University Press, 2018.

O'Keeffe, Georgia. *Some Memories of Drawings*. Albuquerque: University of New Mexico Press, 1988.

Painter, Nell. *Creating Black Americans*. New York: Oxford University Press, 2006.

Painter, Nell. *Old in Art School: A Memoir of Starting Over*. Berkeley, CA: Counterpoint Press, 2018.

Pardee, Hearne. "Hearne Pardee in Conversation with Wayne Thiebaud." *Catamaran*, Vol. 7, Issue 3 (Fall 2019), pp. 113-124.

Peters, Sarah Whitaker. *Becoming O'Keeffe: The Early Years*. New York: Abbeyville Press Publishers, 1991.

Pevny, Ron. *Conscious Living Conscious* Aging. New York: Simon & Schuster, 2014.

Pitiot, Cloé, and Nina Stritzler-Levine, eds. *Eileen Gray*. New York: Bard Graduate Center, 2020.

Powell, Douglas H. *The Nine Myths of Aging*. New York: W. H. Freeman & Co., 1998.

Princenthal, Nancy. *Agnes Martin: Her Life and Art*. New York: Thames and Hudson, 2015.

Purifoy, Noah. *High Desert*. Noah Purifoy Foundation and Steidl Publishers, 2015.

*Quiltmakers of Gees Bend, The*. PBS film by Celia Carey, 2004, https://www.pbs.org/video/alabama-public-television-documentaries-quiltmakers-of-gees-bend/.

Rauch, Jonathan. *The Happiness Curve: Why Life Gets Better After* 50. New York: Picador, 2019.

Remick, Jack. *What Do I Know? Wisdom Essays*. Bellingham, WA: Sidekick Press, 2021.

Renoir, Jean. *Renoir, My Father*. New York: The New York Review of Books, [1958] 1962.

Rewald, John. "Cézanne and his Father." In *Studies in Impressionism*. New York: Harry N. Abrams, Inc., 1985.

Richmond, Lewis. *Aging as a Spiritual Practice*. New York: Penguin Group USA, 2012.

Ringgold, Faith. *Faith Ringgold*. London: Serpentine Galleries and Koenig Books, 2019.

Robertson, N. "Artists in Old Age: The Fires of Creativity Burn Undiminished." *The New York Times*, January 22, 1986, C1.

Robinson, Roxana. *Georgia O'Keeffe*. New York: HarperCollins*Publishers*, 1989.

Roszack, Theodore. *The Making of an Elder Culture: Reflections on the Future of America's Most Audacious Generation*. Gabriola Island, BC: New Society Publishers, 2009.

Rowe, John W., and Robert L. Kahn. *Successful Aging*. New York: Dell/Random House, 1999..

Saar, Betye. *Still Tickin'*. Scottsdale, Arizona: Scottsdale Museum of Contemporary Art, 2017.

Sachs, Harvey. *Rubinstein: A Life*. New York: Grove Press, 1995.

Sacks, Oliver. *Everything in its Place: First Loves and Last Tales*. New York: Alfred A. Knopf, 2019.

Schlenker, Ines. *Marie-Louise von Motesiczky: A Catalogue Raisonné of the Paintings*. Manchester, Vermont : Hudson Hills Press, LLC, 2009.

Sheets, Hilarie M. "You Become Better with Age." *ARTnews* May 20, 1913, http://www.artnews.com/2013/05/20/making-art-after-8/.

Simonton, Dean Keith. *Genius, Creativity, and Leadership: Historiometric Inquiries*. Cambridge, MA: Harvard University Press, 1984.

Simonton, Dean Keith. "Age and Creative Productivity." *International Journal of Aging and Human Development*, Vol. 29, No. 1 (1989), 23–37.

Simonton, Dean Keith. "Creative Productivity: A Predictive and Explanatory Model of Career Trajectories and Landmarks." *Psychological Review* Vol. 104, No. 1 (1997), pp. 66–89.

Simonton, Dean Keith. *Genius and Creativity: Selected Papers*. Greenwich, CT: Ablex Publishing Corporation, 1997.

Simonton, Dean Keith. "Diversifying Experiences and Creative Development," talk at the University of Georgia College of Education, November 11, 2014. YouTube video https://www.youtube.com/watch?v=t2WqOaIKPoc. Accessed November 2019.

Smith, Patti. *Year of the Monkey*. New York: Alfred A. Knopf, 2019.

Sobel, Mechal. *Painting a Hidden Life: The Art of Bill Traylor*. Baton Rouge: Louisiana State University Press, 2009.

Solnit, Rebecca. *Wanderlust: A History of Walking*. New York: Penguin Group, 2000.

Span, Paula. "Ageism is 'A Prevalent and Insidious' Health Threat." *The New York Times*, April 30, 2019, D-7.

Stahl, Stephen M. *Stahl's Essential Psychopharmacology* 3rd Edition. New York: Cambridge University Press, 2008.

Steward, Dana, ed. *A Fine Age: Creativity as a Key to Successful Ageing*. Little Rock: August House Publishers, 1984.

Stravinsky, Igor, and Robert Craft. *Memories and Commentaries*. London and New York: Faber and Faber, 2002.

Ternzio, Stephanie. *The Collected Writings of Robert Motherwell*. Berkeley: University of California Press, 1992.

Terry, Clark, and Gwen Terry. *Clark: The Autobiography of Clark Terry*. Berkeley: University of California Press, 2011.

Tharp, Twyla with Mark Reiter. *The Creative Habit*. New York: Simon & Schuster, 2003.

Tharp, Twyla. *Keep It Moving*. New York: Simon & Schuster, 2019.

Toklas, Alice B. *The Alice B. Toklas Cook Book.* New York: Harper Perennial, 1954.

Tomkins, Calvin. "Painterly Virtues: Alex Katz's Life in Art." *The New Yorker,* August 27, 2018, p. 56–65.

Truitt, Anne. *Daybook.* New York: Pantheon, 1982.

Truitt, Anne. *Turn.* New York: Penguin Books, 1987.

Truitt, Anne. *Prospect.* New York: Scribner, 1996.

Umberger, Leslie. *Between Worlds: The Art of Bill Traylor.* Washington DC: Smithsonian American Art Musuem, 2018.

Valliant, George E. *Triumphs of Experience: The Men of the Harvard Grant Study.* Cambridge, MA: Harvard University Press, 2012.

Volner, Ian. *This Is Frank Lloyd Wright.* London: Laurence King Publishing, 2016..

Weschler, Lawrence. *True to Life: Twenty-Five Years of Conversation with David Hockney.* Berkeley: University of California Press, 2008.

White, Barbara Ehrlich. *The Impressionists Side by Side.* New York: Alfred A. Knopf, Inc. 1996.

White, Eric Walter. *Stravinsky: The Composer and His Works* 2nd Edition. Berkeley: University of California Press, (1966) 1979.

Whiting, Sam. "Wayne Thiebaud, Approaching 98, Takes Stock of the Big Picture." *San Francisco Chronicle,* September 26, 2018.

Woolf, Leonard. *The Journey Not the Arrival Matters.* San Diego: Harcourt Brace Jovanovich, 1969.

Wright, John L. *The Beginning of Love.* Edmonds, WA: Bluestone Books, 2005.

Young, Lucie. *Eva Zeisel.* San Francisco: Chronicle Books, 2003.

Zaiman, Elana. *The Forever Letter: Writing What We Believe for Those We Love.* Woodbury, Minnesota: Llewellyn Publications, 2017.

Zaraska, Marta. *Growing Young: How Friendship, Optimism, and Kindness Can Help You Live to 100.* Appetite/Penguin Random House Canada, 2020.

# Organizations and Institutions

AARP, www.aarp.org.

American Society on Aging, https://www.asaging.org/.

Center on Aging and Work, Boston College School of Social Work, https://www.bc.edu/bc-web/schools/ssw/sites/center-on-aging---work.html.

Diverse Elders Coalition, https://www.diverseelders.org/.

Elderwise, https://www.elderwise.org.

Encore.org

Justice in Aging, https://justiceinaging.org/

Lifetime Arts, https://www.lifetimearts.org

National Council on Aging, https://www.ncoa.org

National Institute on Aging (U.S. Department of Health and Human Services) https://www.nia.nih.gov/

Becca Levy, Yale School of Medicine, https://medicine.yale.edu/profile/becca_levy/.

New England Centenarian Study

Northwest Center for Creative Aging, https://nwcreativeaging.org/.

OATS (Older Adults Technology Services), seniorplanet.org

Dr. Aniruddl Patel, "Creative Aging: Music and the Mind," Live stream of presentation at the Kennedy Center, June 3, 2017, YouTube, https://www.youtube.com/watch?v=Naw3v2OBBY0.

Stanford Center on Longevity, https://longevity.stanford.edu/.

Sage-ing International, https://www.sage-ing.org/.

Senior Planet (from AARP), seniorplanet.org.

Super Aging Study: Correlates of Active Engagement in Life in the Elderly, Northwestern University, Mesulam Center for Cognitive Neurology and Alzheimer's Disease.

World Health Organization campaign against ageism, https://www.who.int/ageing/ageism/en/.

# Index

Cady, Jack, 104
Cage, John, 29
Canetti, Elias, 154
Carstensen, Laura, 16, 17, 62–63, 70, 71, 72, 90
Carter, Elliott, 55, 84, 94, 134
Carter, Jimmy, 77, 78
Casals, Pablo, 42, 67, 73–74, 80
Cash, Johnny, 23–24
Cash, June Carter, 24
Celmins, Vija, 133–134
centenarians, 12, 15, 22, 71. *See also* Asher, Marilee Shapiro; Athill, Diane; Carter, Elliott; Delany sisters; Ferlinghetti, Lawrence; Herrera, Carmen; Hokanson, Randolph ; Kunitz, Stanley; Moses, Anna Mary Robertson; Pellmann, Don; Sharpiro, Harry; Thiebaud, Wayne
Center on Aging and Work (Boston College School of Social Work), 90
Cézanne, Paul, 149
Chandler, Raymond, 131
Cleaves, Emmy, 115
Cognitive Agility Across the Lifespan, 39–40
cognition in older brains, 37–38, 39
Cohen, Gene D., 4, 33, 78, 147–148
Cohen, Leonard, 73, 133
Cole, Larry, 19
connections with others, 50–54, 71–72
Copland, Aaron, 62
COVID-19, 11, 18, 31–32, 48, 50, 59, 69, 118
Crick, Francis, 4
critics, biased, 127–128

Cunningham, Imogen, 55, 72
Cunningham, Merce, 29–30, 95
CVS (pharmacy), 90–91

Dalley, John, 93
Davis, Miles Dewey, 157
deafness, 16, 31
death, 12, 160, 162
DeBaggio, Thomas, 61–62
de Kooning, Willem, 62
Delany, A. Elizabeth ("Bessie"), 36 (photo), 48, 52, 60, 79
Delany, Sarah H. ("Sadie"), 36 (photo), 48, 52, 60, 79
De Lavallade, Carmen, 26
dementia. *See* memory loss
demographics on aging, 11–12, 16–18, 89
dependency, 105
depression, 18, 69–70; of Leonard Cohen, 73; of Martha Graham, 29; of Yayoi Kusama, 161; of May Sarton, 76; of John Wright, 104
Diaz, Albert ("Al"), 126–127
diet, 48–49
Dinesen, Isak, 131
disability, 15–16, 22–30; of Dave Brubeck, 27; of Johnny Cash, 23–24; of Sam Gilliam, 5; of Martha Graham, 16, 29; of Coleman Hawkins, 28; of John Huston, 24–25; of Quincy Jones, 16; of Steven Kuusisto, 16; of Henri Matisse, 16, 25–26; of Anna Mary Robertson Moses, 14; of Pierre-Auguste Renoir, 25; of Sonny Rollins, 69; of Alma Thomas, 15, 23; of Eva Zeisel, 23

# About the Author

Priscilla Long, age 78, 2021. *Photo by Anne Herman*

Priscilla Long is a Seattle-based poet, writer, editor, and longtime independent teacher of writing. She writes science, poetry, history, fiction, and creative nonfiction and essay. She is author of seven books (to date), including the how-to-write manual *The Writer's Portable Mentor*. Her work appears in numerous literary publications, both print and online, and her science column, "Science Frictions," ran for 92 weeks online at *The American Scholar*. She has a Master's of Fine Arts from the University of Washington and serves as founding and consulting editor of HistoryLink.org, the free online encyclopedia of Washington State history.

Of her writing, the novelist Laura Kalpakian said, "She won't be confined by forms. This is what made her recent *Fire and Stone* such a protean, exciting book. Yes, it's a vivid memoir, but she also asks questions of The Past, not simply her own, but the larger anthropological past. Priscilla Long is the enemy of slack thinking, the lazy, the euphemistic. She has a Renaissance mind…"

Priscilla Long grew up on a dairy farm on the Eastern Shore of Maryland.

CPSIA information can be obtained
at www.ICGtesting.com
Printed in the USA
LVHW090709311022
731950LV00006B/225

9 781684 920204